Musics of Many Cultures:

Study Guide & Workbook

Fourth Edition

for

Musics of Many Cultures: An Introduction

(Elizabeth May, Editor)

Dale A. Olsen
The Florida State University

KENDALL/HUNT PUBLISHING COMPANY
4050 Westmark Drive Dubuque, Iowa 52002

Cover images ©Digital Vision

Copyright ©1993, 1995, 2000, 2003 by Kendall/Hunt Publishing Company

ISBN 0-7575-0428-0

All rights reserved. No part of this publication may be reproduced,
stored in a retrieval system, or transmitted, in any form or by any
means, electronic, mechanical, photocopying, recording, or otherwise,
without the prior written permission of the copyright owner.

Printed in the United States of America.
10 9 8 7 6 5 4 3 2

Contents

Introduction		*v*
Preface to the Fourth Edition		*xiii*
Chapter 1	Ethnomusicology: Definitions, Directions, and Problems (*Bruno Nettl*)	1
Chapter 2	Evolution and Revolution in Chinese Music (*Kuo-huang Han and Lindy Li Mark*)	9
Chapter 3	Certain Experiences in Korean Music (*Kang-sook Lee*)	27
Chapter 4	Some of Japan's Musics and Musical Principles (*William P. Malm*)	39
Chapter 5	The Music of Thailand (*David Morton*)	53
Chapter 6	Some Principles of Indian Classical Music (*Bonnie C. Wade*)	67
Chapter 7	Musical Strata in Sumatra, Java, and Bali (*Margaret J. Kartomi*)	83
Chapter 8	Polynesian Music and Dance (*Adrienne L. Kaeppler*)	99
Chapter 9	The Traditional Music of the Australian Aborigines (*Trevor A. Jones*)	115
Chapter 10	Music South of the Sahara (*Atta Annan Mensah*)	129
Chapter 11	Trends in the Black Music of South Africa, 1959–1969 (*John Blacking*)	147
Chapter 12	Anlo Ewe Music in Anyako, Volta Region, Ghana (*Alfred Kwashie Ladzekpo and Kobla Ladzekpo*)	159
Chapter 13	The Music of Ethiopia (*Cynthia Tse Kimberlin*)	171
Chapter 14	Secular Classical Music in the Arabic Near East (*Jozef M. Pacholczyk*)	183
Chapter 15	Classical Iranian Music (*Ella Zonis*)	197
Chapter 16	On Jewish Music (*Abraham A. Schwadron*)	209
Chapter 17	North American Native Music (*David P. McAllester*)	221
Chapter 18	Music of the Alaskan Eskimos (*Lorraine D. Koranda*)	239
Chapter 19	Symbol and Function in South American Indian Music (*Dale A. Olsen*)	255
Chapter 20	Folk Music of South America—A Musical Mosaic (*Dale A. Olsen*)	267

Introduction

Musics of Many Cultures: Study Guide and Workbook for *Musics of Many Cultures: An Introduction* is designed to guide students through the diverse chapters of Elizabeth May's text book for college and university world music classes. The workbook will help both music and nonmusic students to more clearly understand the materials in the book; it will also aid in preparations for examinations.

May's book is very diversely written because there are two dozen contributing authors. The quotation by McAllester in the Editor's Preface — "Ethnomusicologists are concerned with music anywhere in the world and with almost as many approaches to this music as there are scholars" — summarizes why there is such diversity. Well-trained teachers of world music courses can often bring such diversity together, stressing certain concepts and making comparisons that can accomplish stated course objectives. Accompanied by recorded materials, films, slides, and demonstrations, students should be able to gain an in-depth musical and cultural understanding of the nineteen geographic areas presented in *Musics of Many Cultures: An Introduction*. Because the scholars writing these chapters are describing the areas they know best, they have endeavored to be as complete and detailed as possible within the page limitations for each chapter. For students dealing with reading assignments from the book, however, it might be understandably difficult to filter and digest all the facts and concepts presented. Having taught semester courses entitled "Music Cultures of the World I and II" for over twenty years, using May's book since it first became available in 1981, I became aware of the need for a guide to the wealth of information so that students would not be overwhelmed in preparing for their exams. Responding to repeated suggestions from students that I write a study guide for the book, I decided to do so, combining that task with the "Seminar in Ethnomusicology" in the Spring Semester of 1988. My chosen topic, "world music for music educators," was appropriate for the graduate students in the seminar, representing ethnomusicology, historical musicology, music theory, music education, and folklore.

For fifteen weeks six graduate students (Laurie Arizumi, Merri Belland, Karen Brooks, José Lezcano, John Rivest, and Tone Takahashi) and I joined forces to arrive at the instructional design logic and format for a study guide and workbook to accompany Elizabeth May's important book. Weekly projects were completed by the students for individual chapters and portions of chapters. These were discussed and analyzed by members of the seminar. Following their "pilot study" tryouts by a target student audience, all the materials were either edited, rewritten, or completely written by me. Since their inception they have been used and critiqued by over a thousand students between 1988 and 1992. Additionally, most of the chapters for the *Study Guide and Workbook* have been sent to the original authors of *Musics of Many Cultures: An Introduction* for their review and critiques.

Suggested Procedure *Musics of Many Cultures: Study Guide and Workbook* does not replace the text, but is an aid in learning the information in it. The following is a suggested procedure for its use:

1. Read a complete chapter from *Musics of Many Cultures: An Introduction*.
2. Read and work with the corresponding chapter in the *Musics of Many Cultures: Study Guide and Workbook*.
3. Answer the questions without the text first, referring to the text for answers when necessary.
4. Check the answer key given at the end of each chapter. Note — much of the learning process will be hindered if the answers are looked at before trying to figure them out.

5. Review the text as necessary.

Organization I have divided each chapter of *Musics of Many Cultures: Study Guide and Workbook* into subsections that are often indicated by the original authors of *Musics of Many Cultures: An Introduction*. However, when these divisions were not clearly indicated by the authors themselves, I organized each chapter according to the implied organization of topics. Each subsection in *Musics of Many Cultures: Study Guide and Workbook* includes the following parts:

Purpose Rather than presenting a purpose for each complete chapter, *Musics of Many Cultures: Study Guide and Workbook* gives a purpose for each subsection of the chapters. A short statement explains the goal or goals for each subsection.

Guidance This section clarifies the text, expanding upon it only to make it more understandable (but not to add new material). In this section, the information is placed into a broader picture by comparing and contrasting the author's information with what students have already learned about other cultural areas. The chapters in the May book are not written in a consistent manner because of the individuality of the authors. Even though the authors were given a directive to write "informatively, yet simply and easily so that the essays can be read with pleasure by people whose vocabularies have not included the word 'ethnomusicology and musical terminology in general," Elizabeth May continues to explain that "It seems to me unreasonable and constricting to be more restrictive. Cultures and the emphases in them vary greatly as do the perspectives of the various contributors. Part of the value of the book should be in the variety of the contributions. Also I realize that you may want to place your main emphasis on a certain section of the area you are covering" (letter dated May 21, 1975). Thus, the book is not written exclusively as a textbook for music cultures courses. With that in mind, my objective in writing the materials in the guidance sections of the *Musics of Many Cultures: Study Guide and Workbook* is to help the students understand the information, without adding new materials or summarizing the authors' data. Therefore, if an author has written a chapter that is musical in its approach, I have endeavored to make it easier to understand, perhaps by comparing the information with what they already know. If an author's approach has been historical, then I emphasize, in a comparative way, certain historical facts that I think the student needs to know, without heavily emphasizing dates. If the approach is anthropological, then I likewise try to make it understandable by comparing the information to situations with which the students may be familiar.

Terms Because of the wealth of terms included in *Musics of Many Cultures: An Introduction*, I have chosen to carefully select only those terms related to my course objectives. Two types of goals are sought here: *intellectual skills* and *verbal information*. For example, some of the terms are names of countries which the students are asked to identify and locate on a globe; this application of knowledge is an intellectual skill. The second, verbal information, is learning facts or stating information, such as defining a term. Other teachers may wish to select other terms from the text. Often, however, students are overwhelmed with new vocabulary, new concepts, and details that may not be necessary at their level. Additionally, undergraduate, nonmusic majors will have different learning objectives than music majors.

Reading Comprehension This section is intended to assist the student in learning particular ideas by writing them down, or by analyzing whether a statement is true or false. These exercises, intended to give the student practice looking for answers to relevant questions, are carefully geared to the course objectives. The students should use this section as a model for selecting other ideas, trends, sequences of information, comparisons, and so forth, that are based on the objectives of the course.

Listening Exercises Streamed musical and audio examples (RealPlayer is required) of music and dance performances are available on the Internet by going to the following address: http://dolsenmusic.com. I have selected most of these listening and viewing examples to complement the text and provide audio/visual materials that are relevant to the text. While they are not essential for learning the written information in the May book, they are highly recommended because they enable students to learn about the structure of the music (texture, melody, rhythm, tone color, etc.), to hear and often see musical instruments, and to visually and aurally experience many types of cultural contexts for music (such as dance, festivals, concerts, etc.). These constantly updated audio and video examples correspond to the general information provided in the Musical Example boxes in the margins of each chapter. The Listening Form at the end of each chapter can be completed, torn out, and given to your teacher for evaluation, if so required.

Listening Form The Listening Form (printed at the end of this Introduction, and at the ends of each chapter) has been developed to guide critical, active, and careful listening. Students should make multiple photocopies of this form, and use one copy for each example. The listening form is devised to be objective. Students should listen to the selected musical example several times, depending on the length of the example, and place an X, √, or • in the boxes that correspond to the musical characteristics heard. Several boxes under each category may be marked, since musical instruments, voices, and genres are usually characterized by diversity. The student should also write in types when possible, and give native or venacular names when known. An effective way to use the listening form for small ensembles is to draw lines (colored lines work best) from one box to the next (connecting the dots), indicating the characteristics of each particular instrument or voice. If more space is needed, the student can write on the back of the form.

The goal of the listening form is to encourage careful listening rather than to test listening precision. Music should be listened to for enjoyment, and knowing how to listen and what to listen for will increase that pleasure. Since most music is inspired by human emotion, individual musical events will not adhere to one or two areas (as indicated by the boxes), but will be a combination of many of them. The purpose of the form is to develop listening skills so that understanding is created through objectivity and perception; it is not to merely classify music into a series of arbitrary English words. World music should not be described and analyzed with the same vocabulary as European concert music. However, if European terms sometimes seem to work, and if they can be employed objectively, then they should by all means be included in the boxes entitled "other." Each vertical line in the Listening Form is explained as follows:

1. **Performing elements (if vocal).** Listen carefully for the number of singers, and indicate how many are males and how many are females. Under the *group* category, give approximate percentages. The *other* category may refer to alternating choruses (antiphonal), leader and chorus (responsorial), or any other arrangement of interrelationships between performing elements. Explain as briefly and clearly as possible what is heard.

2. **Performing elements (if instrumental).** Using the terms in the Hornbostel-Sachs musical instrument classification system (discussed on p. xii of the text), plus *corpophone* (body sounders, e.g. handclaps, finger snaps, thigh slapping, etc.), mark the appropriate box. Then indicate the specific type (such as bow, lute, zither, harp, lyre for chordophone; edge, single reed, double reed, lip, free for aerophone; etc.) and give the native name. Use as many boxes as necessary.

3. **Texture.** The first line in this category moves from the simple to the complex. Single melody includes unison. *Dense unison* occurs when numerous voices or instruments are playing the same melody with very slight differences in intonation and rhythm. *Heterophony* is when the voices or instruments are playing the same melody with slight or elaborate variation at the same time. *Imitation* means that the same melody is repeated by a different performing element. *Parallelism* occurs when the same melody is performed at different pitch levels simultaneously. *Dis-

phony means separate parts (as in European music with counterpoint).

4. **More texture.** A *drone* (a continuous sound) may be single, double, multiple, steady, or reiterated. The *time indicator* box may be filled in with the name of the the instrument or its classification type, or reference can be made to the performing elements mentioned above. *Chordal* does not refer necessarily to European harmony, but means notes sounding together. *Polyphonic stratification* is the same as *layering*, resulting from many voices or instruments of different tone color or rhythmic character playing together, creating layers of sound. *Colotomy* refers to the texture when particular instruments play particular notes at particular times. When combinations or variables of the above are found, each box should be marked along with the box entitled *combination* or *variable*.

5. **Melodic contour.** A *static* melody is one which does not have much movement, perhaps consisting of one note above and/or below a reciting tone. Many melodies will be a combination of *ascent* and *descent*, as well as *conjunct* (stepwise) and *disjunct* (skips). An *undulating* melodic contour is one that tends to shift or "snake" around, combining many of the previous movements. A *terraced* contour is one that descends slowly, arriving at various plateaus that are static.

6. **Mode or scale.** Mode and scale are not the same thing. A mode is an arrangement of pitches that implies a hierarchy and a mood, while a scale is an arbitrary arrangement of pitches placed in an ascending or descending order. This category of the Listening Form can be optional, since it requires some knowledge of basic ear training. The student should first count the notes that appear within an octave, and determine the principal tone (tonic or foundation tone), assigning it the cipher (number) one (1). The other pitches going up the scale stepwise will be numbered 2, 3, 4, 5, 6, 7, 1, 2, etc. Half steps are indicated by placing a downward (\) diagonal line through the cipher which is flat ($\flat 3$) or an upward (/) diagonal line through the cipher which is sharp ($\sharp 4$). For example, part of a scale containing an augmented second would be written this way: 1 $\flat 2$ 3 4 5. Microtones (e.g., quarter tones), can be indicated by diacritic markings, such as an upward or downward arrow (or + or -) above the cipher.

7. **Meter.** Meter refers to the relationship of strong and weak beats or pulses. Musicians derive this term from rhythm in poetry. *Free meter* means having no particular beat, similar to free verse. *Duple* means two and its multiples; triple means three and its multiples. A common *compound meter* is 6/8, which can be duple and triple combined within one, such as **1** 2 3 **4** 5 6 being also felt as **1** 2 **3** 4 **5** 6. *Additive meter* would be one meter plus another, such as 3 + 2 + 3. *Polymeter* would be several different meters occurring simultaneously.

8. **Speed.** This is a very subjective category, and one that could be determined by the markings on a metronome.

9. **Amplitude.** This term refers to dynamic level, and is also a very subjective category. Scientifically, ratings could be determined by a decibel meter.

10. **Timbre or tone color.** This is perhaps the most subjective category of all, and one for which there are no scientific terms that apply. Acoustitions (physicists who study acoustics), however, can measure overtone structures and determine why certain tone colors exist, but this is out of the range of objectives for the present listening form. A voice is said to be *masked* when the musician purposely alters its sound in order to cover it much like a person wears a mask to cover the face or a costume to cover the body.

11. **Inflections or modifications.** A *vibrato* is like a waver or fluctuation of a musical tone. A *falsetto* usually refers to a man singing in a high voice like a woman, although a woman can also sing in a falsetto. *Yodeling* is employing a type of intermittent falsetto. *Multiphonics* are modifications that occur when a voice or instrument produces more than one note at a time.

12. **Formal structure.** These terms are intended to replace particular terms found in European music

history. *Expanding* replaces through-composed, and means that the formal structure is continuously evolving or expanding. *Reverting* replaces rondo form, and means that a particular theme is constantly referred to or returned to. *Strophic* means that the same melody appears each time a new song text occurs.

13. **Structural or performance techniques.** An *ostinato* is a short melodic, rhythmic, or chordal (or a mixture of them) passage that is repeated many times, while a melody or melodies flow above it. *Responsorial* means call and response, or one musical voice answered by a chorus or group. Antiphonal refers to an individual voice answered by another individual voice, or a group answered by a group. *Elastic* (also *breath*) rhythm means that the basic pulse is slightly interrupted by a slight elongation of time. Vocal music is *syllabic* when each syllable of the text has its own pitch. By contrast, vocal music is *melismatic* when each syllable has many pitches. Sometimes individual parts seem (and are) *nonsynchronous*, that is, they do not match up. A drum may be ahead or behind the rhythm of the melodic line, for example.

Sample Test Questions This section has two goals, of which the first is more important. First, the objectives of the teacher, which should be made evident by stating them, are reflected in the Sample Test Questions. Like the Reading Comprehension Questions, the Sample Test Questions are merely suggestions that fit within my objectives. Many other test questions could also be formulated that would accomplish the same objectives and/or those of other teachers. Second, by working through the Sample Test Questions students will become acquainted with the types of question the teacher will perhaps fabricate. All the Sample Test Questions are multiple choice because other types of tests are not managable for large lecture courses consisting of several hundred students.

Answers to Reading Comprehension Questions The answers to the practice exercises discussed above appear at the end of each chapter, rather than at the end of each Reading Comprehension Questions section. This is so students will not be tempted to simply look at the answers, but will look up the answers in the textbook. Some of the fill-in-the-blank answers are from the section on terms, but others are to be answered by providing the definition of the concept in English. In many cases I require students to be aware of the English meanings of foreign terms, rather than knowing the foreign term itself. True and false questions stress feedback, not only by letting students know when a statement is true, but also by providing the correct phrase when the statement is false. Otherwise, students are memorizing false information.

Answers to Sample Test Questions The answers to the Sample Test Questions are listed in vertical rows. This enables the student to cover the answers to the questions that follow the one that he or she is trying to answer. Some students, of course, will answer all of the questions first and then check the answers, but many will do one at a time.

Listening Form

Student Name_____I.D. Number_____
Course Name _____Course Number _____
Date_____Chapter Number_____Listening Example Number _____
Record or Tape Number_____Name of Culture and Location _____
Name of Performer(s)_____
Instructions: place an X, ✓, or • in appropriate boxes; give types; indicate native names.

performing elements (if vocal)	solo: M/F	duo: M/F	trio: M/F	quartet: M/F	group: M/F	other: M/F
performing elements (if instrumental)	corpophone	idiophone	membrano-phone	aerophone	chordophone	electrophone	other
texture	single melody	dense unison	heterophone	imitation	parallelism	disphony	other
more texture	with drone	with time indicator	chordal	polyphonic stratification	colotomy	combination	variable
melodic contour	static	ascending	descending	conjunct	disjunct	undulating	terraced
mode or scale	number of notes	vernacular	using cipher notation (numbers), indicate the mode or scale in ascending order
meter	free	duple	triple	compound	additive	poly	other
speed	very slow	slow	moderate	fast	very fast	variable	other
amplitude	very soft	soft	moderate	loud	very loud	variable	other
timbre (tone color)	clear	breathy	nasal	open	tight	masked	other
inflections	no vibrato	slow vibrato	fast vibrato	wide vibrato	falsetto	multiphonics	other
formal structure	vernacular name	expanding	reverting	strophic	theme and variations	other
structural or performance techniques	ostinato	responsorial	antiphonal	elastic rhythm	if vocal: syllabic or melismatic	non-synchronous parts	other

Preface to the Fourth Edition

In the ten years since the first edition of *Musics of Many Cultures: Study Guide & Workbook* to accompany *Musics of Many Cultures: An Introduction*, edited by Elizabeth May, many changes have occurred on planet Earth. There have been regime changes, terrible acts of terrorism, natural disasters, wars, billions of human births and deaths, and probably incomparable musical changes. Like previous editions, this fourth edition does not add any new data beyond correcting and updating a few sections from the May chapters when necessary. However, I have added several narratives about some of my experiences in a number of the countries studied.

After more than twenty years, the May book still stands as one of the leading authoritative books on many world musical cultures. While it is impossible for a single book to be comprehensive, the May book is unique in that it comes as close as any one volume can to presenting a large picture of the world's traditional music.

Music, however, is more than reading about music. Apart from the original three 33 1/3 rpm vinyl mini-LPs in the back of the original hardcover and a few of the early paperback versions of the May book, extensive audio examples have not been available for the text. In this fourth edition of *Musics of Many Cultures: Study Guide & Workbook*, I have provided an answer to the question "where are the audio examples?" by incorporating an Internet address that directs owners of this book to my personal website, which contains a directory of and link to hundreds of streamed audio and visual files of music and dance performances from the Florida State University Ethnomusicology Archive. These music and dance examples correspond to the chapters in the May-Olsen books, and function as educational tools to maximize learning. Users of this book should go to the following Internet address before reading each chapter in *Musics of Many Cultures: Study Guide & Workbook*:

http://dolsenmusic.com

In the margins of each chapter are musical example boxes, also identified with the symbol ♪. These boxes provide basic information about corresponding audio and video examples, and direct readers to information found in the active links on the website. The website also contains instructions on how to download media players to receive the streamed examples. Moreover, the website provides many other instructional guidelines, ideas, and information, all intended to make the learning experience interactive and exciting. I graciously thank my graduate assistant, Bragi Thor Vallson for his brilliant help in the designing and construction of the website. All audio and video examples are copyrighted by either Dale A. Olsen or The Florida State University. They cannot be copied without permission from the author.

Finally, a listing (sometimes annotated) of pertinent videos that were not listed in the May textbook is included under the heading Video Viewing. The suggested videos are often available in university music or video libraries, public school libraries or media centers, and public libraries. Moreover, many are commercially available for purchase. Students can gain valuable information by viewing videos; not only do visual materials usually contextualize the musical events and provide details on performance techniques, but they often include explanations of the music and musical contexts by the performers themselves.

Chapter 1

Text Pages 1 – 9

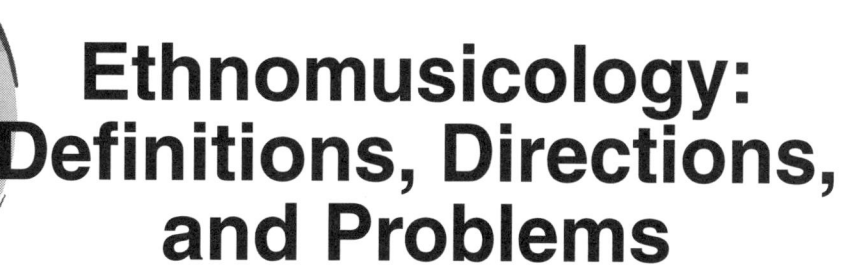

Ethnomusicology: Definitions, Directions, and Problems

Bruno Nettl

Definitions (Text Pages 1–2)

Purpose To introduce the varied meanings of the term "ethnomusicology" and the various ways that ethnomusicologists think about what it is they do.

Guidance There are probably about as many definitions of ethnomusicology as there are ethnomusicologists. Basically, the prefix "ethno" refers to "race" or "culture," and several other uses of that prefix are understood in the words ethnology, ethnobotony, and ethnohistory. The term "ethnic" is derived from the same word root, but it has a slightly different meaning than the prefix "ethno." The middle part of word ethnomusicology, "music," can be defined as humanly organized sound other than speech sound that is capable of some form of communication. The suffix "ology" simply means the study of, or the science of. Thus, ethnomusicology literally means the cultural study of music. Another useful definition, not given in your text, is by Mantle Hood in the second edition of the *Harvard Dictionary of Music* (1972:298): "Ethnomusicology is an approach to the study of *any* music, not only in terms of itself but also in relation to its cultural context." One can also effectively think of ethnomusicology as the anthropology of music. Another field defined as the study of music is musicology, which should also mean the study of any or all music, but is not used in that manner today (although it was at one time). The term "musicology," by itself, usually means historical musicology, which places a greater emphasis upon music in its historical context than as a cultural phenomenon. Also, the most common application of the discipline of historical musicology is to European civilization.

Terms Define or identify the following terms, based on readings from the text and/or other sources.

1. ethnomusicology
2. musicology
3. historical musicology
4. anthropology
5. ethnology

Reading Comprehension Answer the following work questions (answers at end of this chapter):

1. Write out the four definitions of ethnomusicology presented by the author:

    a._____

    b._____

    c._____

    d._____

2. Many ethnomusicologists began as _____, as students of _____, or as _____.

3. The term "ethnomusicology" has been in existence for several hundred years. True or False.

4. Two English terms for what preceded the term "ethnomusicology" are _____ and _____.

Directions (Text Pages 2–8)

Purpose To identify five concepts which ethnomusicologists hold to be important to their discipline, and which explain the various directions that the field has taken.

Guidance The first concept concerns the idea that one of the identifying characteristics of mankind is that it makes music, and that these musics are as varied as are the languages and dialects spoken throughout the earth. Nevertheless, there may be some musical characteristics that are universal, and this possibility is of interest to ethnomusicologists. Still, because the ethnomusicologist is trained to hear minute differences as well as similarities between the innumerable types of music found in the world, figuring out how to describe and analyze the varieties of music is an important goal. The second concept points out the necessity for doing fieldwork. Every ethnomusicologist needs to be trained in the techniques of documenting musical events where they are found in their natural environment. This is often one of the most enjoyable aspects of being an ethnomusicologist, because of the experiences of living with different cultural groups. There are many ways of doing research in the field, and the method chosen is often determined by the research plan. Some ethnomusicologists learn how to perform the music of other cultures while living with them. This technique is similar to learning the language of the group with which you are studying. As one can attempt to become bilingual with the spoken or written language of a foreign culture, one can also attempt to become bimusical, although to do so would probably be secondary to the goals of the research. Nevertheless, one can enjoy the communication between teacher and student, and the depths of human understanding to be gained via learning some of a culture's music while in the field are great. The third concept is about notation, and this is perhaps the most difficult with which to deal. Western notation often does not work for non-Western musics, and much experimentation is constantly taking place to develop a visual notation that actually does describe the subtleties of a culture's music. The fourth concept is one of the most important in ethnomusicology, and the prefix of the name for the discipline, "ethno," directly refers to culture. Since every culture has music, it is important to realize that music can tell us something about a culture that other activities cannot tell us. Music may be like a key towards understanding a culture. Finally, the fifth concept is about the study of music in time, and how music grows, changes, stays the same, or even disappears. What are the processes that cause these developments through time? This concept is related to history, except that it is not written history. The ethnomusicologist often relies on oral history (conducting interviews) in his or her quest to understand what has happened and why.

Terms Define or identify the following terms, based on readings from the text and/or other sources.

6. fieldwork

7. notation or transcription of music

8. Seeger solution

9. Hipkins solution

10. Laban solution

11. acculturation

Reading Comprehension Answer the following work questions (answers at end of this chapter):

5. List, in summary form, the five characteristics of the field of ethnomusicology:

a._____

b._____

c._____

d._____

e._____

6. Westernization, modernization, urbanization are types of culture contact included under the term _____.

Problems (Text Pages 8–9)

Purpose To consider the difficulties and problems that confront ethnomusicology as a discipline, while suggesting how ethnomusicologists are scholars who have great respect for and love of the music and people they study.

Guidance Perhaps because of the youthfulness of ethnomusicology as a scientific discipline, it is still lacking in basic theory. This is because of the tremendous diversity of the musics and cultures in the world, because of the variety of approaches of ethnomusicologists themselves, and because of the abstract nature of music and what it means, what it does, and how it does it.

Reading Comprehension Answer the following work questions (answers at end of this chapter):

7. Ethnomusicologists have data on all the world's music. True or False.

8. A constant problem in ethnomusicology is the difficulty in achieving a proper balance between the observations of the _____ with the understanding of the _____ who has grown up in the culture.

9. Ethnomusicologists have not yet figured out an effective way to study music as a part of culture. True or False.

10. Ethnomusicologists have called the attention of _____ to the multitude of phenomena around the world on which they might draw for inspiration.

Sample Test Questions

Multiple choice questions. Only one answer is correct.

1. Mantle Hood has formulated three solutions to the problem of transcribing or notating non-Western music. Which is *not* one of them: a.

Hood Solution, b. Seeger Solution, c. Laban Solution, d. Hipkins Solution.

2. Which term means something quite different from what ethnomusicology is actually about: a. comparative musicology, b. musical ethnology, c. historical musicology, d. anthropology of music.

3. Which of the following best describes how an ethnomusicologist obtains his or her materials for research: a. through fieldwork, b. from recordings, c. out of books, d. by bringing an informant to the home, office, or studio for an interview and recording session.

4. Ethnomusicologists seem to be torn between which two ideals: a. unity of mankind and variety of musical phenomena, b. music as a universal language and mankind as a universal species, c. the unity of music and the diversity of mankind, d. music as language and language as music.

5. Ethnomusicologists are always interested in music as a phenomenon produced by a(n) a. composer, b. artist, c. musician, d. culture.

Answers to Reading Comprehension Questions

1. a. The study of a music foreign to one's own; b. The study of contemporary musical systems; c. The study of music *in* and *as* culture; d. The comparative study of musical systems and cultures

2. musicians, musicology, anthropologists

3. False: it has been around for only about twenty-five years

4. comparative musicology, musical ethnology

5. a. the interest in universals balanced by appreciation of infinite variety, b. the emphasis on fieldwork, c. the possibility of notating and analyzing music visually and verbally, d. the insistence that music can be understood only in its cultural context, e. the interest in processes

6. acculturation

7. False: there are what seems to be an infinite number of cultures in the world, and it is seemingly impossible to have data on all of them

8. outsider, insider

9. True

10. composers

Answers to Sample Test Questions

1. a   2. c   3. a   4. a
5. d

Listening Form

Student Name_____ I.D. Number_____
Course Name _____ Course Number _____
Date_____Chapter Number_____Listening Example Number _____
Record or Tape Number_____Name of Culture and Location _____
Name of Performer(s)_____
Instructions: place an X, ✓, or • in appropriate boxes; give types; indicate native names.

performing elements (if vocal)	solo: M/F	duo: M/F	trio: M/F	quartet: M/F	group: M/F	other: M/F
performing elements (if instrumental)	corpophone	idiophone	membrano-phone	aerophone	chordophone	electrophone	other
texture	single melody	dense unison	heterophone	imitation	parallelism	disphony	other
more texture	with drone	with time indicator	chordal	polyphonic stratification	colotomy	combination	variable
melodic contour	static	ascending	descending	conjunct	disjunct	undulating	terraced
mode or scale	number of notes	vernacular	using cipher notation (numbers), indicate the mode or scale in ascending order
meter	free	duple	triple	compound	additive	poly	other
speed	very slow	slow	moderate	fast	very fast	variable	other
amplitude	very soft	soft	moderate	loud	very loud	variable	other
timbre (tone color)	clear	breathy	nasal	open	tight	masked	other
inflections	no vibrato	slow vibrato	fast vibrato	wide vibrato	falsetto	multiphonics	other
formal structure	vernacular name	expanding	reverting	strophic	theme and variations	other
structural or performance techniques	ostinato	responsorial	antiphonal	elastic rhythm	if vocal: syllabic or melismatic	non-synchronous parts	other

Chapter 2

Text Pages 10 – 31

Evolution and Revolution in Chinese Music

Kuo-huang Han and Lindy Li Mark

Introduction to Chapter (Text Pages 10–11)

Purpose To introduce basic sociocultural concepts that underlie the historical context of Chinese music, and to present the authors' research plan.

Guidance Historically, music in China was embedded strongly in socio-ideological contexts. Music was mostly programmatic (i.e., for painting a musical picture or evoking other sensory forms) or symbolic (i.e., for expressing philosophical ideas, or ritual and/or social behavior) rather than aesthetic (i.e., for enjoyment in itself). In general, these concepts still apply to modern Chinese music. The authors discuss four kinds of conflicts that have led to the development of Chinese music, creating the diversity of Chinese musical forms and effecting changes in China's musical history. The terms "China" and "Chinese music" are meant to include both Taiwan and the People's Republic of China (and also Hong Kong), and all of the various traditional musics found within them, excluding the certain musics of particular ethnic minorities, such as Islamic and Korean enclaves and the Taiwan native people. Chinese terms in this chapter are romanized with the older Wade Giles system. When appropriate (e.g., under Terms), the newer and official pinyin romanizations are included in parentheses.

Terms Define or identify the following terms or areas, based on readings from the text and/or other sources.

1. Find People's Republic of China, Republic of China (Taiwan or Formosa), and Hong Kong on a globe and locate Peking (Beijing), Tibet or Tibetan Plateau, Mongolia, Yellow River, great wall of China, and Gobi Desert. Notice the proximity that China has with Korea, Japan,

Southeast Asia, India, Russia, and try to imagine possible trade routes between the Middle East and China. Compare China's size with Europe and the United States of America.

2. programmatic music

3. absolute music

4. symbolic music

Reading Comprehension
Answer the following work questions (answers at end of this chapter):

1. In traditional China, music was embedded in _____ and _____ contexts.

2. The notion of "absolute music" in traditional China was quite prevalent. True or False.

3. In traditional China music was mostly _____ or _____.

4. The music of Taiwan and that of China share the same musical heritage. True or False.

Acoustic Theory in Chinese History
(Text Pages 11–13)

Purpose To survey the acoustical theories of Chinese music.

Guidance Acoustics is the study of sound. In contrast to ancient Greece, where musical acoustics was the concern of mysticism, musical acoustics in ancient China was associated with politics. This was probably because it was necessary to have certain instruments such as bells and blown tubes (panpipes) be in tune for governmental functions. Three ancient sources about Chinese scale systems are important to remember for their antiquity and their similarity to Greek scales (it us usually thought that European music derived from Greek music). These are the *Rites of the Chou Dynasty* (the earliest, from about 400 B.C.), the *Discourses on the State* (also from about 400 B.C.), and the *Chronicles of the House of Lü* (about 240 B.C.). The basis for the pitches referred to or explained in these literary sources is called the "cycle of fifths," or sometimes the "circle of fifths." Also the term "overblown fifths" is used. As explained in footnote 3, a length ratio of 3:2 also explains the concept of relationships between tubes. This concept is difficult to understand without a demonstration using a set of closed tubes, whereby the notes can actually be produced. You can experiment with a 50 inch length of 3/4 inch diameter plastic tubing. Begin by cutting a piece 12 1/2 inches long (pitch C), next cut a piece at 8 3/8 inches (pitch G), then 11 1/4 inches (pitch D), another at 7 1/2 inches (pitch A), and a last one at 10 1/4 inches. Place a cork in the end of each and blow across the top. The lowest pitch you can produce is the fundamental; the next pitch you produce by overblowing is the fifth plus an octave. When you arrange the pipes in a descending order of length you have a raftpipe (panpipe) that plays the Chinese pentatonic scale. The complexity of acoustics continues when you understand that this system of fifths is actually like a spiral, which means infinity. In other words, you could go on making pipes for the rest of your life, and if they were correctly made according to acoustic theory, you would never repeat the first note (this is what a closed system means). This discovery was made in antiquity by Greek and Chinese scholars at about the same time. Another discovery that occurred at about the same time in Europe and China is called "equal temperament." This is a system whereby all the twelve notes of the chromatic scale are slightly out of tune in order to accommodate playing them together in chordal sequences. Today our ears (really our brains) have accepted this out of tune equal temperament as being in tune.

Terms Define or identify the following terms, based on readings from the text and/or other sources.

5. Rites of the Chou Dynasty

6. Discourses on the State

7. Chronicles of the House of Lü

8. yellow bell

9. great tone

10. forest bell

11. resonating bell

12. cycle of fifths

13. pentatonic scale

14. Complete Book of Rules for Music

15. Book of Pitches

16. lü

Reading Comprehension Answer the following work questions (answers at end of this chapter):

5. In ancient China, music was from the beginning associated with _____.

6. The earliest reference to scale intervals is found in (English name) _____.

7. The fundamental or lowest pitch was called (English name) _____.

8. Theoretically, pentatonic scales could be constructed upon any of the (Chinese and English terms) _____ or _____.

9. According to the Chronicles of the House of Lü, the construction of a set of twelve pitch pipes or tubes was based on the method of the _____.

10. By the _____ century the practice of tuning court instruments to standard pitches well established.

11. An important element of the state ideology was that music could influence the _____ and _____ order.

12. Each new dynasty had restandardized the pitch measurements, although the same names and terminologies were used. True or False.

13. The discovery of a method of equal temperament by prince Chu Tsai-yü in 1584 is unique to Chinese acoustic history. True or False.

Historical Survey (Text Pages 13–16)

Purpose To place Chinese musical instruments, ideas about music, and cultural contexts for music, into a Chinese historical perspective, based on the three major periods called ancient, middle ancient, and late historical.

Guidance The Ancient Period (from the Stone Age to about 250 B.C.). There are three ways to obtain some understanding about music from this lengthy period. First, through a study of actual musical instruments excavated by archaeologists we can understand something about the complexity of ancient Chinese music, especially by examining the tuning of instruments with fixed pitch, such as stone chimes. Second, a study of musical instruments and musical activity as shown in pictures or carved in stone yields information of cultural significance. Third, ancient historical writings in China provide important types of musical information. One can appreciate the antiquity of musical thinking in China (for example, the instrument classification system, the relationship of instruments to the seasons, months, directions, and metaphysics, the relationship of music to government, and so forth) by comparing it with Europe at that time. Practically nothing is known about music during the European stone age, for example, and not until the Etruscan and Greek civilizations do musical events appear in painting and sculpture, and not until the Greek and Roman periods do historical accounts appear that explain anything about music.

The Middle Ancient Period (from about 250 B.C. to 907 A.D.). Information is obtained about this period by the same methods as for the Ancient Period, that is, through archaeology, music iconography, and historical writ-

---

♪

Music Example

pipa
(p'i-p'a)

chordophone

plucked lute

ings. The latter has revealed that music was divided into three types or divisions: ritual music, secular music, and folk music. The chronological list on text page 14 indicates that many dynasties or kingdoms existed during this period, and music was an important and frequent part of the royal courts. Because of the large number of dynasties during the Middle Ancient Period it is difficult to grasp a feeling of unity of musical development that would define this period as unified. Instead, we see musical activities expanding, with influences from outside cultures via trade, and with the development of governmental musical establishments and court ensembles of enormous sizes.

The Late Historical Period (from 907 A.D. to 1911). This period saw a return to certain ancient ideas about music, especially those associated with Confucianism (which originated in the sixth century B.C.) and the ch'in, the zither type of chordophone that was a part of the typical Confucian scholar-gentleman. Nevertheless, the p'i-p'a, a lute type of chordophone that was originally introduced from the Middle East, remained more popular than the ch'in because it was louder and flashier (see Figure 2-3). Chinese drama, which was an early form of opera, became very popular during this period, and two styles existed, the northern and the southern. These were differentiated in three ways: northern style = p'i-p'a (lute), seven tones, one singer; southern style = ti (transverse flute, pronounced *dee*), five tones, many singers. These two styles merged during the 1500s into the K'un opera style. Later, Peking opera, from north-central China, became so popular during the 1800s that it was called the national style.

Music Example
qin (ch'in)
chordophone
plucked zither

Terms Define or identify the following terms, based on readings from the text and/or other sources.

17. p'i-p'a (pipa)

18. ch'in (qin)

19. shêng (sheng)

20. se

21. Pear Garden

22. Confucianism

23. Yuan drama

24. K'un opera

25. Peking opera (Beijing)

26. Tang dynasty and the Tang emperor

Reading Comprehension Answer the following work questions (answers at end of this chapter):

14. Chinese musical instruments had been classified into _____ categories according to the materials from which they were made by the _____ century _____.

15. List the categories of musical instruments:

    a._____, b._____,

    c._____, d._____,

    e._____, f._____,

    g._____, h._____,

16. During the sixth century B.C., musical art was considered a necessary part of the education of a gentleman. True or False.

17. The three major divisions of music that were recognized during the first part of the Middle Ancient Period by the ministry of music were _____, _____, and _____.

18. Give the Chinese names of the following thousand year old musical instruments that were recently excavated by archaeologists in China:

    a. seven-string zither without fret studs called _____,

    b. a twenty-two-pipe mouth organ called _____, and

    c. a twenty-five-string zither called _____.

19. A pear-shaped plucked lute known as the _____ was introduced into China from _____ during the sixth century A.D.

20. During the early Late Historical Period (Sung dynasty) the ch'in was revived and its popularity far surpassed that of the p'i-p'a. True or False.

21. In the northern style of Yuan drama, the _____ was the main accompanying instrument.

22. In the southern style of Yuan drama, the _____ was the main accompanying instrument.

23. The most popular Chinese opera style during the nineteenth century, and which became the national style, was K'un opera. True or False.

24. The emperor of the _____ dynasty became known as the patron deity of musicians and actors.

25. A music academy established in 714 (during the T'ang dynasty) was called the _____.

Traditional Music Today (Text Pages 16–22)

Purpose To describe the most important traditional musical styles and instruments found today in China, using the categories of ritual music, modern classical music, folk song and minstrel music, and theater music.

Guidance *Ritual Music:* The celebration of Confucius' birthday on September 28 in Taiwan is the only occasion when music can be heard that may sound something like ancient Chinese court ritual music. The instruments, costumes, music, rhythm, and dance used during this Taiwanese government-supported ritual are derived from the ritual court musics of several Chinese dynasties, with the tuned stone chimes and bronze bells being the oldest (from possibly 1000 years B.C.). This type of music is no longer heard in the People's Republic of China, since the Republican Revolution of 1911 ended many traditional musical styles, especially those associated with religion.

Modern Classical Music: Classical Chinese music today is often a mixture of classical, folk, and popular styles. Musical instruments are also mixed together, including those that traditionally played classical solos with those that performed in opera. One ancient instrument that continues to be played alone is the ch'in, a zither chordophone (see Figure 2-2). The modern instrument, still with seven strings (usually metal today, rather than silk), has thirteen inlayed markings or studs along the strings to indicate finger placement. The ancient instruments (i.e., pre-Han Dynasty) did not have such markings. Since the ch'in has no frets and no bridges to raise the strings, the musician presses the desired string completely down with his left hand fingers (touching the wood underneath it) while plucking it with his or her right hand fingers. Additionally, many types of harmonics (lightly touching the string with the left hand fingers), vibratos, and slides are produced. The ch'in is a very subtle and very soft sounding instrument. The cheng (pronounced with an upward intonation), another zither, has sixteen strings of metal (some had 13 and today some have 22) that are raised from the wooden body by an equal number of movable bridges shaped like an inverted V (see Figure 2-1, left). The musician plucks the strings with his or her right hand (using little plectrums on his or her fingers) while often pressing the desired string on the left side of the bridge to achieve a vibrato and/or sliding effect. The erh-hu or nan-hu (see Figure 2-1, middle for a variant), a popular Chinese fiddle or violin, is unique because the hairs of the bow pass between the two metal strings of the instrument, and cannot be removed unless the bow or the instrument is disassembled. The small resonating chamber of the instrument is usually covered with reptile skin, and its sound is very nasal. Another instrument whose sound is nasal (at least when compared with its Western counterparts) is the ti or ti-tzu, a bamboo transverse or horizontal flute. A special hole between the mouthpiece hole and the fingerholes is covered with a very thin piece of bamboo skin. This skin buzzes like the skin on a kazoo when the instrument is played. These characteristics of tone color alteration (the reptile skin on the fiddle and the bamboo skin on the flute) give the instruments great carrying power, enabling them to be heard during performances of opera, or outside. Both instru-

---

♪

Music Example

zheng (cheng)

chordophone

plucked zither

♪

Music Example

erhu (erh-hu)

chordophone

bowed lute

♪

Music Example

dizi (ti-tzu)

aerophone

horizontal flute

ments were common in Chinese folk music. Another outdoor instrument is the sona, a double reed instrument like the oboe. This loud instrument originated in the Middle East, and a very similar aerophone is the zurna from Turkey (sona and zurna are almost the same word). The shêng (one is pictured in the very back-center of Figure 2-4) is a mouth organ or harmonica with over twenty pipes that stick straight up out of a gourd windchest (it is classified as a gourd instrument, even though its pipes are made from bamboo). Each of the pipes has a single reed cut into it where it is inserted into the windchest, making the instrument a multiple single-reed aerophone (or a multiple clarinet; the Western harmonica or blues-harp is also a multiple single-reed aerophone). Finally, the yang chin, a hammered dulcimer (front-center of Figure 2-4), is very similar to the Appalachian hammered dulcimer found in the United States. This shows how some musical instruments have migrated, in this case from Persia or Iran east to China and north to Europe and finally to the United States of America.

Folk Song and Minstrel Music: One of the popular musical instruments played by minstrels or wondering singers is the san-hsien, a three-stringed lute. This instrument should be remembered because it migrated to Japan via Okinawa, where it is known as the shamisen in Japan and jamisen in Okinawa; both terms, like the name san-hsien, mean three-strings. All three instruments are covered with skin and are therefore somewhat similar to the American banjo.

Theater Music: Peking opera is the most widely known of Chinese operatic styles. The authors discuss the style, performance practice, and the function of the instrumental ensemble in Peking opera. It is interesting to contrast the authors' descriptions of Peking opera with European opera because the conventions are so very different. On the one hand Peking opera can be very subtle (for example, the 26 ways to laugh or the 39 ways to stroke the beard), while on the other hand it can be very outgoing (for example, the use of acrobatics and percussion punctuation).

Terms Define or identify the following terms, based on readings from the text and/or other sources.

27. be able to identify the musical instruments in the pictures

28. cheng (zheng)

29. erh-hu or nan-hu (erhu)

30. ti or ti-tzu (dizi)

31. sona (souna)

32. san-hsien

33. yang chin (yang qin)

34. hsiao or tung hsiao (xiao or dongxiao)

Music Example

sheng

aerophone

mouth organ

Music Example

yangqin (yang ch'in)

chordophone

hammered dulcimer

Evolution and Revolution in Chinese Music 17

Reading Comprehension Answer the following work questions (answers at end of this chapter):

26. The only occasion in the People's Republic of China during which ancient court ritual music is heard is the celebration of Confucius' birthday. True or False.

27. The traditional Chinese classical sixteen-stringed instrument known as the _____ is a _____ type chordophone with _____ bridges.

28. The strings of the ch'in, a _____ type chordophone with _____ bridges, are tuned to one of several _____ modes.

29. The Chinese transverse flute known as the _____ has a hole that is covered with _____, which functions like the buzz on a kazoo.

30. The shêng is an instrument with many _____ made from _____; it is classified in China as a _____ instrument because of the material of its body.

Contemporary Chinese Music (Text Pages 22–26)

Purpose To describe the musical situation in mainland China since the Republican Revolution, and the present state of music in Taiwan and Hong Kong.

Guidance There are four periods of history in mainland China in the twentieth century that affected the way music developed there: (1) from the Republican Revolution of 1911 until (2) the founding of the People's Republic of China in 1949, which lasted until (3) the Cultural Revolution from 1966–69, giving way to (4) the modern age to the present. Generally speaking, traditional Chinese music was considered less and less desirable by the government during the first three periods, and European musical concepts and musical instruments gained in popularity. It is an interesting paradox that traditional Chinese music and musical instruments were not acceptable to the communist government, while European ideas were. While the compositions during much of this time are very Western sounding, and range from art songs (the English translation of the German lieder) to symphonies, most music since 1945 has been composed by committees of composers whereby no single individual takes the credit. This is all part of the concept of music for the masses. The Cultural Revolution, however, was a very bleak time for the arts, and the only compositions written were eight revolutionary operas and ballets, in which the singers and dancers are dressed in military fatigues or peasant clothing, and the themes are always about the working masses triumphing over the feudal and bourgeois (capitalist) elite.

The musical situation in Taiwan and Hong Kong has been a contrast to that found in mainland China, largely because composers have been free to do what they want to do. Music in Taiwan, especially, has expressed nationalism (based on folk themes and/or other conventions that depict national pride) because of its long struggle to portray itself as free China. Avant-garde or very modern music has also appeared, often based on traditional Chinese musical, textual, or programmatic ideas. In these ways, twentieth-century Chinese music throughout the People's Republic of China and the Republic of China (Taiwan) has been closely associated with politics and promoting social values, sort of like it had centuries earlier.

In 1993 my wife and I spent about a month in Hong Kong and the People's Republic of China (PRC). At that time we heard several concerts in Hong Kong by the Hong Kong Philharmonic Orchestra, performances of traditional music in the civic center, and snatches of traditional music in various places in Kowloon, on the mainland. Hong Kong is a huge ultra modern city, and encountering traditional music in traditional settings is not easy. Excellent traditional music study opportunities are possible at several universities, especially the Chinese University of Hong Kong, where there is an excellent program in ethnomusicology.

We encountered more traditional music in Beijing than in Hong Kong. I gave several lectures at the Central Conservatory of Music, where I had the opportunity to hear several of its faculty members perform. One moving experience in particular was at the apartment of the yangqin professor, who gave us a private concert that was fascinating. Such virtuosity and musicianship! All the traditional Chinese musical instruments are taught at the Central Conservatory of Music in Beijing, and all the professors are among the best in China. Another memorable experience in Beijing was at the Temple of Heaven. When we were there, a film was being made, and numerous musicians playing souna, erhu, and percussion accompanied several men performing the famous lion dance. We thought they were making an art film about traditional Chinese music and dance, but they were making a cigarette commercial! I never did find out what type of cigarettes the commercial was being made for, and I knew I would never see it on television.

Another great center for Chinese music in the PRC is Shanghai, where a type of music known as "southern silk and bamboo" (page 19 in textbook) originated. The Shanghai Conservatory of Music is very famous, not only for traditional music, but for learning Western classical music as well. Shanghai is China's most modern city, after Hong Kong, and it is becoming the financial center of this country of a billion, if not all of East Asia. Like Tokyo, Shanghai has just about everything anybody would want, and finding traditional music can be a difficult task without knowing the right people to guide you.

Terms Define or identify the following terms, based on readings from the text and/or other sources.

35. Republican Revolution

36. Cultural Revolution

37. Mao Tse-tung

38. Chiang Ching

Reading Comprehension
Answer the following work questions (answers at end of this chapter):

31. The purpose of the arts in a socialist country was outlined during a speech in May 1942 by _____.

32. One of the outcomes of the founding of the People's Republic in 1949 was large-scale research of _____.

33. Beginning in 1945 musical creativity in the People's Republic of China was done by _____ of _____.

34. Much of the music composed in Taiwan and Hong Kong uses new techniques to express_____.

35. In general, people in Taiwan and Hong Kong prefer _____ _____ music.

Video Viewing

1. Dizi—flute, with ensemble [erhu, sheng, yangqin, and pipa]: "Gusuxing" ("Trip to Suzhou") (3-1). *The JVC Video Anthology of World Music and Dance*, East Asia III, Volume 3, China 1 (VTMV-33).

2. Pipa—lute solo: "Shimian maifu" ("Ambush on all sides") (3-2). *The JVC Video Anthology of World Music and Dance*, East Asia III, Volume 3, China 1 (VTMV-33). This composition is often translated as "The Great Ambuscade."

3. Erhu—bowed fiddle with yangqin: "Erquan yingyue" ("The moon reflected in a spring") (3-3). *The JVC Video Anthology of World Music and Dance*, East Asia III, Volume 3, China 1 (VTMV-33).

4. Zheng—zither solo: "Yuzhou changwan" ("The fisherman singing in the evening") (3-4). *The JVC Video Anthology of World Music and Dance*, East Asia III, Volume 3, China 1 (VTMV-33).

5. Instrumental ensemble: "Chunjiang huayueye" ("A beautiful moonlit night by the river in springtime") (3-5). *The JVC Video Anthology of World Music and Dance*, East Asia III, Volume 3, China 1 (VTMV-33).

6. Instrumental ensemble: "Meihuacao" ("Plum blossoms") (3-7). *The JVC Video Anthology of World Music and Dance*, East Asia III, Volume 3, China 1 (VTMV-33).

7. Dongxiao—flute solo: "Huainian" ("Nostalgia") (3-8). *The JVC Video Anthology of World Music and Dance*, East Asia III, Volume 3, China 1 (VTMV-33). This vertical flute, from Fujien in southern China, is related to the Japanese shakuhachi.

8. From *jingju*—Beijing opera: "Bawang biefi" ("The King's parting with his favorite") (3-10). *The JVC Video Anthology of World Music and Dance*, East Asia III, Volume 3, China 1 (VTMV-33).
9. From *Chuanju*—Sichuan opera: "Baishezbuan" ("The white snake"), 3-11. *The JVC Video Anthology of World Music and Dance*, East Asia III, Volume 3, China 1 (VTMV-33).
10. *No. 17 Cotton Mill Shanghai Blues: Music in China.* Beats of the Heart series. Jeremy Marre, director and producer.

Sample Test Questions

Multiple choice questions. Only one answer is correct.

1. While the term "symbolic music" is used to express philosophical ideas, ritual, and social behavior, which term is used to express music that evokes other sensory forms? a. absolute, b. programmatic, c. meditative, d. social.

2. Like Pythagoras, the ancient Chinese metaphysical musicians discovered that: a. harmony is to music what beauty is to nature, b. the origin of music is mankind's imitation of nature, c. pitches derived from the cycle of fifths did not form a closed system, d. the tritone was indeed the "devil in music."

3. Which characteristic is *not* a part of traditional Chinese music? a. the notion of absolute music, b. it was embedded in social and ideological contexts, c. it was mostly programmatic, d. it was largely symbolic.

4. The fundamental pitch of Chinese music is called: a. Forest Bell, b. Yellow Bell, c. Bronze Bell, d. Old Standard, e. Mean Tone.

5. Which instrument is vastly different from the other three? a. sheng, b. cheng, c. ch'in, d. p'i-p'a.

6. The ch'in was originally associated with which ideology? a. Buddhism, b. Taoism, c. Hinduism, d. Islam, e. Confucianism.

7. The ch'in is classified in ethnomusicology as: a. plucked lute chordophone, b. struck zither chordophone, c. plucked zither chordophone, d. bowed lute chordophone, e. string instrument.

8. China's own classification of the ch'in is: a. wood, b. bamboo, c. silk, d. metal, e. gourd.

9. One of the techniques of playing the ch'in is: a. striking its wooden body with the plectrum, b. using harmonics, c. striking the drone strings while playing the melody strings, d. pressing the strings in back of the bridges to bend the tones.

10. The bow used to play the erh-hu: a. is made from cat gut, b. shows Western influence, c. is made from human hair, d. passes between the two strings, e. also strikes the body of the instrument to produce a percussive effect.

11. Chinese musical instruments are classified into how many categories according to the traditional Chinese manner? a. 4, b. 5, c. 6, d. 8, e. 10.

12. The sheng is classified as what according to the traditional Chinese manner? a. wood, b. bamboo, c. gourd, d. metal, e. silk.

13. The instrument pictured in Figure 2-1, text page 18 (extreme left), was classified historically according to the traditional Chinese manner as? a. wood, b. bamboo, c. gourd, d. metal, e. silk.

14. Although it was developed half a century earlier in China than in Europe, the equal tempered scale: a. remained theoretical and dormant, b. was used only in ritual music, c. was used only in Chinese opera, d. was employed by the philosophical Chinese musicians only.

15. In the People's Republic of China, most works, especially recent ones, are created by: a. composers designated by the government, b. national treasures, c. folk musicians, d. committees of composers, e. women, which shows that socialism has no sex discrimination.

16. In historical Chinese literature, professional musicians and actors were considered: a. rich, b. sacred beings, c. strange, d. lowly and unworthy of mention, e. elite.

17. Which type of instrument was not found in late neolithic archaeological sites in China? a. 25-stringed zither, b. stone chimes, c. pottery ocarina, d. bronze bells.

18. The main accompanying instrument in the northern style of Yuan drama is the: a. ch'in, b. ti, c. p'i-p'a, d. sheng, e. cheng.

19. Which of the following is *not* one of the trends first introduced by Mao Tse-tung and realized with the founding of the People's Republic in 1949? a. the return to folk tradition, b. the emphasis on rigorous training in performance, c. the implication of the electronic medium, d. the combination of Western and Chinese elements, e. the infusion of political content in program music.

20. The Chinese hammered dulcimer yang chin: a. is an instrument from the Appalachian mountains that was introduced by Pete Seeger during his tour of China in the 1950s, b. was imported into China from Persia during the eighteenth century, c. is an ancient Chinese instrument that was popular in northern China during the Han dynasty, d. is an important instrument in Peking opera, e. is used only for Chinese mountain music.

21. The instrument in Figure 2-2, text page 19, is the: a. ch'in, b. p'i-p'a, c. cheng, d. erh-hu, e. ti.

22. The instrument in Figure 2-2, text page 19, is developed from prototypes : a. from the Middle East, b. from the north, c. indigenous to China, d. from Japan, e. from Korea.

23. The instrument in Figure 2-3, text page 19, is the: a. ch'in, b. p'i-p'a,

c. cheng, d. erh-hu, e. ti.

24. The instrument in Figure 2-3, text page 19, is developed from prototypes: a. from the Middle East, b. from the north, c. indigenous to China, d. from Japan, e. from Korea.

25. In which area or group have Chinese musicians *not* kept pace with international trends: a. Chinese communities overseas, b. Hong Kong, c. People's Republic of China, d. Republic of China.

Answers to Reading Comprehension Questions

1. social, ideological
2. False: although it exists, it is not nearly as common as program music
3. programmatic, symbolic
4. True
5. politics
6. Rites of the Chou Dynasty
7. yellow bell
8. lü or chromatic pitches
9. cycle of fifths
10. third century B.C.
11. cosmic, social
12. True
13. False: it was also discovered in Europe at about the same time, although some scholars maintain the Europeans learned it from the Chinese
14. eight, third, B.C.
15. a. metal, b. stone, c. silk, d. bamboo, e. gourd, f. pottery or earth, g. leather, h. wood
16. True
17. ritual music, secular music, regional or folk music
18. a. ch'in, b. shêng, c. se
19. p'i-p'a, Central Asia
20. False: the p'i-p'a remained more popular than the ch'in because it could play louder and was more virtuoso
21. p'i-p'a
22. ti
23. False: it was the Peking opera
24. T'ang
25. Pear Garden
26. False: while the statement is true for Taiwan, the People's Republic of China does not celebrate Confucius' birthday
27. cheng, zither, movable
28. zither, no, pentatonic
29. ti or ti-tzu, bamboo skin

30. pipes, bamboo, gourd
31. Mao Tse-tung
32. folk music
33. committees of composers
34. nationalism
35. popular

Answers to Sample Test Questions

1. b	2. c	3. a	4. b
5. a	6. e	7. c	8. c
9. b	10. d	11. d	12. c
13. e	14. a	15. d	16. d
17. a	18. c	19. c	20. b
21. a	22. c	23. b	24. a
25. c			

Listening Form

Student Name_____ I.D. Number_____
Course Name _____ Course Number _____
Date_____Chapter Number_____Listening Example Number _____
Record or Tape Number_____Name of Culture and Location _____
Name of Performer(s)_____
Instructions: place an X, ✓, or • in appropriate boxes; give types; indicate native names.

performing elements (if vocal)	solo: M/F	duo: M/F	trio: M/F	quartet: M/F	group: M/F	other: M/F
performing elements (if instrumental)	corpophone	idiophone	membrano-phone	aerophone	chordophone	electrophone	other
texture	single melody	dense unison	heterophone	imitation	parallelism	disphony	other
more texture	with drone	with time indicator	chordal	polyphonic stratification	colotomy	combination	variable
melodic contour	static	ascending	descending	conjunct	disjunct	undulating	terraced
mode or scale	number of notes	vernacular	using cipher notation (numbers), indicate the mode or scale in ascending order
meter	free	duple	triple	compound	additive	poly	other
speed	very slow	slow	moderate	fast	very fast	variable	other
amplitude	very soft	soft	moderate	loud	very loud	variable	other
timbre (tone color)	clear	breathy	nasal	open	tight	masked	other
inflections	no vibrato	slow vibrato	fast vibrato	wide vibrato	falsetto	multiphonics	other
formal structure	vernacular name	expanding	reverting	strophic	theme and variations	other
structural or performance techniques	ostinato	responsorial	antiphonal	elastic rhythm	if vocal: syllabic or melismatic	non-synchronous parts	other

Chapter 3

Text Pages 32 – 47

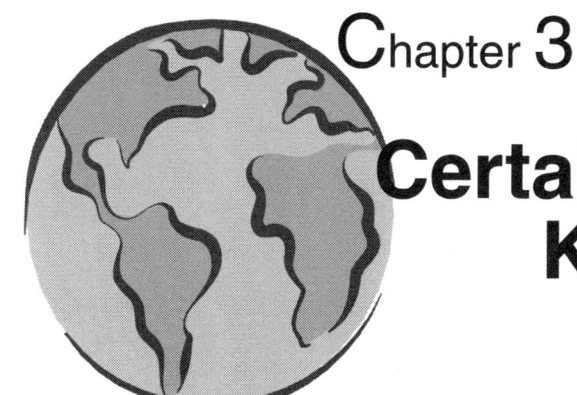

Certain Experiences in Korean Music

Kang-sook Lee

Introduction to Chapter (Text Pages 32–33)

Purpose To introduce several very basic geographical, historical, and cultural points relating to Korean music, and to discuss, by way of introduction, the diverse categories of Korean music.

Guidance This chapter is musical in its approach; that is, much of the material consists of musical analysis of certain areas of Korean music. As the title indicates, preparations are made for the reader to have certain experiences in Korean music, and as the author further states, he feels that one must have a basic understanding of Korean tonal materials to understand the language of Korean music. He relates the learning experience as a music-grammar one; that is, as one must learn the grammar of a language in order to thoroughly understand the language, so too one must learn the music-grammar of a culture in order to thoroughly understand that culture's music. While this approach is valid, it differs from many of the other approaches in this book. This one is more musicological, while others are anthropological, and still others are historical.

Many terms are introduced in this section, and most of them end with the suffix "ak," the Korean word for music. (It is interesting that the last chapter did not make very much of the Chinese word for music, which is "yüeh.") The two most important concepts are the following two major categories: music for the ruling class (chong-ak) and music for the common man (sok-ak). The three major types of music for the ruling class are (1) Confucian ritual music (a-ak), (2) court music that originated from China during the T'ang and Sung dynasties (t'ang-ak), and (3) court music that originated in Korea (hyang-ak). Sometimes the two types of court music are simply categorized into three types: ritual, banquet, and military music. The music for the common man (sok-ak) has a number of categories that a person (in the West) would not think of as being categorized together, especially music of the shamans, the Buddhists, the farmers, the folk, and the classical vocal and instrumental forms known as p'ansori and sanjo. Nevertheless, they are all separate from the first category because they were not a part of the ruling class.

Terms Define or identify the following terms or areas, based on readings from text and/or other sources.

1. Find Korea on a globe and locate Seoul, South Korea and North Korea. Notice Korea's proximity to China and Japan.

2. ak

3. music for the ruling class

4. music for the common man

5. a-ak

6. t'ang-ak

7. p'ansori

8. sanjo

Reading Comprehension Answer the following work questions (answers at end of this chapter):

1. The two categories of Korean traditional music (English terms) can be divided into music for the_____ _____ and for the _____.

2. Improvisation is a characteristic of sanjo. True or False.

3. The Pomp'ae, a song of praise to Buddha, has been designated as Korea's national cultural treasure. True or False.

4. List the six forms of music included in the category of sokak:

   a._____,

   b._____,

   c._____,

   d._____,

   e._____.

Certain Experiences in Korean Music   29

Instruments (Text Pages 33–35)

Purpose   To introduce the student to five of the more popular musical instruments in Korea.

Guidance   Many of the musical instruments found today in Korea are similar to those in China (and Japan). The kayagum, for example, resembles the Chinese cheng and the Japanese koto, the changgo is similar to the Japanese san no tsuzumi, the haegum resembles the Chinese hu-chin (of which the erh-hu is an example), the p'iri is similar to the Japanese hichiriki, and the taegum is similar to the Chinese dizi. The kayagum has movable bridges, enabling the musician to change tunings and tone quality by moving them. Like the similar zithers, the zheng and the koto, the musician can produce a vibrato or wavering of the tone by rapidly pressing a string on the left side of a bridge. This is especially important in the kayagum because of the characteristic wide vibrato of Korean music. The kayagum is usually placed across the lap of the musician as he or she sits cross-legged on the floor. The changgo plays with the kayagum (or another solo instrument) during performances of sanjo. It is placed horizontally in front of the drummer and played with a stick on its right head, and with the fingers on its left. The haegum is nearly identical to the Chinese bowed fiddle, which is generically called the hu-chin (you can also see linguistic similarity as "hae" and "hu" mean "barbarian," and "gum" and "chin" mean "instrument"). Like the erh-hu from China, the haegum is played with a bow that is permanently placed between its two strings, and the strings are touched (not pressed or squeezed down completely onto the fingerboard as with the European fiddle). Three of the p'iri oboes are used in court music, like the Japanese hichiriki. Finally, the Korean horizontal flute (taegum) is similar to the Chinese dizi only because it also has a membrane that buzzes like a kazoo while played. The smaller varieties of horizontal flute, however, do not have membranes.

> ♪
>
> *Music Example*
>
> *kayagum & changgo duet*
>
> *chordophone and membranophone*
>
> *plucked zither and hourglass drum*

Terms   Define or identify the following terms, based on readings from text and/or other sources.

9. kayagum

10. changgo

11. haegum

12. p'iri

13. taegum

14. be able to recognize the pictures of the above instruments.

Reading Comprehension   Answer the following work questions (answers at end of this chapter):

5. There are more than _____ different Korean musical instruments in existence today.

6. The most popular instrument in Korea, a 12-stringed zither, is the _____.

7. The hourglass-shaped changgo drum is struck by _____ on its right head and by _____ on its left.

8. A two-stringed bowed instrument is the _____.

9. The taegum has a buzzing membrane like the Chinese ti. True or False.

10. The p'iri with a flared bell is associated with Korean opera. True or False.

Modes and Melody (Text Pages 35–37)

Purpose To discuss two of the Korean musical modes and how melody can create tension and release.

Guidance A musical mode is somewhat like a musical scale, except that the latter is simply a list of the pitches from lowest to highest, while the former implies a hierarchy of tones, where some are more important than others, and where a particular note must go to another particular note. Whereas a scale is a list, a mode is a scheme. The pitches of traditional non-Western cultures do not correspond to the Western equal-tempered tuning system (i.e., they cannot be precisely played on the piano). The author employs the cents system to explain his point. With the cents system there are 100 cents or divisions in each half step of the Western equal-tempered scale (for a total of 1200 cents to the octave). Therefore, whereas a major second (e.g., from *do* to *re*, as in the pitches to the word "country" in "My Country 'tis of Thee") in Western music has 200 cents (equal to two half steps), a corresponding major second in Korean music is smaller, containing perhaps 135 cents (this is flexible). Therefore, our ears (brains) have to be flexible enough to accept Korean music in terms of itself, and not compare it to Western music. Likewise, Korean melodic usage must be understood in terms of itself. Here the author discusses the term "wavering tone," which is similar to (and is heard by Westerners as) a wide vibrato. The difference is that a vibrato is often thought of in Western music as an ornament or decorative embellishment, while the Korean wavering tone is essential to Korean music. In reality, however, within certain Western musics, such as opera and other classical singing forms, vibrato is also essential. No singer of Western opera, for example, would ever sing an aria or a song without using a vibrato. Although the author chooses to, we must not constantly try to rationalize the validity of non-Western music by comparing it to Western music. Korean music, for example, is a truly unique characteristic of the highly individualized Korean society.

Terms Define or identify the following terms, based on readings from text and/or other sources.

15. mode

16. vibrato

17. straight tone

18. wavering tone

Reading Comprehension Answer the following work questions (answers at end of this chapter):

11. The major second in Western equal-tempered tuning contains 200 cents, whereas an equivalent interval in Korean tuning might contain _____ cents.

12. Leonard Meyer says that sensitivity to a certain kind of music is a _____ behavior.

13. There are only two modes in Korean music. True or False.

14. Korean traditional musicians can hear several tones as a single tone. True or False.

Rhythm (Text Pages 37–38)

Purpose To acquaint the student with one important Korean rhythmical concept.

Guidance The author compares a Korean musical idea, termed "elastic rhythm," with Western musical practice. He argues that Western musicians, conditioned to metronomes (mechanical devices that produce consistent beats), have a difficult time comprehending Korean rhythm, which is based on the Korean individual's inner or psychological metronome. This so-called "psychological meter" comes from subdivisions of the duration of a long breath exhalation. The result is elastic rhythm, an intermittent use of free meter. An example from sijo, an indigenous vocal genre, uses superimposed 5-beat and 8-beat patterns with a pulse that is so slow (about two seconds per beat) that the rhythm can be described as nonmetrical or elastic. There are other types of meter commonly found in Korean music that are unfortunately not discussed by the author. One very important meter, found in sanjo, is a medium to fast compound double/triple that approximates the Western concept known as 6/8 time.

Terms Define the following terms based on the reading from your text.

19. elastic rhythm

20. nonmeter

Reading Comprehension Answer the following work questions (answers at end of this chapter):

15. The concept (in English) of rhythm in Korean music where the time between two beat reference points is not always the same is called _____ and/or _____ rhythm.

16. The Korean music student measures the time it takes to slowly _____ _____, using this duration to represent a 5-beat pattern.

17. Write the fraction that can be used to describe another common meter in Korean music: _____.

Harmonic Texture (Text Pages 38–40)

Purpose To acquaint the student with the Korean concept of musical texture.

Guidance The author implies that without an understanding of Korean "harmonic" theory (the way tones work together), Korean music may not be appreciated. As in many other non-Western musics, especially those of the Far East, the term "heterophony" applies. The excellent definition of heterophony in the text can be shortened to mean simply "music that is almost in unison." Korean ensemble music is based on a complex system that creates tension by combining certain portions of melodies heterophonically, and then release by ending together on a sustained tone that has waver or wide vibrato added. While it is preferable to restrict the terms "harmony" and "harmonic" to Western usage, the author substantiates their use here with the words "tones that result in a pleasing sound to a listener." This is, of course, a culture-bound statement because one listener may hear the tones as pleasing and another as displeasing. It is perhaps clearer to simply use the term "texture" to discuss the relationship of tones that sound together. The author's notation helps to graphically clarify heterophony in Korean music, although there is one printing error in Example 3-6. The instrument name at the beginning of the top musical staff should read taegum (obviously the typesetter misread the original script). The author mentions Schenkerian analysis, a system devised by Mr. Schenker that reduces a melodic line into its most basic parts; it is, as it were, an abstraction of the melody.

Terms Define the following term based on the reading from your text.

21. heterophony

Reading Comprehension Answer the following work questions (answers at end of this chapter):

18. When the voice line sustains only one or two long tones, _____ is used by an accompanying instrument to complement and reinforce inner musical coherence.

19. Korean "harmony" or texture can be described in a chordal sense. True or False.

Form (Text Pages 40–43)

Purpose To acquaint the student with one of the most important and popular formal structures of Korean music—sanjo.

Guidance In terms of popularity, sanjo is to Korean classical instrumental music what sonata form is to Western classical instrumental music. Beyond that, no comparisons should be made. Sanjo is instrumental music of a particular type for a solo instrument (which gives the performance its name) and the changgo drum. The author discusses sanjo as it is performed on the kayagum; the name is, therefore, kayagum sanjo. While kayagum sanjo is the most common arrangement, others could be taegum sanjo, komungo (a bass zither) sanjo, and so forth. In each case the structure of the sanjo is similar, and the changgo is always used. Several of the author's points should be stressed. First, sanjo is comprised of six movements or sections that are played continuously, without a break. Secondly, the movements differ from one another because their speeds or tempi, as well as their rhythmic patterns, differ. Sanjo begins slowly and gradually increases in speed and rhythm as each movement is played. It is in some of the movements of sanjo where you can feel the compound duple/triple (6/8) meter that is a characteristic of much Korean music. The author uses the term "tightening and loosening" to explain the flexibility and variety within sanjo, a technique that builds and releases tension. Thirdly, sanjo is improvised, and involves much musical, visual, and aural interaction between the melodic instrumentalist and the changgo drummer. Sanjo is rhythmically, melodically, and ornamentally very subtle, complex, and exciting.

Terms Define or identify the following terms, based on readings from text and/or other sources.

22. sanjo

23. improvisation

Reading Comprehension Answer the following work questions (answers at end of this chapter):

20. Sanjo is characterized by having _____ movements that are played _____ pause.

21. Sanjo movements are characterized by variety of _____ and _____.

22. A thirty minute sanjo performance may be simplified and reduced to seven minutes while still retaining a sense of musical movement and change. True or False.

23. The tempo or speed of sanjo begins fast and gradually slows until it reaches the end. True or False.

24. Each sanjo subsection (sections of a movement) has an equal number of beats. True or False.

Video Viewing

1. Hyangak—court music: "P'yojongmanbangjigok" (1-1). *The JVC Video Anthology of World Music and Dance*, East Asia I, Volume 1, Korea 1 (VTMV-31).
2. Kayagum pyongch'ang—song with kayagum: "Sae-t'aryong" ("Song of the Birds") (1-5). *The JVC Video Anthology of World Music and Dance*, East Asia I, Volume 1, Korea 1 (VTMV-31).
3. Chongak: taegum solo: "Sangyongsan" from "P'yongjo hoesang" (1-6). *The JVC Video Anthology of World Music and Dance*, East Asia I, Volume 1, Korea 1 (VTMV-31).
4. P'ansori—sung narrative with drum: "Hungboga" (2-5). *The JVC Video Anthology of World Music and Dance*, East Asia II, Volume 2, Korea 2 (VTMV-32).
5. Nongak—farmer's band (2-8). *The JVC Video Anthology of World Music and Dance*, East Asia II, Volume 2, Korea 2 (VTMV-32).

Sample Test Questions

Multiple choice questions. Only one answer is correct.

1. Korean court music, a subcategory of chong-ak or music for the ruling class, includes: a. ritual music, b. banquet music, c. military music, d. Imperial shrine music, e. all the above.
2. Korean sokak or music for the common man includes all the following except: a. shaman music, b. folk songs, Confucian music, d. sanjo, e. p'ansori.
3. Korean p'ansori, or song in drama, is an opera-like production consisting of: a. spoken description of dramatic content, b. songs, c. physical motion, d. a and b, e. all the above.
4. The Korean word for music is: a. ak, b. sanjo, c. p'iri, d. gum, e. sijo.
5. Korean chong-ak and a-ak can be used interchangeably to refer to: a. Buddhist music, b. lyric song, c. farmer music, d. music for the ruling class, e. opera.
6. The Korean kayagum is a(n): a. idiophone, b. membranophone, c. chordophone, d. aerophone.
7. (Refer to Figure 3-2 on page 34 of text) Where is this instrument positioned when played? a. on the musician's shoulder, b. vertically in

front of the performer, c. horizontally in front of the musician, d. on the musician's lap, e. suspended from a rack.

8. (Refer to Figure 3-3 on page 34 of text) Pitch is modified during performance on this instrument by: a. bowing lightly or strongly, b. pressing the string to be modified, c. pressing the string below the bridge, d. loosening or tightening the tuning pegs, e. increasing or decreasing the tension of the bow string.

9. Which Korean instrument is similar to a Chinese instrument: a. kayagum, b. haegum, c. taegum, d. a and b, e. all the above.

10. The Korean concept of the wavering tone: a. is ornamental in practice, b. is essential in expressing dramatic change, c. is an embellishment, d. is an individualistic practice, e. is only used in vocal music.

11. One way that tension/release patterns in Korean music can be accomplished is through contrast between: a. perfect and imperfect pitch relationships, b. loud and soft volume, c. straight and wavering tone, d. dissonant and consonant chords, e. solo and ensemble.

12. The distance between each two beat-referential-point is different in Korean music; this is known as: a. heterophony, b. wavering tone, c. elastic rhythm, d. tightening and loosening.

13. The simultaneous use of slightly or elaborately modified versions of the same melody by two (or more) performers is known as: a. heterophony, b. wavering tone, c. elastic rhythm, d. tightening and loosening.

14. The technique whereby the tone fluctuates, involving more than one note around the essential note is known as: a. heterophony, b. wavering tone, c. elastic rhythm, d. tightening and loosening.

15. The principle whereby all the movements of Korean sanjo differ from one another, and where all the rhythmic patterns also vary, is known as: a. heterophony, b. wavering tone, c. elastic rhythm, d. tightening and loosening.

16. Korean students of traditional music practice beat patterns by: a. watching and listening to a metronome, b. counting varied intervals of time, c. watching a conductor, d. slowly exhaling and tapping on their legs, e. beating a drum.

17. Recordings of Korean sanjo for foreign markets often: a. present the whole performance, b. include Westernized tunes, c. completely omit the first movement, d. abbreviate each of the six movements, e. perform the music much faster than during a Korean concert.

18. Korean sanjo is basically: a. composed, b. improvised, c. heterophonic, d. colotomic, e. idiophonic.

19. Which instrument is not related to the others: a. haegum, b. cheng, c. koto, d. kayagum.

20. The accompanying instrument in Korean kayagum sanjo is: a. haegum, b. taegum, c. changgo, d. a-ak, e. p'iri.

Answers to Reading Comprehension Questions

1. ruling class, commoner
2. True
3. True
4. a. shaman music, b. Buddhist music, c. folk songs, d. farmers' music, e. dramatic song called p'ansori, f. instrumental solo music called sanjo
5. sixty
6. kayagum
7. a stick, fingers
8. haegum
9. True
10. False: it is associated with ancient military music
11. 135
12. learned
13. False: there are a number of Korean modes
14. True
15. elastic, nonmetric
16. exhale
17. 6/8
18. heterophony
19. False: it literally means the way tones work together
20. six, without
21. rhythmic patterns, tempi or speed
22. True
23. False: just the opposite happens
24. False: the beats vary from section to section, and this is determined by the different schools of playing sanjo

Answers to Sample Test Questions

1. e	2. c	3. e	4. a
5. d	6. c	7. c	8. b
9. e	10. b	11. c	12. c
13. a	14. b	15. d	16. d
17. d	18. b	19. a	20. c

Listening Form

Student Name_____ I.D. Number_____
Course Name _____ Course Number_____
Date_____ Chapter Number_____ Listening Example Number _____
Record or Tape Number_____ Name of Culture and Location _____
Name of Performer(s)_____
Instructions: place an X, ✓, or • in appropriate boxes; give types; indicate native names.

performing elements (if vocal)	solo: M/F	duo: M/F	trio: M/F	quartet: M/F	group: M/F	other: M/F
performing elements (if instrumental)	corpophone	idiophone	membranophone	aerophone	chordophone	electrophone	other
texture	single melody	dense unison	heterophone	imitation	parallelism	disphony	other
more texture	with drone	with time indicator	chordal	polyphonic stratification	colotomy	combination	variable
melodic contour	static	ascending	descending	conjunct	disjunct	undulating	terraced
mode or scale	number of notes	vernacular	using cipher notation (numbers), indicate the mode or scale in ascending order
meter	free	duple	triple	compound	additive	poly	other
speed	very slow	slow	moderate	fast	very fast	variable	other
amplitude	very soft	soft	moderate	loud	very loud	variable	other
timbre (tone color)	clear	breathy	nasal	open	tight	masked	other
inflections	no vibrato	slow vibrato	fast vibrato	wide vibrato	falsetto	multiphonics	other
formal structure	vernacular name	expanding	reverting	strophic	theme and variations	other
structural or performance techniques	ostinato	responsorial	antiphonal	elastic rhythm	if vocal: syllabic or melismatic	non-synchronous parts	other

Chapter 4

Text Pages 48 – 62

Some of Japan's Musics and Musical Principles

William P. Malm

Introduction to Chapter (Text Page 48)

Purpose To introduce Japanese music by making general comparisons of its historical development with the development of music in Europe.

Guidance This chapter is historical in its organization, and musical in its approach; that is, much of the material consists of placing various types of Japanese music into a Japanese historical context, while at the same time describing them as living traditions. The introduction explains how one can see a certain historical parallel between European music and Japanese music, in that they had similar forces from the outside that influenced their development. Music in Western civilization, for example, was influenced by the Greek and Islamic cultures, and Japanese music was influenced by the Chinese and Korean civilizations. Also, both Europe and Japan have derived much of their inspiration for musical development from religion: Europe from Christianity and Japan from Buddhism. However, while Western composers have constantly redefined musical elements and introduced new ideas while abandoning many older forms, many Japanese composers have been inspired to emulate their ancient traditions.

Terms Define or identify the following terms or areas, based on readings from text and/or other sources.

1. Find Japan on a globe and locate Nara, Kyoto, and Tokyo (formerly Edo). Notice the proximity that Japan has to China and Korea.

2. Buddhism

3. Chinese T'ang dynasty

Reading Comprehension Answer the following work questions (answers at end of this chapter):

1. Surviving musical traditions in Japan have their origins in which Japa-

nese historical period: _____.

2. The development of Western and Japanese music shares what two influences: _____ and _____.

3. Before the twentieth century, two of the countries Japan imported music from were:

   _____ and _____.

4. The chronicled length of Western and Japanese music history are about the same. True or False.

5. Japanese music is all based on Islamic and Greek traditions. True or False.

Ancient Japanese Court Music (Text Pages 48–50)

Music Examples

gagaku ensemble (shô, ryuteki, hichiriki, gakusô, gaku-biwa, kakko, shoko, taiko)

court orchestra

Purpose To trace some of the history of gagaku, the court music of Japan, and describe its form, instruments, and tonal system.

Guidance Japanese word for music is "gaku." Gagaku means elegant or refined music, and is the traditional music of the Emperor's royal court. Because of royal patronage since the sixth century, gagaku has survived to become (along with its Korean counterpart a-ak) the oldest orchestral music in the world. Gagaku as performed today may to a certain degree resemble some ancient forms, although there is no way to prove it. Gagaku has two forms determined by its function: one is to play for listening only (kangen), and the other is to play for dancing (bugaku). The listening form uses a full orchestra, while the dancing form excludes the chordophones. In addition, there are two other forms determined by origin: one is from China (tôgaku; the prefix "tô" means "T'ang"), and the other is from Korea (komagaku; koma refers to an ancient part of Korea). The instruments differ slightly in these two forms of music. In general, gagaku uses a multi-single reed mouth organ aerophone, the shô, which is very similar to the Chinese mouth organ (sheng); this instrument plays high chords that seem to hover above the melody. The flutes in gagaku are horizontal instruments that do *not* have membranes; they play with double reed aerophones that do *not* resemble the Chinese sona. The chordophones include the biwa lute and the gakusô (sô, like a koto) zither. The biwa developed from the Chinese p'i-p'a, while the sô developed from the Chinese se; these words in their respective languages are linguistically similar, pointing to the biwa's and gakusô's derivations from Chinese instruments. Likewise, one of the membranophones (san no tsuzumi) used in gagaku is related to the Korean changgo drum. The scales used in gagaku are based on pentatonic forms or cores, although they differ from the Chinese pentatonic scale somewhat (in the notation in Example 4-1, the whole notes indicate the pitches of the scales that form pentatonic cores). Before a gagaku piece is performed in a particular mode or chô, a composed warm up piece (netori or introduction) is performed by the entire orchestra. The author writes that this evokes the mood of the piece, and it is valuable to consider the words "mood" and "mode" as being related in that a mode is not really a scale (which is like a list of pitches in ascending order), but is rather an arrangement of pitches chosen by the culture to evoke a particular feeling.

Terms   Define or identify the following terms, based on readings from text and/or other sources.

4. gagaku

5. gaku

6. tôgaku and T'ang derived music

7. komagaku and Korean derived music

8. shô and relationship to sheng

9. biwa and relationship to p'i-p'a

10. gakusô (sô or koto) and relationship to se (cheng)

Reading Comprehension   Answer the following work questions (answers at end of this chapter):

6. When gagaku music is played to accompany dance (known as bugaku), what group of instruments is left out? _____ .

7. The two basic scales in gagaku are based on _____ _____ cores.

8. The clappers (shakubyôshi) are used by the lead singer in Shinto religious compositions (kagura) to _____ the entrances of the unison chorus and the formal divisions of the piece.

9. Shô performance technique is identical to that of the Chinese sheng and other similar instruments played in Asia. True or False.

10. The chordophones in gagaku play the melody. True or False.

Medieval Narratives and Theatricals
(Text Pages 50–53)

Purpose   To describe the history, instruments and characteristics of the medieval Japanese theatrical form called noh (nô) or noh drama, and in the process introduce six important aphorisms or profound statements about Japanese music and one about all music.

Guidance   Japanese noh (the "h" after an "o" in the Romanization of Japanese indicates that it is a long "o"; other forms of writing that character are to use either "ô" or "o", which are all pronounced the same way) drama and its music (nohgaku or nôgaku) are probably quite different from their ancient prototypes. Popular entertainments associated with religious events form the basis of noh. Its present rather esoteric form was introduced by the Zen Buddhist-inspired Kannami and his son Zeami in the late fourteenth and early fifteenth centuries. Nohgaku is influenced by Buddhist singing, and noh plots are often based on Buddhist themes. In the author's discussion the following six profound statements (aphorisms) are made about Japanese music: (1) improvisation plays almost no role; (2) notation is only a memory aid, and the real knowledge about musical traditions is held and dispersed by authorized teachers; (3) the sound of a small group (chamber music) is more desirable than that of a large group (orchestra); (4) the actual physical aspect of making music is as important as the music and the performer itself; (5) often not many musical sounds are used, but they have a great effect; and (6) a three-part structure called jo (slow introduction), ha (scattering or sudden outburst of energy), and kyû (rushing towards the end or focusing of the energy) is often found as an aesthetic concept. In addition, the author points out that although music is *not* an international language, the many types of music in the world are similar to languages and, because they are logically structured, they can be learned. This reinforces one of the statements made by Bruno Nettl in Chapter 1.

Terms

Define or identify the following terms or people, based on readings from text and/or other sources.

11. noh drama

12. nohgaku

13. Kannami and Zeami

14. hayashi

15. jo-ha-kyû

Reading Comprehension

Answer the following work questions (answers at end of this chapter):

11. Noh drama grew out of various forms connected with _____.

12. The noh actors' parts are divided into _____ sections and actual _____.

13. Melodies of noh songs are categorized into _____ and _____ types.

Some of Japan's Musics and Musical Principles   43

14. Much Japanese music, and especially nohgaku, is improvised. True or False.

15. The drum calls in noh are used to _____ and control the entire ensemble in lieu of a conductor.

16. The hayashi is situated in an orchestra pit in front of the noh stage. True or False.

17. Noh melodies are centered around three pitches designated as low, middle, and high. True or False.

18. The musical secrets of a school's tradition are passed on by old manuscripts. True or False.

19. Noh texts are sung by a few main actors and a unison chorus. True or False.

20. The three-part Japanese structural and aesthetic concept is called _____ _____ _____; give the English meaning or explanation for each of the three parts, in their proper order:

   a. _____,

   b. _____,

   c. _____.

Edo Period Instrumental and Theatrical Music
(Text Pages 53–59)

Purpose   To acquaint the student with three important instruments of the seventeenth through the nineteenth centuries—the koto, the shakuhachi, and the shamisen—and two popular dramatic forms of the same time period—bunraku and kabuki.

Guidance   The koto (a zither-type chordophone) was an early instrument in gagaku, and was once also played by blind male musicians. In the past it was also a favorite musical instrument of royal court ladies, and today, along with the piano, it is a status symbol for cultured young woman preparing for marriage. The koto is related to the Chinese cheng and the Korean kayagum, and it probably developed from the cheng and the native Japanese wa-gon, a Shinto zither also with movable bridges. The two major schools (ryû) of koto, the Ikuta and the Yamada (the term "Kengyô" is an honorific title given to blind koto masters; in Japan, as in China, a person's last name appears first), differ in that the latter features more vocal styles than the former. Nevertheless, a basic repertory exists that can be performed either solo, in duet with another koto or with a shamisen, or in trio with koto, shamisen (the classical musicians prefer the term sangen), and shakuh-

♪

Music Examples

koto

chordophone

plucked zither

> **Music Examples**
> *shakuhachi*
>
> *aerophone*
>
> *vertical flute*

achi (this is called sankyoku style, or music for three instruments).

The shakuhachi, an end-blown, vertical, flute-type aerophone of bamboo, was an instrument of certain Zen Buddhist priests of Japan. It also became a favored instrument of the samurai warrior class. The shakuhachi has its origin in China, but it does not have a membrane like some Chinese and Korean flutes. The main school (ryû) of shakuhachi, the aristocratic Kinko school, to a certain degree strives to maintain profound Buddhist philosophical ideals with its solo music, whereas the newer Tôzan school caters to the common man and teaches to large groups. The music, teaching techniques, and performance practice of these two schools reflect a basic difference in economics and social class.

The shamisen is a 3-stringed, skin-covered, box-shaped, lute-type chordophone associated with many musical genres in Japan, such as the entertainment world of the geisha, the diverse world of folk music, classical solo (with voice) and ensemble performances with koto and shakuhachi, and the dramatic musics of the bunraku and kabuki theaters.

Terms
Define or identify the following terms, based on readings from text and/or other sources.

16. koto

17. Ikuta ryû

18. Yamada ryû

19. shakuhachi

20. Kinko ryû

21. Tôzan ryû

22. shamisen

23. sankyoku

24. bunraku

25. kabuki

> **Music Example**
> *shamisen (sangen)*
>
> *chordophone*
>
> *plucked lute*

Reading Comprehension
Answer the following work questions (answers at end of this chapter):

21. Most of the koto literature performed today comes from the _____ period.

22. The ensemble of koto, shakuhachi, and shamisen is called _____.

23. The shamisen developed out of an instrument from China called the _____.

24. Shamisen music can be divided into two basic types: _____ and _____.

25. Each koto and shakuhachi school has its own system of written memory aids (form of notation). True or False.

26. The koto has a lower string which creates sawari, a buzzing sound. True or False.

27. The Edo period puppet theater of Japan is called _____.

28. The Edo period melodramatic theater with live actors is called _____.

29 Accompanying musicians for the kabuki theater can be placed either onstage or off stage in a small room. True or False.

30. The main instruments pictured in Figures 4-4 and 4-5 of the text book (back row) are _____.

Music Since Meiji (Text Pages 59–60)

Purpose   To discuss how music in Japan has changed since 1868 with the opening of Japan to Western culture.

Guidance   For several centuries, Japan had an isolationist policy, imposed by its shogun military dictators. In July of 1853, however, that policy began to unfold when American Commodore Matthew Perry entered the Tokyo (then Edo) bay with his black ships. Perry was finally allowed to come ashore at Yokohama on March 8, 1854, and thus began an awakening of Japan by the United States that resulted in an end to Japan's feudalistic military rule and an eventual restoration of the Emperor as the supreme ruler. This Emperor was named Meiji, and his rule began in 1868 and lasted until 1913, when the Taisho period began. In 1926, the Showa period began, lasting until the death of Emperor Hirohito in 1987. Thus, each period coincides with a particular Emperor.

Just as Japan had eagerly absorbed Chinese culture many centuries ago, musical ideas of Western civilization began to be adopted in the Meiji period and have flourished up to the present. The opening of Japan to the West has vastly changed a culture that had kept so many ancient traditions intact. Certain religious values and concepts, foods, dress, and music underwent Westernization. Today in Japan folk music, traditional music (hôgaku), new traditional music, and Western-type classical music, jazz, and pop are found side by side. There are also progressive ensembles that feature traditional Japanese instruments playing compositions based on current Western compositional techniques, and large koto ensembles performing arrangements of works by Handel, Vivaldi, Mozart, Debussy, and others. Popular culture in Japan often tends to mix Eastern and Western musical

---

♪

Music Example

sankyoku ensemble (koto, sangen, shakuhachi)

music for three instruments

ideas, and Japanese music has even influenced Western rock and new age groups. Western rock bands such as Rush and Dire Straits, for example, employ shakuhachi and koto sounds produced on their Japanese synthesizers, and some rock groups (Hiroshima, for example) play actual Japanese instruments along with the usual Western ones.

Walking the streets of Kyoto, Nara, Tokyo, Hirosaki, or any city and town in Japan, can be a musical experience, if you are lucky. More often than not, the only music you will hear is American or Japanese pop. Each locale, however, has its musical nooks and crannies, such as Buddhist temples, live houses (like bars or coffee houses where music is performed), museums, and theaters. Some of my favorite places to find traditional culture and music is the flea market at Tôji Temple in Kyoto (where they always have old used shakuhachi flutes for sale), the Shamisen Live House in Hirosaki (where you can hear tsugaru shamisen), the bunraku theater in Tokyo, and especially the temples in Nara, where there is often Buddhist or Shinto chanting. I particularly like the countryside, where music is not common, but the clanking of the bamboo irrigation tubes is a music of sorts. I have heard wonderful folk music and seen folk dancing in Sado Jima, a very remote island in the Sea of Japan, off the west coast of Honshu. I have heard and seen excellent performances of Ainu (indigenous people) music and dance in Hokkaido, done for tourists, but done very well. Japan is a fascinating place, and the people are fast paced, but very friendly. The author of this chapter, Dr. Malm, once told me (rather tongue in cheek, I think) that Japan is not a far eastern culture, but a far western one. While that observation is true in many ways, I would say that Japan is what you want it to be, and like any modern country in the twenty-first century, it has nearly everything for everyone.

Terms   Define or identify the following terms or people, based on readings from text and/or other sources.

26. Meiji Restoration

27. hôgaku

28. Miyagi Michio

29. Takemitsu Toru

Reading Comprehension   Answer the following work questions (answers at end of this chapter):

31. The period when Japan began to modernize, beginning in 1868, and which had a tremendous effect on its music, is the _____ period.

32. The last name of the best-known composer of modern koto music (according to the text book) is _____.

33. The Japanese aesthetic of "maximum effect from a minimum amount of material" has been accomplished by Toru Takemitsu using the _____.

34. Traditional and Western musical forms exist side-by-side in modern Japan. True or False.

35. It is impossible to mix such different musical systems as the Japanese and the Western to create a performable music. True or False.

Video Viewing

1. *Discovering the Music of Japan*, BFA.
2. *Gagaku*, University of Oklahoma.
3. *The Japanese Sounds of Music—Sukiyaki and Chips.* Beats of the Heart series. Jeremy Marre, director and producer.

Sample Test Questions

Multiple choice questions. Only one answer is correct (answers at end of this chapter):

1. The main religion in Japan that has influenced music since the sixth century is: a. Christianity, b. Shintoism, c. Buddhism, d. Hinduism, e. Islam.

2. What sources reveal music to have existed in Japan as early as the third century A.D.? a. Korean, b. Chinese, c. archaeological, d. a and b, e. b and c.

3. Gagaku has been influenced directly by all of these countries except: a. China, b. Iran, c. Manchuria, d. Korea, e. India.

4. In jo-ha-kyu, the "ha" means: a. introduction, b. scattering, c. rushing to the end, d. ending, e. warm up.

5. How do we know for sure that certain stringed instruments were played as melodic instruments by courtiers (court musicians) in the 11th century? a. they are played melodically in gagaku, b. it is written in the Emperor's diary, c. it is described in Murasaki's novel *The Tale of Genji*, d. they are played that way in China and Korea, e. the notations have dates on them.

6. Partbooks for gagaku instruments: a. were only memory aids, and were not strictly notated, b. were quite detailed, c. were in Western notation, d. were written only recently, e. do not exist.

7. The tonal system of gagaku is based on ancient Chinese and: a. Russian sources, b. Islamic sources, c. Buddhist sources, d. Hindu sources, e. Christian sources.

8. In jo-ha-kyu, the "jo" means: a. introduction, b. scattering, c. rushing to the end, d. ending, e. warm up.

9. The literal translation of noh is: a. drama, b. religious play, c. elegant

music, d. accomplishment, e. opera.

10. Which is *not* characteristic of the noh drama and other Japanese musical genres? a. chamber rather than orchestral sound, b. emphasis on not only what is played but also how it is played, c. jo-ha-kyu form, d. maximum effect from a minimum amount of sonic material, e. improvisation.

11. The vocal interjections in noh (yo-ho) function to: a. combine with the drums to create a perceivable pattern, b. cue the actors, c. add comedy to the serious theme, d. warm up the voice in preparation to sing, e. give the singers their pitch.

12. Biwa players took the Chinese san-hsien and reconstructed it into its Japanese counterpart, the shamisen, by changing: a. the oval shape to rectangular, b. the skin from snake to cat or dog, c. the bone finger picks to a large plectrum, d. the lower string to create a buzz, e. all the above.

13. What ensemble accompanies the bunraku puppet theater? a. nagauta ensemble, b. shamisen and narrator, c. sankyoku, d. hayashi, e. koto and shakuhachi.

14. The "slide rule" effect in Japanese music can best be described as: a. sympathetic vibration of strings, b. a gradual rise in pitch, c. two units rhythmically out of synchronization, d. additive meter, e. non-conventional harmony.

15. In jo-ha-kyu, the "kyu" means: a. introduction, b. scattering, c. rushing to the end, d. ending, e. warm up.

16. Japanese puppet theater is called: a. kabuki, b. noh, c. gagaku, d. bunraku, e. sankyoku.

17. What medium is especially adaptable to the modern Japanese composer's sensitivity to texture, timing and musical gesture? a. fusion jazz, b. string quartets, c. woodwind quintets, d. electronic music, e. orchestral music.

18. The ensemble in Figure 4-5 of your text book is playing what kind of music? a. nohgaku, b. gagaku, c. bunraku, d. sankyoku, e. kabuki.

19. The ensemble in Figure 4-2 of your text book is playing what kind of music? a. nohgaku, b. gagaku, c. bunraku, d. sankyoku, e. kabuki.

20. The ensemble in Figure 4-1 of your text book is playing what kind of music? a. nohgaku, b. gagaku, c. bunraku, d. sankyoku, e. kabuki.

Answers to Reading Comprehension Questions

1. Nara period
2. foreign cultures, religion
3. China, Korea

4. True
5. False: it is based on Chinese, Korean, and native Japanese traditions
6. strings (chordophones)
7. pentatonic
8. signal
9. False: the shô plays chords, while the sheng and others play melodies, drones, and occasional chords
10. False: they play stereotyped rhythmic passages
11. religious events
12. recitative, songs
13. lyrical, strong
14. False; there is very little improvisation in Japanese music
15. signal
16. False: in noh drama the hayashi sits on stage, behind the action of the actors
17. True
18. False: they are passed on by certified teachers
19. True
20. jo-ha-kyu: jo = slow introduction, ha = the scattering or sudden outburst of energy, kyu = rushing towards the end or focusing of the energy
21. Edo period
22. sankyoku
23. san-hsien
24. lyrical, narrative
25. True
26. False: the shamisen does, but not the koto
27. bunraku
28. kabuki
29. True
30. shamisen
31. Meiji period
32. Miyagi
33. synthesizer
34. True
35. False: it is very possible, and has been done by many Japanese composers, including Takemitsu.

Answers to Sample Test Questions

1. c
2. e
3. b
4. b
5. c

6. a
7. c
8. a
9. d
10. e
11. a
12. e
13. b
14. c
15. c
16. d
17. d
18. e
19. a
20. b

Listening Form

Student Name _____ I.D. Number _____
Course Name _____ Course Number _____
Date _____ Chapter Number _____ Listening Example Number _____
Record or Tape Number _____ Name of Culture and Location _____
Name of Performer(s) _____
Instructions: place an X, ✓, or • in appropriate boxes; give types; indicate native names.

performing elements (if vocal)	solo: M/F	duo: M/F	trio: M/F	quartet: M/F	group: M/F	other: M/F
performing elements (if instrumental)	corpophone	idiophone	membranophone	aerophone	chordophone	electrophone	other
texture	single melody	dense unison	heterophone	imitation	parallelism	disphony	other
more texture	with drone	with time indicator	chordal	polyphonic stratification	colotomy	combination	variable
melodic contour	static	ascending	descending	conjunct	disjunct	undulating	terraced
mode or scale	number of notes	vernacular	using cipher notation (numbers), indicate the mode or scale in ascending order
meter	free	duple	triple	compound	additive	poly	other
speed	very slow	slow	moderate	fast	very fast	variable	other
amplitude	very soft	soft	moderate	loud	very loud	variable	other
timbre (tone color)	clear	breathy	nasal	open	tight	masked	other
inflections	no vibrato	slow vibrato	fast vibrato	wide vibrato	falsetto	multiphonics	other
formal structure	vernacular name	expanding	reverting	strophic	theme and variations	other	
structural or performance techniques	ostinato	responsorial	antiphonal	elastic rhythm	if vocal: syllabic or melismatic	non-synchronous parts	other

Chapter 5

Text Pages 63 – 82

The Music of Thailand

David Morton

Introduction to Chapter (Text Page 63)

Purpose To introduce the topic of Southeast Asian traditional art music.

Guidance This chapter discusses the history, organology (musical instruments), and construction of the art music (classical music) from Thailand. It can broadly be used to represent the art musics of Southeast Asia as a whole, since the countries of Thailand, Burma, Laos, Vietnam, and Cambodia share many musical characteristics. The author, a composer, discusses Thai music in an analytical and objective manner. He explains his attraction to the art music of Southeast Asia, and how the lack of materials (books, recordings, and scores) about Thai music specifically led him to visit Thailand and investigate Thai music. He describes his first encounter with a live traditional Thai musical ensemble.

History (Text Pages 63–66)

Purpose To trace the cultural history of Thailand and relate it to the development of Thai music.

Guidance Until the latter part of the 1200s the Thai people inhabited the Canton district of southern China, and culturally the Thai and the Chinese were very similar. The Mongol invasion and conquest of China between approximately 900 and 1300 A.D. caused the Thai to migrate southward, spreading into the present regions of Laos, Vietnam, Burma, and Thailand. This helps us to understand why there are musical similarities within these countries. Several historical reasons for the differences among much of the musics of Southeast Asia and China were the influences of regional civilizations such as the Khmer of present Cambodia and outside civilizations such as the Javanese to the south.

Terms Define or identify the following terms or areas, based on readings from text and/or other sources.

1. Locate the region of Southeast Asia on a globe.

2. Thailand (old name is Siam)

3. Laos

4. Burma

5. Cambodia

6. Vietnam (old name is North Vietnam and South Vietnam)

7. Khmer

8. India

9. Java

Reading Comprehension Answer the following work questions (answers at end of this chapter):

1. What great ancient kingdom, captured by the Thai in 1450, influenced Thai music?

   _____.

2. One of the only ways we can know anything about Khmer music is through _____.

3. Until the thirteenth century, the musics of the Thai and Chinese people were virtually the same. True or False.

4. Study the picture in Figure 5-1, and list the four musical instrument types from left to right:

   _____, _____,

   _____, _____.

Thai Musical Instruments (Text Pages 66–69)

Purpose To identify the cultural background and physical characteristics of Thai musical instruments.

Guidance The author discusses the four sources for Thai musical instruments and divides them into the following four main categories: (1) melodic percussion, or struck idiophones with fixed pitch, (2) strings, or chordophones, (3) winds, or aerophones, and (4) rhythmic percussion, or idiophones and membranophones without fixed pitches.

Several instruments are in the first category, and a common type is the xylophone ("xylon" is Greek for wood, and the marimba, which has African origins, is the common xylophone used in America). Another is the metallophone, probably derived from Javanese music (a common metallophone in America is the vibraphone or vibraharp, commonly known as "vibes").

The gong circle known as *khong wong lek* is one of the most unique metallophones in the world. You can see several in Figures 5-3 and 5-4, as they are used in the pi-phat and mahori ensembles. A prototype can be seen in the sculpture in Figure 5-1.

There are two types of chordophone found in Thailand, the two-stringed bowed lute that is similar to the Chinese (the hu-chin in China, which includes the erh-hu) and Korean models, and the three-stringed "spiked fiddle" (the fingerboard, like a spear that pierces the body of the lute and comes out the end to rest on the floor) which has its origin in the Middle East (both types can be seen in Figure 5-4, the Chinese type in the back and the Middle Eastern type in the front). Another important distinction between the northern Chinese fiddle and the Middle Eastern type is that the former has its tuning pegs coming in from the back of the top part of the finger board, and the latter has its tuning pegs coming in from the side of the top part of the finger board (carefully compare the pictures in Figures 2-1, 3-3, 5-4, and 7-6). Besides the jakhe zither in Thailand, the Vietnamese have a zither that is nearly identical to the Chinese cheng, and the Burmese have a harp tradition that has very ancient roots.

There are two types of aerophone that should be remembered: the pi and the khaen. The pi is an "oboe" type of instrument except that rather than a double reed, a quadruple reed consisting of four layers that beat together is used. Like oboe-types throughout the world, the pi is mostly used for outdoor performances. One of the court orchestra types, the pi-phat, derives its name from the pi because it is an outdoor orchestra in which the pi plays the melody. The khaen is a multitubed, single reed aerophone (mouth organ) that is related to the Chinese sheng and the Japanese shô. Unlike those instruments, however, the pipes of the khaen extend below the gourd wind chest as well as above it (look at Figure 5-2). For Western students, the music of this instrument is usually the most interesting of Southeast Asian music.

In the final category is a set of idiophones, the ching (whose name is onomatopoeic, i.e., derived from the sound it makes), and several membranophones. In the latter group of instruments it is possible to determine their origins because of their construction techniques, as the author has explained. It is often possible to use the physical characteristics of musical instruments to understand migration patterns of people or to understand about trade routes, military conquests, religious intrusions, and so forth. Can you think of other instances in which musical instruments can suggest to us that type of information? Finally, be aware of the fact that the two court orchestra ensembles, the pi-phat and the mahori, are functional because the former is an outdoor orchestra (it uses the loud sounding pi quadruple reed "oboe") while the latter is an indoor orchestra (it uses the soft sounding bowed lutes and vertical flute-type aerophones).

Terms Define or identify the following terms or areas, based on reading from text and/or other sources.

10. pi

♪

Music Example

khong wong lek

idiophone

gong circle

♪

Music Example

khaen

aerophone

mouth organ

11. khaen (*can*)

12. ching

13. pi-phat

14. mahori

15. khong wong lek (khawng wong lek)

16. metallophone

17. xylophone

18. spiked fiddle

Reading Comprehension Answer the following work questions (answers at end of this chapter):

5. Most of the instruments used in Thai music can be traced to the following four sources:
   _____, _____,
   _____, _____.

6. List the four main categories of principal instruments of traditional Thai music:
   _____, _____,
   _____, _____.

7. The most important folk instrument, which consists of a number of long thin bamboo tubes, each with a free metal reed, is the _____ _____ .

8. The Thai instruments with Khmer origin were probably derived from models from _____ and _____ .

9. Thai instruments from China are mostly _____ and _____, or, using ethnomusicological classification are _____-phones and _____-phones.

10. Two instruments, a three-stringed "spiked fiddle" and a goblet-shaped drum are derived from _____ .

11. The two main types of Thai melodic percussion instruments are _____ _____ and _____ _____ .

12. An ancient harp tradition is today found in which Southeastern Asian country _____ .

13. One of the principal Thai ensembles, which consists of melodic and rhythmic percussion instruments and the pi, is called _____; it plays for indoor functions. True or False.

14. Thai membranophones that are Chinese in origin are characterized by _____ _____.

15. Thai membranophones that are Middle Eastern in origin are characterized by _____ _____.

16. Thai membranophones that are Indian and Southeast Asian (Khmer) in origin are characterized by _____ _____.

The Fundamentals of Thai Music (Text Pages 69–79)

Purpose To acquaint the student with the elements of Southeast Asian music, and specifically those of the music of Thailand.

Guidance The author's very detailed and analytical discussion of Thai music is organized into the following six categories: texture (text pages 69–70), tuning (text pages 70–71), melody (text pages 71–72), rhythm (text pages 72–73), modality (text pages 73–75), and form (text pages 75–78).

Texture: The term "polyphonic stratification" is explained in such a way as to be perhaps confused with heterophony. Linear texture could perhaps be explained by using the following continuum:

unison - heterophony - imitation - polyphonic stratification - disphony

(Disphony is separate parts or counterpoint). Looked at this way, heterophony bleeds into polyphonic stratification, and where one ends and the other begins is a moot point. Indeed, music cannot so easily be categorized into clear-cut frameworks. The idea of "layering," however, is an important one for understanding much non-Western music.

Tuning: In Southeast Asia two common tuning systems (scales) are the Chinese pentatonic, and the pentatonic tuning system discussed by the author, which is based on five pitches chosen from the total seven equidistant pitches within the octave. It must first be realized that the second scale (the Thai scale) cannot be approximated on the piano, nor can it be accurately notated with Western notation. Thus, if you sing any of the notations in this chapter, you will not grasp the Thai tuning. If you sing the notations (or play them on any Western instrument), they will sound like Western or Chinese music, and not Thai music. This is a type of complexity for which words and Western notation are of little use for explanation. It is essential to listen to the music and to hear the tunings of the instruments.

Melody: The author explains that the motivic melodic style is older, while the lyric melodic style is newer. The notations in Examples 5-4 and 5-5 clarify their differences.

Rhythm: Likewise, rhythmic structure can be best appreciated through listening. Essential to Southeast Asian rhythmic structure is the metrical pulse that is outlined by the small cymbals known as the ching. The open sound (ching) and the closed sound (chap) alternate in patterns that provide the basis for the form of the music. The author explains how the system of emphasis places the strong beat at the end of the phrase, which is just the opposite of the use of emphasis (what we feel as a down beat) in Western music. A close analogy, however, is Jamaican reggae music, which emphasizes beats two and four, rather than beats one and three.

Modality: This concept is related to tuning in that you must understand the tuning before modality can be understood. The music of Southeast Asia may be based on any one of the five pitches of the pentatonic scale. These can shift (move from one to another) during a composition, and the practice has been termed "metabole" by a French ethnomusicologist.

Form: The basic concept is that the ching forms the basis for Southeast Asian music. Three sections are standard when considering overall form: slow, medium, and fast.

Terms Define or identify the following term, based on the readings from text and/or other sources.

19. polyphonic stratification

Reading Comprehension   Answer the following work questions (answers at end of this chapter):

17. The texture of Thai traditional music is based on a technique that Mantle Hood has termed _____.

18. Thai instruments of fixed pitch are tuned to an _____ system of seven pitches per octave.

19. The older style of Thai melodies may be termed _____, while the newer style may be considered _____.

20. The _____ (small cymbals) alternate between _____ or _____ sounds and _____ or _____ sounds.

21. There seem to be indications that the Indian raga system left some appreciable marks on Thai music. True or False.

22. The Thai system of emphasis places the strong beat on beat one. True or False.

Other Kinds of Thai Music and Conclusion
(Text Pages 79–80)

Purpose To complement Thai mainstream traditional music with other music, dance, and theatrical forms in Thailand.

Guidance In addition to the musics discussed in the main body of this chapter, music is also used to accompany traditional Thai theater and dance. There are also many folk songs in Thailand, and the author classifies them into chant-like songs where the words seem to be more important than the music, and what he calls "true" songs, where the melody seems to be more important than the words. Often vocables are used by singers (vocables are sung syllables, such as "fa, la, la" in English). Another genre of music is popular song, which reveals a mixture of pentatonicism with Western harmonies. The author's final discussion is about musical change, and it is important to understand that traditional music in many cultures, especially where it was a part of royal courts, is often forgotten about when governments modernize or change in other ways (as in China). Traditional music has often served a purpose that has little relevance today. It is usually replaced by some type of popular music that displays many Western characteristics, such as harmony, lyrical melodies, rhythms, and so forth.

Terms Define or identify the following terms or areas, based on readings from text and/or other sources.

20. chant-like songs

21. true songs

22. vocables

Reading Comprehension Answer the following work questions (answers at end of this chapter):

23. In traditional Thai theater, the actors have an active role in singing. True or False.

24. Thai dance is almost entirely derived from _____ culture, in which dance postures and hand positions are extremely important.

25. Vocal style in Thai traditional music is similar to other Asian vocal styles in that there is little or no vibrato, and pitches other than those of the fixed tuning system are used. True or False.

26. When the standard ensembles are used for ceremonies, they play any kinds of music. True or False.

27. In the chant-like Thai folk songs, the vocal line is more in the nature of _____.

28. Many Thai have begun to learn how to play traditional music as a hobby. True or False.

29. Royal musicians were highly paid and had great freedom in the past. True or False.

30. The Thai language restricts melody, and _____ such as "oh" and "ah" are often sung.

Video Viewing

1. Dan tranh—zither ensemble: "Treo len nui thien thai" ("Climbing Mt. Thien Thai") (Vietnam) (6-6). *The JVC Video Anthology of World Music and Dance*, Southeast Asia I (VTMV-6).
2. Wedding ceremony (Cambodia) (6-15. *The JVC Video Anthology of World Music and Dance*, Southeast Asia I (VTMV-6).
3. Khon—masked dance-drama: "Prince Rama's fight with the Devil King Thosakanth," from the *Ramakian* (Thailand) (7-3). *The JVC Video Anthology of World Music and Dance*, Southeast Asia II (VTMV-7).
4. Jakhe—three-string zither, with ensemble "Lao Phaen" (Thailand) (7-5). *The JVC Video Anthology of World Music and Dance*, Southeast Asia II (VTMV-7).
5. So sam sai—bowed lute solo: "Khaek mon" (Thailand) (7-7). *The JVC Video Anthology of World Music and Dance*, Southeast Asia II (VTMV-7).
6. Molam—song and dance genre (*khaen*) (Thailand) (7-9). *The JVC Video Anthology of World Music and Dance*, Southeast Asia II (VTMV-7).
7. Saung performance (Burma) (7-15). *The JVC Video Anthology of World Music and Dance*, Southeast Asia II (VTMV-7).
8. *Two Faces of Thailand—A Musical Portrait*. Beats of the Heart series. Jeremy Marre, director and producer.

Sample Test Questions

Multiple choice questions. Only one answer is correct.

1. During which Chinese dynasty did peoples of the southern territory of China begin to develop an organized culture in which one integrated group became known as the Thai: a. T'ang, b. Han, c. Sung, d. Mongol.

2. The music of the Khmer culture probably contained elements from: a. Laos, b. Burma, c. India, d. Japan, e. Indonesia.

3. Thai music today contains elements from all but which one of the following cultures: a. Chinese, b. Javanese, c. Indian, d. Japanese, e. Khmer.

4. The Southeast Asian pi is an aerophone with: a. single reed, b. double reed, c. triple reed, d. quadruple reed, e. flute mouthpiece.

5. The front part of Thai and Burmese zithers was carved to represent the head of what animal: a. fish, b. bird, c. crocodile, d. snake, e. tiger.

6. Which is not a traditional Southeast Asian idiophone: a. gong circle, b. xylophone, c. gong chimes, d. gong-kettles, e. stone chimes.

7. Bowed lutes in Southeast Asia have how many strings: a. one, b. two, c. three, d. a and b, e. b and c.

8. Which Southeast Asian court music ensemble has an outdoor function: a. gagaku, b. mahori, c. nohgaku, d. pi-phat, e. sanjo.

9. Which Southeast Asian court music ensemble has an indoor function: a. gagaku, b. mahori, c. nohgaku, d. pi-phat, e. sanjo.

10. Which Southeast Asian musical instrument is a folk instrument: a. ching, b. khaen, c. pi, d. jakhe, e. ti.

11. The Southeast Asian ching belongs to which category: a. melodic percussion idiophone, b. rhythmic percussion idiophone, c. melodic percussion membranophone, d. rhythmic percussion membranophone, e. none of the choices.

12. The Southeast Asian xylophone belongs to which category: a. melodic percussion idiophone, b. rhythmic percussion idiophone, c. melodic percussion membranophone, d. rhythmic percussion membranophone, e. none of the choices.

13. The Southeast Asian gong chimes belong to which category: a. melodic percussion idiophone, b. rhythmic percussion idiophone, c. melodic percussion membranophone, d. rhythmic percussion membranophone, e. none of the choices.

14. The Southeast Asian khaen belongs to which category: a. melodic percussion idiophone, b. rhythmic percussion idiophone, c. melodic percussion membranophone, d. rhythmic percussion membranophone, e. none of the choices.

15. Thai traditional music is always in which meter whenever a steady tempo is observed: a. triple, b. duple, c. single, d. compound duple (6/8), e. nonmeter.

16. The metrical pulse of Southeast Asian music is outlined by the: a. khaen, b. ching, c. pi, d. gong circle, e. xylophone.

17. When groups of four pulses are played in Thai music, the strong pulse is on which beat: a. first, b. second, c. third, d. fourth, e. fifth.

18. In Thai theater where are the singers? a. since they are the actors they are on stage, b. there are no singers, c. behind the stage, d. off to the side of the stage.

19. Which statement best describes Thai court musicians of the past: a. they were highly paid, b. they were treated as royalty, c. they were servants, d. they were treated as gods, e. they were slaves.

20. Today the music most often heard in Southeast Asian cities is: a. khaen, b. popular, c. court, d. folk, e. theater.

Answers to Reading Comprehension Questions

1. Khmer
2. the carvings of musical instruments on the buildings of ancient Angkor
3. True
4. gong, wind instruments, gong-circle, laced drums
5. China, Khmer models, other foreign sources, original Thai
6. melodic percussion, strings, winds, rhythmic percussion
7. khaen
8. India, Indonesia
9. strings, winds, chordophones, aerophones
10. Middle East
11. bars of wood and of metal (xylophones and metallophones), sets of tuned gongs (gong chimes or sets of gong-kettles)
12. Burma
13. pi-phat, False: it plays for outdoor functions
14. their heads are stretched tightly over the ends of the body and permanently fastened with pegs or nails
15. goblet-shaped bodies
16. their heads are stretched tightly over the ends of the body and are laced together across the entire wooden body
17. polyphonic stratification
18. equidistant
19. motivic, lyric
20. ching, open or undamped, closed or damped
21. False: there is no evidence
22. False: it occurs on beat four
23. False: the actors mime the parts which are sung by soloists who sit at the side of the stage
24. Khmer
25. True
26. False: they play music that is specific for the occasion
27. heightened speech
28. True

29. False: they were actually servants
30. vocables

Answers to Sample Test Questions

1. b
2. c
3. d
4. d
5. c
6. e
7. e
8. d
9. b
10. b
11. b
12. a
13. a
14. e
15. b
16. b
17. d
18. d
19. c
20. b

Listening Form

Student Name_____I.D. Number_____
Course Name _____ Course Number_____
Date_____Chapter Number_____Listening Example Number _____
Record or Tape Number_____Name of Culture and Location _____
Name of Performer(s)_____
Instructions: place an X, ✓, or • in appropriate boxes; give types; indicate native names.

performing elements (if vocal)	solo: M/F	duo: M/F	trio: M/F	quartet: M/F	group: M/F	other: M/F
performing elements (if instrumental)	corpophone	idiophone	membranophone	aerophone	chordophone	electrophone	other
texture	single melody	dense unison	heterophone	imitation	parallelism	disphony	other
more texture	with drone	with time indicator	chordal	polyphonic stratification	colotomy	combination	variable
melodic contour	static	ascending	descending	conjunct	disjunct	undulating	terraced
mode or scale	number of notes	vernacular	using cipher notation (numbers), indicate the mode or scale in ascending order			
meter	free	duple	triple	compound	additive	poly	other
speed	very slow	slow	moderate	fast	very fast	variable	other
amplitude	very soft	soft	moderate	loud	very loud	variable	other
timbre (tone color)	clear	breathy	nasal	open	tight	masked	other
inflections	no vibrato	slow vibrato	fast vibrato	wide vibrato	falsetto	multiphonics	other
formal structure	vernacular name	expanding	reverting	strophic	theme and variations	other	
structural or performance techniques	ostinato	responsorial	antiphonal	elastic rhythm	if vocal: syllabic or melismatic	non-synchronous parts	other

Chapter 6

Text Pages 83 – 110

Some Principles of Indian Classical Music

Bonnie C. Wade

Introduction to Chapter (Text Page 83)

Purpose To examine basic cultural concepts of the music of India.

Guidance The author writes that Hindustani or North Indian music is better known in America than Karnatak or South Indian music, primarily because "Hindustani music is most widely available in [this]... country..." This fact is due to the popularity of the sitar in America and Europe as performed and recorded by Ravi Shankar. From his performances in concerts, with the Beatles (including Shankar's teaching of George Harrison, and the latter's performances as well), on the Verve jazz label, and with Andre Previn, through his teaching at UCLA and in Marin County, California, Ravi Shankar has been heard by millions of Americans. Unfortunately (because it negates its real meaning as artistic music with religious basis), North Indian music became a household sound in hippy pads from San Francisco to London and was often associated with American and European counterculture (this perhaps culminated in Woodstock in the 1960s). In the 1970s North Indian music found a place in the new age movement with performers like John McLaughlin on sitar and Collin Walcott on tabla. In order to truly understand the music of India, however, it is necessary to go beyond these nontraditional versions. One must understand it in terms of the culture that produces it, and in terms of the musical elements that make it up; and, most importantly, one must listen carefully to how the music unfolds.

Terms Define or identify the following terms or areas, based on readings from the text and/or other sources.

1. Find the Indian subcontinent on a globe and compare the details of the map on text page 84 with the details on a globe. Compare India's size with Europe, the United States of America, and China. Called a subcontinent because of its separation from the Asian land mass by the Himalayan Mountains, India lies between the Near East and the Far East. Try to imagine the route that the Islamic invaders must have taken

to reach North India.

2. Hindu

3. Muslim and Islam

4. Hindustani

5. Karnatak (or Carnatic)

6. Ravi Shankar

7. Indus River

Reading Comprehension Answer the following work questions (answers at end of this chapter):

1. Musicians in the Indian classical tradition often offer _____ before practicing or performing music.

2. Indian folk music includes _____ songs, music and dance for _____, and _____ songs for the many religious ceremonies and personal worship.

3. The subcontinent of India is quite large, and it therefore encompasses a wide variety of folk musics and cultural differences. True or False.

4. The classical music of North India is called _____.

5. The classical music of South India is called _____.

6. The north part of India was ruled by _____ from the _____ century through the _____ century.

Hindustani Music—Ensembles and Instruments
(Text Pages 83–85)

Purpose To identify some musical instruments of North Indian or Hindustani music and describe how they are used.

Guidance Musical instruments in Hindustani music play a very important role whether the performance is for voice or for instruments alone. There are always three essential elements that constitute the texture of Hindustani music: melody, drone, and drumming. Some stringed instruments or chordophones, such as the sitar (pictured on text page 85) and sarod (pictured on text page 89), have drone strings that are plucked at the same time that the musician plays the melody. Even then, and along with other instruments that do not have drone capabilities, a drone instrument such as the tambur lute (pictured on text page 94), provides a continuous drone. A wind instrument or aerophone that is prominent both in folk and classical music is the shehnai, a conical double reed oboe that has its origin in the Near East (known as the zurna in Turkey, it is also related to the Chinese sona; all these terms are linguistic cognates, giving further evidence to their connection). The author mentions the technique of circular breathing, which is a method often applied by wind instrument players whereby the performer breathes through his nose while continuing to expel air through his mouth. The musician's cheeks act as a windbag, and the sound produced on the instrument is continuous. The most common skin drum or membranophone in Hindustani music is the tabla, which is actually a set consisting of a single-headed drum called the bayan (played with the left hand) and another, the dayan (played with the right hand). Color photographs of the Indian instruments drawn in your textbook reveal the chordophones to be often impressive works of visual as well as musical art. In addition, photographs of the instruments being played will give you an idea of the sizes of the instruments and their playing techniques. A movie, such as "Discovering the Music of India," is an ideal way to see some of the instruments in action.

Music Example

sitar

chordophone

plucked lute

Terms Define or identify the following terms, based on readings from the text and/or other sources. Be able to identify the picture of the instrument if it is included in the book.

8. drone

9. sitar

10. sarod

11. tambur

12. tabla (dayan and bayan)

13. bin

14. sarangi

Music Example

tabla (tabla and bayan)

membranophone

two piece drum and bols (voice)

Reading Comprehension Answer the following work questions (answers at end of this chapter):

7. List the three elements that make up an ideal ensemble texture in Hindustani music: _____, _____, and _____.

8. Two plucked lute-type chordophones of the Hindustani tradition are the _____ and the _____.

9. Some solo or melodic stringed instruments have their own drone capabilities. True or False.

10. The predominant drum used in North India, which consists of a set of two membranophones beaten with the hands of one player, is a _____.

11. When two solo instruments play in the same performance selection, they never play in unison. True or False.

12. Since Indian music is an ensemble tradition, improvisation is never employed. True or False.

Hindustani Music—Melody (Text Pages 85–89)

Purpose To examine some of the basic concepts and principles of melody in classical North Indian music.

Guidance The term "raga" (in the south) or "rag" (in the north) in India refers to the materials from which melody is made. It is closely related to the term "rasa" which means mood or sentiment. As the author explains, the concept of raga is very definitive as to which notes can or cannot be included in a performance selection. Likewise, gamaks or ornamentations are carefully theorized about and practiced.

Terms Define or identify the following terms, based on readings from the text and/or other sources.

15. raga

16. rag

17. gamak

18. rasa

19. sa

Reading Comprehension Answer the following work questions (answers at end of this chapter):

13. A single raga encompasses _____ and _____ ideas about _____.

14. A Hindustani rag includes a selection of _____, often a distinctive _____ shape, usually a pitch hierarchy, sometimes characteristic _____ on certain pitches, and an association with an _____ of the day, perhaps a _____ of the year, and also with an emotional state of _____.

15. A rag (or raga) is a tune. True or False.

16. When a performer chooses a particular rag, no other pitches than those of that rag can be used. True or False.

17. Rags with many distinctive specifications allow the greatest flexibility for improvisation. True or False.

18. In Hindustani classical music, much of the ornamentation used by a performer is predetermined. True or False.

19. In some rags, certain gamaks must be used on certain pitches. True or False.

20. In classical Indian music, the moods of ragas and the content of _____ _____ are equally a part of the Indian aesthetic theory or _____.

21. Even today a rag must be performed during a particular time of day or for a certain season. True or False.

22. In Rag Bageshri (and therefore in the tune "Balma mori") (Ex. 6-1), the pitch Re always occurs in descending melodic motion. True or False.

23. The seven pitches in Hindustani music are called by the syllables _____ _____ _____ _____ _____ _____ _____ .

24. In "Balma mori" (Ex. 6-1) pitch Sa, the most important pitch in Rag Bageshri, is found in every line of the melody. True or False.

Hindustani Music—Meter (Text Pages 89–91)
Drumming (Text Pages 91–93)

Purpose To examine some of the basic concepts and principles of rhythmic order and drumming in classical Indian music.

Guidance All music cultures have some type of rhythmic order that can be referred to as meter, a term borrowed from rhythm in poetry. Duple meter seems to be basic to humankind, related, perhaps, to life itself (day and night, female and male, up and down, left and right, etc.). Triple meter may have been introduced into Europe by the Catholic Church as a musical symbol of the Trinity, although this is largely speculative. Many other cultures have meters of much more complexity than groupings of two or three counts, and they are often conceptualized, given names, and arranged into types that could be referred to as rhythmic modes (as there are melodic modes). The Near East, India, Korea, ancient Japan, Southeast Asia, and medieval Europe have employed such principles of rhythmic ordering, and the Indian system called tal (tala in South India) may suggest a relationship to the medieval European system known as talea. The rhythmical ordering system in Indian classical music is manifested by the drummer, other percussionists who may also be playing, the melodic performer, and the audience. This section of the chapter makes it very clear that, although improvised, the drummer must be aware of the elaborate structures in the musical performance. All improvised music has some type of structure.

Terms Define or identify the following terms, based on readings from the text and/or other sources.

20. bol

21. tal (or tala)

22. tintal

23. sam

Reading Comprehension Answer the following work questions (answers at end of this chapter):

25. In a performance of Indian music, the audience may keep track of the tal by counting on their fingers. True or False.

26. In the classical Hindustani music tradition, stress is put on _____ accompaniment, _____ theory, and _____ by every performer.

27. Drumming plays only a secondary role in the performance of Hindustani classical music. True or False.

28. For each drum stroke in Hindustani music, there are one or more _____ _____ called _____.

29. In learning Hindustani drumming, one only needs to learn how to play the patterns. True or False.

30. When put into the framework of tal in Hindustani music, drumming sequences are combined with others to form _____.

31. In Hindustani improvisation, musical ideas are brought to an end on count _____ of the next _____ of the tal(a).

Hindustani Music—Structure: Principles of Improvisation (Text Pages 93–96)
Speed (Text Pages 96–97)
Compositions (Text Pages 97–101)

Purpose To introduce the basic structural concepts of Hindustani music—how improvisation is conceived, how speeds (tempi) of sections vary, and what types of compositions are most important. Additionally, historical-cultural observations of musical training and performance are made.

Guidance It is important to understand the elements of musical construction of Hindustani music. All the types are conceptualized in an arch form as depicted on page 97, and the first half of each form is slower and freer than the second half. Improvisation pervades all forms. It is important to realize that even within the first and second halves, the music gradually increases in intensity. Such an increase in intensity (often, but not always, manifested as an increase in speed) is a characteristic of many types of music around the world, such as European sonata form, Near Eastern taqsim, Iranian daramad, Japanese gagaku, and others.

Terms Define or identify the following terms, based on readings from the text and/or other sources.

♪

Music Example

sitar and tabla duet

alap and gat

---

24. alap

25. jor

26. jhala

27. gat

28. dhrupad

29. khyal

30. thumri

Reading Comprehension Answer the following work questions (answers at end of this chapter):

32. In India, different types of concerts will always include the same types of music. True or False.

33. The major selection in a Hindustani instrumental concert can be regarded as a study in musical _____.

34. In Indian music, the composer is the same as the performer. True or False.

35. In alap, the Hindustani musician begins to perform very _____ and intensely, but in _____ rhythm.

36. The intent in alap is to build a climax on the psychological effect of ___ _____.

37. The jhala of Hindustani music is _____- and _____-oriented, and is built in anticipation of the _____ and utilization of a _____.

38. Once a Hindustani musician begins his performance, he maintains a constant speed throughout each section of his music. True or False.

39. Thumri compositions in Hindustani music are different from other types of music because improvisation does not stress _____ or _____, but rather _____, as the artist tries to express the feeling in the poetry.

40. The faster second section of the improvisation shifts focus from "pure rag" in floating rhythm to rag plus an _____ _____ _____.

41. The Hindu reverence for music as a sacred art that characterized pre-Muslim India was maintained in the Muslim courts. True or False.

42. For centuries, the study of music among Muslims in North India has been a_____ affair.

43. The European attitude toward Indian culture helped to uplift music in the eyes of upper-class Indians. True or False.

Karnatak Music (Text Pages 101–104)

Dance Example

Bharata Natyam

South India

Purpose To introduce the unique aspects of South Indian or Karnatak music by comparing them to the music types and characteristics of the Hindustani tradition.

Guidance The musical systems of North and South India have a similar theoretical basis. The main differences between the Hindustani and Karnatak musical traditions as discussed by the author can be attributed to the fact that northern India was subjected to foreign incursions and influences, most notably from the Near East and Central Asia (Mogul invasion), from as early as the twelfth century and continuing consistently through the sixteenth century. Those acculturative forces greatly affected the development of Hindustani music, while Karnatak music developed in a calmer atmosphere. Recall the footnote number 6 on page 85, and you will understand why the spellings of certain instruments and terms for concepts differ slightly between the Persian-influenced Hindi language of the north and the Sanskrit language of the south (tambur in the north and tambura in the south, for example). The important membranophone of Karnatak music, the mridangam, is not pictured; the drawing of the pakhavaj on page 91, however, is nearly identical to the mridangam.

Terms Define or identify the following terms, based on readings from the text and/or other sources.

31. ghatam

32. kanjira

33. mridangam

34. ragam

35. tanam

36. pallavi

37. kriti

38. Bharata Natyam

39. vina

40. tambura

41. melakarta system

Reading Comprehension Answer the following work questions (answers at end of this chapter):

44. Hindustani and Karnatak music stem from the same ancient tradition. True or False.

45. In Karnatak music, less importance is given to _____ or _____ shape for distinguishing ragas, when compared to Hindustani music.

46. Ornamentation is used less profusely in Karnatak music than Hindustani music. True or False.

47. A small musical device such as a _____ (in English) may make a particular Karnatak raga unique.

48. The Karnatak concept of rasa and the way it is carried out are exactly the same as in Hindustani music. True or False.

49. A major difference between the Karnatak and Hindustani systems is that a great deal more attention is paid to classification in the southern tradition. True or False.

50. Acceleration of the rate of tala counts in Karnatak music is not permitted. True or False.

51. Two types of performances in Karnatak musical tradition are the (English words) _____ -oriented and the _____- oriented.

52. A major distinction between the Karnatak and Hindustani cultures is the close relationship between _____ music and _____ music in the south.

53. In Hindu Indian thought, _____, like music making, has been considered an act of _____.

54. A Western _____ is usually one of the instruments that accompanies vocal compositions in Karnatak music.

55. The principal solo instruments in Karnatak music are the (English word) _____ and the _____.

Video Viewing

1. Rudra-vina—plucked zither solo (13-1). *The JVC Video Anthology of World Music and Dance*, South Asia III, India 3 (VTMV-43).
2. Sitar—plucked lute solo (13-2). *The JVC Video Anthology of World Music and Dance*, South Asia III, India 3 (VTMV-43).
3. *Raga: Ravi Shankar*. Produced and directed by Howard Worth. Mystic Fire Video 76329.

Sample Test Questions

Multiple choice questions. Only one answer is correct.

1. In India, religion is often linked to or associated with: a. evangelism, b. music, c. sacrifices, d. industrialism, e. social status.

2. Which type of music is most enjoyed and practiced by the Indian people: a. Western, b. film, c. religious, d. folk, e. rock.

3. The most common Indian music that Westerners hear is that which comes from: a. North India, b. South India, c. central India, d. east India, e. west India.

4. The classical music tradition from South India is called: a. Hindustani, b. Muslim, c. Karnatak, d. Farsi, e. Mogul.

5. The classical music tradition from North India is called: a. Hindustani, b. Muslim, c. Karnatak, d. Farsi, e. Mogul.

6. In some Hindustani performances, a solo instrument is supported by another melody instrument, most often the: a. tambur, b. vina, c. bayan, d. tabla, e. sarangi.

7. One essential element in every Indian musical ensemble is a: a. tambourine, b. pot for burning incense, c. drone, d. bouquet of flowers, e. conductor.

8. Which Hindustani instrument is used primarily to produce the drone effect? a. sitar, b. sarangi, c. bin, d. tambur, e. violin.

9. The tabla is: a. a single-headed metal drum, b. a double-headed wooden drum, c. a set of drums played by one player, d. a single-headed wooden drum, e. c and d.

10. Which Indian instrument has been traditionally associated with outdoor performances and with folk music and has been brought into the forefront as a classical solo instrument? a. shehnai, b. tambur, c. bin, d. sarod, e. sitar.

11. In theory, a Hindustani musician should perform in how many octaves in the course of improvising on a rag? a. 1, b. 2, c. 3. d. 4, e. it does not matter because it is not a theoretical concept.

12. A Hindustani rag includes: a. an association with an hour of the day or season of the year, b. an emotional state of mind, c. a distinctive melodic shape of selected pitches, d. ornamentation on certain pitches, e. all of the above.

13. Interval sizes in Indian music: a. are the same as in Western music, b. are all equal in space, c. are equal in ascending melodic shapes only, d. can be larger or smaller than those in Western music, e. do not exist.

14. Rags are often classified as: a. morning rags, b. midday rags, c. late afternoon rags, d. night rags, e. all the above.

15. In Hindustani drumming, each stroke has: a. a specific hand motion before the stroke is made, b. one or more verbal syllables, c. a counterpart with the melody or solo instrument that is always playing, d. two beats, e. none of the above.

16. Bols are interpreted on the tabla: a. with one hand, b. with one or both hands, c. on left- or right-handed drums, d. on both drums at the same time, e. all of the above.

17. Today, the most commonly used tal in Hindustani music is: a. tintal, b. taltal, c. dektal, d. quetal, e. fulanodetal.

18. Emphasis on melody in Hindustani music is a feature of which musical section? a. jor, b. jhala, c. alap, d. tal, e. a and b.

19. The jor section of a Hindustani instrumental alap gradually: a. decreases the rhythm of a composition, b. quadruples the rhythm, c. changes the tal of a composition, d. signals a change in rasa, e. increases the rhythm and pulse of the improvisation.

20. What happens when the improvisation reaches its release of tension and the focus of the performance is shifted from "pure rag"? a. the tabla enters, b. the song begins, c. the musician suddenly plays low notes, d. the rhythm begins to pulsate.

21. A basic tempo characteristic of classical Hindustani music is: a. slow-fast-medium, b. slow-fast, c. fast-slow-fast, d. medium-slow-fast, e. fast.

22. Count one, which is both the beginning and the end, is known as: a. Pa, b. Sam, c. Tin, d. Sa, e. Ma.

23. The main feature of thumri is the: a. text, b. vocal range, c. instrumental accompaniment, d. performer's ability to adhere to the rag, e. improvisation of an interesting melodic line.

24. In Hindustani music, dhrupad is associated with the pomp and grandeur of the: a. family,
    b. Hindu priests, c. wedding ceremony, d. Mogul courts, e. king.

25. In Hindustani music, thumri can be thought of as which type of music? a. opera, b. religious,
    c. light classical, d. classical, e. jazz.

26. The Karnatak melakarta system specifies that there are how many melody types? a. 5, b. 10,
    c. 72, d. 150, e. an infinite number.

27. Karnatak classical music is often associated with: a. death, b. fertility, c. prosperity, d. dance,
    e. art.

28. The principal melody making medium in Karnatak classical music is the: a. sitar, b. violin,
    c. tambura, d. voice, e. harmonium.

29. Kriti is: a. an instrumental genre, b. a vocal genre, c. unaccompanied religious chant, d. performed only on the flute, e. performed by female singers only.

30. The premier classical dance style of all of India is: a. Kabuki, b. Bharata Natyam, c. Pallavi,
    d. Melakarta, e. Kriti.

Answers to Reading Comprehension Questions

1. prayers
2. work, festive occasions, devotional
3. True
4. Hindustani
5. Karnatak
6. Muslims, thirteenth, nineteenth
7. melody, drone, drumming
8. sitar, sarod
9. True
10. tabla
11. False: they alternate or play in unison
12. False: improvisation is central to the tradition
13. musical, extramusical, melody
14. pitches, melodic, ornamentation, hour, season, mind

15. False: it is a mode
16. True
17. False: rags with few specifications
18. True
19. True
20. song texts, rasa
21. False: it was flexible even for a maharajah, and today recordings, radio broadcasts, and concerts have caused the time of day or season concept to be disregarded
22. True
23. Sa, Re, Ga, Ma, Pa, Dha, Ni
24. True
25. True
26. percussion, metric, improvisation
27. False: it plays a primary role
28. verbal syllables, bol
29. False: the process also involves learning to speak drumming patterns in bols
30. compositions
31. one, cycle
32. False: concerts included different types of music
33. contrast
34. True
35. slowly, freely floating
36. constantly rising pitch register
37. speed, rhythm, drum, meter
38. False: acceleration takes place within unmetered alap and also in the metered portion of the performance as the rate of the tal counts picks up
39. rag, tal, text
40. increasingly pulsating rhythm
41. True
42. family
43. False: the European attitude did nothing to uplift music
44. True
45. ornamentation, melodic
46. False: it is used less
47. slur
48. False: while the concept is the same, the way it is carried out is not.
49. True
50. True
51. improvisation, composition
52. dance, concert
53. dancing, worship
54. violin

55. flute, vina

Answers to Sample Test Questions

1. b	2. d
3. a	4. c
5. a	6. e
7. c	8. d
9. e	10. a
11. c	12. e
13. d	14. e
15. b	16. e
17. a	18. c
19. e	20. d
21. b	22. b.
23. a	24. d
25. c	26. c
27. d	28. d
29. b	30. b

Listening Form

Student Name_____ I.D. Number_____
Course Name _____Course Number _____
Date_____Chapter Number_____Listening Example Number _____
Record or Tape Number_____Name of Culture and Location _____
Name of Performer(s)_____
Instructions: place an X, ✓, or • in appropriate boxes; give types; indicate native names.

performing elements (if vocal)	solo: M/F	duo: M/F	trio: M/F	quartet: M/F	group: M/F	other: M/F	
performing elements (if instrumental)	corpophone	idiophone	membrano-phone	aerophone	chordophone	electrophone	other
texture	single melody	dense unison	heterophone	imitation	parallelism	disphony	other
more texture	with drone	with time indicator	chordal	polyphonic stratification	colotomy	combination	variable
melodic contour	static	ascending	descending	conjunct	disjunct	undulating	terraced
mode or scale	number of notes	vernacular	using cipher notation (numbers), indicate the mode or scale in ascending order
meter	free	duple	triple	compound	additive	poly	other
speed	very slow	slow	moderate	fast	very fast	variable	other
amplitude	very soft	soft	moderate	loud	very loud	variable	other
timbre (tone color)	clear	breathy	nasal	open	tight	masked	other
inflections	no vibrato	slow vibrato	fast vibrato	wide vibrato	falsetto	multiphonics	other
formal structure	vernacular name	expanding	reverting	strophic	theme and variations	other	
structural or performance techniques	ostinato	responsorial	antiphonal	elastic rhythm	if vocal: syllabic or melismatic	non-synchronous parts	other

Chapter 7

Text Pages 111 – 113

Musical Strata in Sumatra, Java, and Bali

Margaret J. Kartomi

Introduction to Chapter (Text Pages 111–113)

Purpose To explore the musical styles of Indonesia by examining the cultural influences that have shaped musical expression in Sumatra, Java, and Bali.

Guidance The musical cultures of Indonesia are as diverse as are the geographic regions that make up that multi-islanded country. This chapter focuses on three of the most populated islands of Indonesia: Sumatra, Java, and Bali (see Figure 7-1 on text page 112). Because of geographical, religious, and historical reasons, there is no single regional or homogeneous Indonesian style of music. The author suggests that the music culture of each region can be examined through four strata that exist, in part, because of geographical isolation. The four strata are identified as elements that have affected religion and other aspects of culture, and that, in turn, have influenced Indonesian musical expression. The first is identified as an "animist artistic stratum," which, as the oldest, can be seen as the tradition of spirit and ancestor worship. The second stratum of influence is the result of the introduction of Indian philosophies and art to Indonesian culture. The third stratum, which brought change in many areas (but not Bali), came about through the introduction of Islam and Muslim-influenced art forms. The fourth stratum resulted through contact with Portuguese nationals.

The author suggests that although common traits are not completely obvious, similarities in musical expressive culture do exist in Indonesia. For example, there are similar languages and folk traditions between islands, as well as shared historical experiences. Religious artistic expressions suggest similarities between the islands, and there are common shared musical instruments, ensembles, and vocal forms. The people of Indonesia enjoy a communal life style, and music is important in their daily lives. Musical instruments such as gongs, kettles, bamboo flutes, and two-headed drums can be seen as common elements amidst diversity.

Terms Define or identify the following terms or areas, based on readings from the text and/or other sources.

1. On a globe locate Indonesia and the following islands: Sumatra, Java, Bali, and Borneo. Also locate the Middle East, Portugal, and the Netherlands (Dutch people).

2. musical strata

3. Balinese barong dance

4. wayang kulit

5. gamelan

6. long fingernail dance

7. kroncong

Reading Comprehension Answer the following work questions (answers at end of this chapter):

1. The three factors that have prevented the growth of any one specific Indonesian musical style are_____, _____, and _____.

2. Instruments such as gongs, kettles, bamboo flutes, and two-headed drums are unifying musical elements in the midst of Indonesian diversity. True or False.

3. In Indonesia there are similar musical instruments, ensembles, and vocal forms found in the musical cultures of each region. True or False.

4. Balinese leather puppet plays known as _____ are based on epics of _____ and _____ origin.

5. The Balinese barong dance is an example of _____ due to the influences of Indian beliefs being absorbed by animist beliefs in Indonesia.

6. Gamelan instruments are venerated as holy objects because of Islamic influence. True or False.

7. A solo vocal form accompanied in Western harmonies by plucked strings and violin or flute is called_____; this is an example of syncretism produced by which two influences:_____ _____ and _____.

Sumatra (Text Pages 113–117)

Purpose To introduce the basic musical styles of Sumatra and to show how they developed.

Guidance On the island of Sumatra, music cultures are distinguished by language and religion. Three major factors influence the variety of music found in this part of Indonesia: Christianity, Islam, and indigenous religious beliefs. In addition, many of the smaller islands off the coast of Sumatra have contrasting music cultures, formed by the native peoples scattered throughout those areas. In Sumatra ancient indigenous musical traditions often have combined with those from the outside (especially Islamic and Portuguese), resulting in interesting musical forms not found in other parts of the world.

> ♪
> *Music Example*
>
> *talempong ensemble*
>
> *idiophones*
>
> *Sumatra, Indonesia*

Although there is much variety among the musics of Sumatra, two common characteristics may be seen. First is the use of sets of idiophonic percussion instruments that are beaten in complex interlocking fashion (not unlike American bell ringers) at unusually loud intensities; second is the concept of varied rhythmic (the author uses the term "tone") densities, whereby different sets of instruments play layers of rhythms that are multiples of each other. The talempong ensemble is the greatest exponent of these two characteristics. The talempong, the Minangkabau (a region in west Sumatra) equivalent of the gamelan, consists of large and small bronze-knobbed kettle gongs (these gongs are like inverted shallow bowls or kettles, with a convex knob or nipple in the center that is struck with a mallet). There is regional variety in the size of the instruments, their tunings, and their ensemble combinations. Talempong ensembles perform at festivals and ceremonies, for dances, during interludes in randai theater, and are heard on local radio stations.

Muslim and pre-Muslim influences can be seen in randai theater, where the stories are based on Muslim moral tales. Western influences can also be seen, such as in the modern Minangkabau songs with poetic texts. These are often accompanied by violins (biola [viola] is Portuguese for a European chordophone, here the violin) and guitars, along with more traditional instruments such as the tambourine and drums.

Terms Define or identify the following terms or areas, based on readings from the text and/or other sources.

8. On a map locate the province of West Sumatra, where the Minangkabau region is found.

9. talempong ensemble

10. biola (viola)

11. tambourine

12. concept of interlocking parts (rhythmic patterns)

Reading Comprehension Answer the following work questions (answers at end of this chapter):

8. The _____ ensemble is the Minangkabau (West Sumatra) equivalent of the _____ ensemble found in Java and Bali.

9. Randai, or Manangkabau theater, is an art form that combines Muslim and pre-Muslim characteristics. True or False.

10. Modern Minangkabau songs often include such Western chordophones as the _____ (known as _____ in Sumatra), and the _____, along with the tambourine and drums.

11. Even Sumatra is so diverse that the people of one of the small islands off its coast sing in an ancient choral fashion. True or False.

12. Talempong ensembles are almost never heard in Sumatra today due to European and other Western musical traditions. True or False.

13. Two of the most important musical principles upon which talempong ensemble playing is based are _____ and _____.

Java (Text Pages 117–126)

Purpose To identify the musical cultures of Java, and to recognize the varied influences which have shaped the musical cultures of the island.

Guidance Java is a smaller and more densely populated island than Sumatra. Note the location of the island in Figure 7-1 on page 112 of the text. There are three main cultural-linguistic areas in Java: Sundanese, Central Javanese, and East Javanese. As mentioned in the introduction to this chapter, Islamic influence is felt in many regions of Java, especially in the north.

The gamelan (which means orchestra) is the principal ensemble in Java, and the diagram in Figure 7-3 indicates the positions of the instruments and their players (the front of the orchestra is at the top of the figure). There are two scales, pelog and slendro, used in Javanese music, and there are separate instruments to play in each scale (the marks P and S indicate these in the diagram). The notation in Example 7-4 of the text, however, does not explain an important difference between pelog and slendro, for many of the notes are indicated as being the same in the Western staff. This is not usually the case, however, because both scales are constructed from different sets of microtones that cannot be notated accurately with the Western staff (neither can they be accurately rendered on a piano). The notation in Example 7-4, for example, suggests that the E to G in both pelog and slendro are the same, which is not true. The pelog interval may contain 230 cents, while the slendro interval may contain 250 cents. In addition, while E to F in Western music would contain 100 cents (in equal temperament, like on a piano), the E to F in pelog could contain more or less 125 cents. Although the pitches within a particular gamelan would always be the same within a particular scale, another gamelan would be different. In other words, an instrument from one gamelan cannot be used in another gamelan. Thus, each gamelan is slightly different, and each is unique, with its own name, history, maker, and sentiment.

Although there are many types, the most common Javanese gamelan is made up of the following four groups of instruments: (1) the "colotomic" gongs and gong kettles (text page 119); (2) the melodic idiophone instruments (text pages 119–120); (3) the melodic vocal tone instruments and voices (text page 120); and (4) the membranophones (text pages 120–121). The term "colotomic" is an important one to remember because it can be used to explain musics of many cultures. "Colotomy" refers to the concept when a particular instrument plays a particular note or notes at a particular time. Used as an adjective, you can say that the great gong has a colotomic function because it plays its particular pitch on the last beat of each cycle. The smaller colotomic instruments play their particular notes also at particular times (again, not unlike American bell ringers). The melodic idiophonic instruments are explained as playing fast notes (high degree of density), which are like variations upon basic melodies (sometimes called skeleton, nuclear theme, or nuclear melody; see footnote 5) played by the slower and larger instruments. Some of them play in an interlocking fashion, although this is not as much of a characteristic as will be found in the music of Bali. These melodic idiophones are played loudly, and the style is often referred to as "strong." The third group, by contrast, sounds soft, and because such instruments as the bamboo flute (suling) and the bowed lute (rebab) have flexibility, like the human voice, their soft musical elaborations are referred to as vocal tones. Also included in this group are singers and a female soloist. During a gamelan piece the music will often alternate between the strong and soft styles. Included in both the strong and soft styles are metallophones known as gender, and xylophones known as gambang (Figure 7-10), which play fast notes that are constantly moving variations and elaborations. During the soft style the rebab (Figure 7-6) is the leader, but during the strong style the drummer is the leader (Figure 7-7).

Terms Define or identify the following terms, based on readings from the text and/or other sources.

13. gamelan

14. slendro

15. pelog

16. gong

17. gongan

18. nuclear melody, skeleton (balungan)

19. colotomy

20. strong style vs soft style

21. vocal tone instruments

22. gender

23. bonang (Figure 7-5)

24. rebab (Figure 7-6)

25. wayang kulit (Figure 7-8)

26. wayang orang (Figure 7-9)

27. double gamelan

Reading Comprehension
Answer the following work questions (answers at end of this chapter):

14. Most Javanese musical instruments are idiophones made from _____ _____.

15. In antiquity the Javanese made large metal musical instruments that were probably magically used for _____.

16. A major musical achievement of the Javanese is the orchestra known as a _____.

17. Gongan can be thought of as long time units that are defined by the great gong during certain gamelan performances. True or False.

18. The gamelan in its modern form contains over 200 instruments with hundreds of singers and dancers who are capable of entertaining the entire evening. True or False.

19. The most important instrument of the gamelan, and one which plays on the last note of the cycle, is called the _____ in English; this manner of playing a particular note or notes at a particular time is referred to as _____ by ethnomusicologists.

20. Wayang kulit are all night _____ _____.

21. Sometimes two gamelan orchestras are played together during theatrical performances to create a double gamelan. True or False.

22. Two dimensional puppets made from _____ are used in wayang kulit to explore man's relationship with _____ _____, _____ and the _____.

23. The two scale systems in Javanese music are _____ and _____.

24. Two styles of playing in Javanese gamelan are known in English as ____ _____ and _____.

25. In the style of playing Javanese gamelan that is contemplative, three additional performing elements are used, which are (in English) _____, _____ and _____.

26. List four things the dhalang or puppeteer does while performing:

    a. _____,

    b. _____,

    c. _____,

    d. _____.

27. The Muslims in Java highly approve of gamelan music. True or False.

28. An important type of Sundanese small ensemble includes which two instruments (in English): _____ and _____.

Bali (Text Pages 126–129)

Purpose To examine the musical culture of Bali through the development of distinctive musical forms, the use of instruments, and the traditional artistic life which supports them.

Guidance Bali is the smallest of the three Indonesian islands explored in the text; see Figure 7-1 on text page 112 for a comparison of their sizes. Bali lies just east of Java, and because of this close proximity the Javanese culture has greatly influenced the culture of Bali. The advent of tourism, however, has caused the most changes in the arts. Today, gamelan performances and trance dances are frequently performed at coastal tourist hotels, as well is in villages for local entertainment and functional events.

Balinese gamelan sounds different from Javanese gamelan, mainly because the overall effect is more brilliant and exciting. The Javanese say that Balinese gamelan is too loud, and the Balinese say that Javanese gamelan puts them to sleep. There are several reasons for the brilliance of

---

♪

Music Examples

instruments of the gamelan gong kebyar

idiophones and membranophone

Balinese gamelan gong kebyar

> ♪
>
> *Music Example*
>
> *gamelan gong kebyar ensemble*
>
> *Balinese gamelan gong kebyar*

> ♪
>
> *Music, Dance, and Theater Examples*
>
> *Balinese topeng and kecak*
>
> *Bali, Indonesia*

sound and richness of tone color of Balinese gamelan. First, wooden mallets are most often used to strike the metal keys or slabs of the idiophones; and second, the leading metal keyed instruments are played in nearly identical twins, except that the very similar metal keys are slightly "out-of-tune" with each other. When they are struck together to produce the "same" note, therefore, the resulting sound shimmers because beat frequency interference waves are created. The effect is not unlike the mechanical vibrato added to the vibraphone in American jazz (as in the Modern Jazz Quartet, for example).

The three most common types of gamelan orchestras in Bali are the gamelan angklung, the gamelan gong, and the gamelan gong kebyar. The first type is a small orchestra that can be carried during processions; the second is a traditional large orchestral used for traditional events; and the third is a large type for which modern music is being composed annually. In general, Balinese gamelan music features an extensive use of interlocking parts, and many of the smaller instruments consist actually of two halves, with a total of two players who interlock their notes (this is called kotekan). This interlocking technique is also seen in the performance of kecak, when a chorus of several hundred men alternate the chanting of the syllable "cak" (pronounced "chahk"), creating an interlocking mass of sound that is an imitation of an army of monkeys.

Terms Define or identify the following terms, based on readings from the text and/or other sources.

28. barong

29. kecak

30. gamelan angklung

31. gamelan gong kebyar

32. kotekan

Reading Comprehension Answer the following work questions (answers at end of this chapter):

29. The music culture of Bali flourishes because practically all areas of the island's rich folklife have religious significance. True or False.

30. The Balinese _____ is the mythical creature used as a symbol of goodness in the Calonarang drama, a trance dance.

31. The most famous trance dance choir in Bali is the _____, originally performed to appease the gods during all kinds of emergencies.

32. A twentieth century development of the gamelan, for which music is composed annually, is the_____ _____ _____.

33. Balinese puppet theater music is the same as Javanese because it is also accompanied by a complete gamelan. True or False.

34. The lead instruments in a Balinese gamelan are constructed in _____ which are intentionally slightly "_____-_____"; and when their nearly identical pitches are sounded together, the effect is like a _____.

35. Bali was very isolated until the year _____ when which European country gained control of the island: _____.

Video Viewing

1. Wayang—shadow puppet play (Central Java) (10-2). *The JVC Video Anthology of World Music and Dance*, Southeast Asia V, Indonesia 2 (VTMV-10).
2. Gamelan degung—small court ensemble (Sunda, Java) (10-3). *The JVC Video Anthology of World Music and Dance*, Southeast Asia V, Indonesia 2 (VTMV-10).
3. Tembang Sunda Cianjuran—song with instrument ensemble [suling, kacapi indung, kacapi rincik] (Sunda, Java) (10-4). *The JVC Video Anthology of World Music and Dance*, Southeast Asia V, Indonesia 2 (VTMV-10).
4. Gamelan—instrument ensemble (gong kebyar): "Sekar jupun" (Bali) (9-1). *The JVC Video Anthology of World Music and Dance*, Southeast Asia IV, Indonesia 1 (VTMV-9).
5. Baris—warriors' dance drill (Bali) (9-3). *The JVC Video Anthology of World Music and Dance*, Southeast Asia IV, Indonesia 1 (VTMV-9).
6. Kebyar trompong—seated dance with gong set (Bali) (9-5). *The JVC Video Anthology of World Music and Dance*, Southeast Asia IV, Indonesia 1 (VTMV-9).
7. Kecak—men's chorus (Bali) (10-1). *The JVC Video Anthology of World Music and Dance*, Southeast Asia V, Indonesia 2 (VTMV-10).

Sample Test Questions

Multiple choice questions. Only one answer is correct.

1. A basic element of cultural unity, which lends strength to Indonesian musical traditions, is the preservation of: a. musical instruments, b. spirit and ancestor worship, c. vocal expressions, d. religious art forms, e. the isolation of being an island nation.
2. Common Indonesian musical elements include: a. similar musical instruments, ensembles, and vocal forms, b. use of gongs, kettles, bamboo flutes, and two-headed drums, c. similar use of harmony,

rhythm and language for songs, d. a and b, e. a and c.

3. Islam has *not* been a musical influence in which part of Indonesia: a. Bali, b. Java, c. Sumatra, d. a and b, e. a, b, and c.

4. Important musical principles in Sumatra include: a. interlocking parts, b. varied tone densities, c. rhythmic interest in proportion to density, d. all of the above, e. none of the above.

5. Bronze orchestras in the Minangkabau region of Sumatra are: a. more complex than in Java and Bali, b. less complex than in Java and Bali, c. equal to those in Java and Bali, d. are the most complex in all of Indonesia, e. not found.

6. The great gong is: a. the most revered instrument of the gamelan, b. said to be where the great spirit of the orchestra resides, c. is worshiped daily, d. a and b, e. b and c.

7. The all night puppet plays depict stories of: a. Indonesian origins, b. Indian origins, c. Muslim origins, d. a and b, e. a and c.

8. A popular form of theater in Java is the wayang orang, which has: a. living actors/dancers, b. accompaniment by a double gamelan, c. plots from the same sources as the puppet theater, d. a and c, e. a, b, and c.

9. Performance of trance dances like the hobby horse dance and the rain-inducing ceremony are examples of: a. Islamic influences, b. Hindu influences, c. indigenous influences, d. Christian influences, e. Buddhist influences.

10. The Balinese barong is: a. a type of gamelan ensemble, b. a mythical animal, c. a trance state, d. an indigenous musical instrument, e. a puppeteer.

11. The Balinese trance choir dance called kecak uses fast interlocking patterns of vocal sounds such as: a. cak, b. shouts, grunts, and hisses, c. hup, d. a and b, e. a and c.

12. The instruments of most Balinese gamelan ensembles: a. are unique to Bali, b. are similar to Javanese ensembles, c. have changed radically due to tourism and do not exist at all in the original form, d. are made of bronze and used only for religious temple ceremonies.

13. The most important ceremonial gamelan in Bali is: a. gamelan gong kebyar, b. gamelan slendro, c. gamelan pelog, d. gamelan gong, e. gamelan angklung.

14. If, during a performance of Javanese wayang kulit, the dhalang wishes to change from a slendro to a pelog piece: a. each player will simply retune his instrument, b. each player will move from his slendro to his nearby pelog instrument, c. a different set of musicians will be called in, d. that would never happen.

15. What is the reason for the technique of interlocking parts in the music of Indonesia: a. it makes the notation easier to write, b. it makes possible the performance of fast melodies without great effort, c. it is a religious belief in the power of dualism, d. it was sanctioned by the emperor.

16. Figure 7-8 (page 124 of text) is a leading actor in: a. wayang kulit, b. wayang orang, c. wayang pelog, d. wayang gamelan, e. wayang slendro.

17. Figure 7-9 (page 125 of text) is a leading actor in: a. wayang kulit, b. wayang orang, c. wayang pelog, d. wayang gamelan, e. wayang slendro.

18. The instrument in Figure 7-6 (page 123 of text) has its origins in: a. China, b. ancient Indonesia, c. India, d. Middle East, e. Europe.

19. The instrument in Figure 7-5 (page 122 of text) has its origins in: a. China, b. ancient Indonesia, c. India, d. Middle East, e. Europe.

20. The musician playing the instrument in Figure 7-6 (page 123 of text) is the leader of which style gamelan: a. Balinese trance dance, b. Javanese strong, c. Javanese soft, d. Balinese gong kebyar, e. he is never a leader.

21. The musician playing the instrument in Figure 7-7 (page 123 of text) is the leader of which style gamelan: a. Balinese trance dance, b. Javanese strong, c. Javanese soft, d. Balinese gong kebyar, e. he is never a leader.

22. The musician playing the instrument in Figure 7-5 (page 122 of text) is the leader of which style gamelan: a. Balinese trance dance, b. Javanese strong, c. Javanese soft, d. Balinese gong kebyar, e. he is never a leader.

23. Which statement is most correct for what happens during Hindu processions along the roads and paths in Bali: a. no music is heard, b. cassette tapes are played, c. gamelan orchestras wait along certain stopping points on the road and play when the procession arrives, d. musicians carry and play instruments of the gamelan while processing, e. oboes and drums, which are outdoor instruments, accompany the procession, playing as they go.

24. In which culture of Indonesia are certain gamelan instruments constructed to be intentionally "out of tune"? a. Sumatra, b. Java, c. Bali, d. a and c, e. none of the above.

25. No two gamelan orchestras are tuned exactly alike because of the Javanese: a. inability to hear tuning differences, b. belief that nothing should be reproduced exactly, c. makers who are not unionized, d. predilection for pitch variability and nonequidistant intervals, e. bamboo instruments which are nearly impossible to keep in tune.

Answers to Reading Comprehension Questions

1. geography, religion, history
2. True
3. True
4. wayang kulit, Indian, Indonesian
5. syncretism
6. False: it is indigenous (i.e., animistic)
7. kroncong, Portuguese, Indonesian
8. talempong, gamelan
9. True
10. violins, biola, guitar
11. True
12. False: they are heard at ceremonies, on radio, at dances, and at theater
13. interlocking parts, varied tone (rhythmic) densities
14. bronze
15. rainmaking
16. gamelan
17. True
18. False: a gamelan has from 70–80 instruments, a small chorus, and a female singer
19. great gong, colotomy
20. puppet plays
21. True
22. leather, man, nature, supernatural
23. pelog, slendro
24. soft, strong
25. female soloist, bowed lute, bamboo flute
26. manipulates the puppets, chants and sings the story, plays percussion instruments with his foot, controls the gamelan and singers
27. False: they disapprove
28. zither and bamboo flute
29. True
30. barong
31. kecak
32. gong kebyar
33. False: it is accompanied by a quartet of gender
34. pairs, out-of-tune, shimmering vibrato
35. 1906, Netherlands (Dutch people)

Answers to Sample Test Questions

1. b
2. d

3. a
4. d
5. b
6. d
7. d
8. e
9. c
10. b
11. d
12. b
13. d
14. b
15. b
16. a
17. b
18. d
19. b
20. c
21. b
22. e
23. d
24. c
25. d

Listening Form

Student Name_____I.D. Number_____
Course Name _____Course Number _____
Date_____Chapter Number_____Listening Example Number _____
Record or Tape Number_____Name of Culture and Location _____
Name of Performer(s)_____
Instructions: place an X, ✓, or • in appropriate boxes; give types; indicate native names.

performing elements (if vocal)	solo: M/F	duo: M/F	trio: M/F	quartet: M/F	group: M/F	other: M/F
performing elements (if instrumental)	corpophone	idiophone	membranophone	aerophone	chordophone	electrophone	other
texture	single melody	dense unison	heterophone	imitation	parallelism	disphony	other
more texture	with drone	with time indicator	chordal	polyphonic stratification	colotomy	combination	variable
melodic contour	static	ascending	descending	conjunct	disjunct	undulating	terraced
mode or scale	number of notes	vernacular	using cipher notation (numbers), indicate the mode or scale in ascending order
meter	free	duple	triple	compound	additive	poly	other
speed	very slow	slow	moderate	fast	very fast	variable	other
amplitude	very soft	soft	moderate	loud	very loud	variable	other
timbre (tone color)	clear	breathy	nasal	open	tight	masked	other
inflections	no vibrato	slow vibrato	fast vibrato	wide vibrato	falsetto	multiphonics	other
formal structure	vernacular name	expanding	reverting	strophic	theme and variations	other	
structural or performance techniques	ostinato	responsorial	antiphonal	elastic rhythm	if vocal: syllabic or melismatic	non-synchronous parts	other

Chapter 8

Text Pages 134 – 136

Polynesian Music and Dance

Adrienne L. Kaeppler

Introduction to Chapter (Text Pages 134–136)

Purpose To acquaint the student with the geographic location of the major island groups of Polynesia, to identify the four categories for understanding Polynesian music, to introduce the basic musical styles of several Polynesian cultures and to show the basic differences and similarities between them, and to discuss how social structure and religion are related to Polynesian music.

Guidance Polynesia must be viewed in a geographic context along with Melanesia and Micronesia. The map on page 135 gives you a rough idea of where Polynesia and Melanesia are, but a more thorough map is *Islands of the Pacific*, published in 1974 by the National Geographic Society as a supplement to the article "Pacific Islands and Discoverers," which appeared in *National Geographic*, December 1974, Vol. 146, No. 6. That map clearly delineates the islands that make up the three Oceanic cultural areas, and it also gives their political affiliation and some descriptive data. The reverse side of the National Geographic map details some of the prehistory, history, and ethnology of the Pacific. Your author points out on page 136 that Polynesia forms a triangle, with Hawaii in the north, New Zealand in the west, and Easter Island in the east. She continues to explain that there are three subdivisions of Polynesia, including east, west, and the outliers. You may be confused, however, when she includes the islands at the points of the triangle into east Polynesia. Her divisions, therefore, must be understood as cultural rather than entirely geographic, although only New Zealand falls outside of her geographic framework. By pinpointing the islands she mentions on the National Geographic map, you will better understand the subdivisions, keeping in mind that New Zealand is included because of cultural similarities with the other islands of east Polynesia. The Polynesian outliers are pocket areas where Polynesian cultural traits are found, even though they are located in Micronesia (Nukuoro Atoll and Kapingamarangi Atoll) or Melanesia (Tikopia, Anuta, and Ontong

Java). Often, these pocket areas retain more pure Polynesian musical characteristics than do the "mainstream" Polynesian islands.

Songs texts (the lyrics or words) form the basis for much of the music in Polynesia, and the music is, in fact, organized to fit the words. Likewise, dance is organized to fit or strengthen the words. The musical characteristics explained by Burrows (quoted on page 134) can be best understood when the terms he uses are looked up in the introduction to this Study Guide. Generally he is saying that Polynesian vocal music is either of an epic nature (almost recited rather than sung) or of a smaller type, based on stanzas or verses. The rhythm of the music is determined by the natural rhythm of the words used, and is, therefore, irregular, since words are irregular unless they are used in poetry. The exceptions to this are when the songs are short and consist of verses, or when dancing is employed. Then the rhythm of the music may fall into a pattern. Tonality is a term that should be employed only for Western (i.e., European or American) music. He means, rather, that melodies are simple, and often only one tone is emphasized over others. The melodies are based on either one or two notes, or they form the contour of an arch (i.e., moving gradually higher and then gradually lower). All music has structure. Here Barrows explains that the structure exists in one of three possible ways: 1) one uncomplicated phrase (which he calls a "simple progression"), 2) one short phrase or motive that is repeated with slight variations, and 3) the alternation of two contrasting short phrases or motives. When people sing together, it is usually in two parts, as a duet, with one part being a repetition of one note as a drone, while the other sings a melody (this is referred to as bordun by Barrows) or else both sing the melody in unison with variation at the same time (this is called heterophony).

A great deal of variety is found in Polynesian music, not only between island groups, but also in the individual island cultures. Four categories have been developed by the author for examining Polynesian music (defined on page 134): traditional music, evolved traditional music, folk music, and airport art music. These categories are useful for analysis only in context of the entire social/cultural environment.

Polynesian music is in essence a vocal music, and Polynesian people have a reputation for using music in a variety of performance situations. In Polynesia both the social structure and religion use music regularly to express solidarity. Songs for work, games, derision, and laments are considered part of the ordinary lifeways of the people. The music used to honor chiefs and gods is the most formal and structured. Social organization is based on lineage and/or religious practice, depending on the island group.

Terms   Define or identify the following terms or areas, based on readings from text and/or other sources.

1. Locate Polynesia on a globe

2. North Pacific

3. East Polynesia

4. West Polynesia

5. Polynesian Outliers

6. traditional music

7. evolved traditional music

8. folk music

9. airport art music

10. Locate Melanesia and Micronesia on a globe, and notice their proximity to Polynesia.

Reading Comprehension Answer the following work questions (answers at end of this chapter):

1. Polynesian music requires analysis involving _____, _____, _____, and _____.

2. Text is the most important component in the study of Polynesian music. True or False.

3. There is little variety in Polynesian music between island groups. True or False.

4. The four categories of Polynesian music are _____, _____, _____, and _____.

5. Folk music in Polynesia is that music which has pre-European antecedents. True or False.

6. Performances with dangerous fire or knives are often included in the analysis category identified as airport art music. True or False.

7. Many outside observers of Polynesian music suggest the categories of _____ and _____ for analysis, but these have resulted in a too simplistic approach to a complex musical culture.

8. The views of Polynesians about their music should be considered in any serious analysis of their music. True or False.

9. The islands of Polynesia form a triangle with _____ at the north, _____ _____ at the east, and _____ at the west.

10. Social structure and _____ are important contexts for music in Polynesia.

West Polynesia—Tonga (Text Pages 136–142)

Music and Dance Examples

'otuhaka, ma'ulu'ulu, lakalaka, and tau'alunga

ensembles from Tonga

Music Example

hiva kavala

male trio from Tonga

Purpose To identify many of the traditional functions or evolved traditional functions of music found in Tonga today. The survey is based on a three part analysis of poetry, music, and movement, which takes into consideration structure, sentiment, and function of music in west Polynesia.

Guidance The ancestors of the Polynesians, who originated generations ago in Asia, arrived in Tonga from eastern Melanesia at least by the twelfth century B.C. Eventually Polynesians inhabited all the major island groups. West Polynesia is one of the three major cultural subdivisions, and besides Tonga, it includes Samoa, the Ellice Islands, Uvea, Futuna, Niue, and Tokelau.

Traditional functions or evolved traditional functions of the music of Tonga are closely related to their social/cultural contexts. Tongan music essentially includes poetry and bodily movement and is primarily secular rather than religious. Four basic genres or types of Tongan music are children's game songs, mourning songs, work songs, and narrative songs, all categorized as traditional or evolved traditional music. Two additional types are found in Tonga: the ceremonial dance songs and "sweet songs"; the latter are examples of acculturated folk music.

For several weeks during the summer of 1998, my wife and I lived in Nuku'alofa, the capital of the Kingdom of Tonga. We had been invited to attend the eightieth birthday celebrations of the king, and it was a wonderful opportunity to see and hear traditional dances and music every day and night. *Lakalaka* was one of the most impressive types of dancing and singing. I was fascinated as I watched the women dancers on one end of the line use very graceful upper body movements, including arm, hand, and head gestures, while the men at the other end of the line jumped up, rolled around, and used very exaggerated body movements that were in complete contrast to the women. In the very center of the dance line (which sometimes included several hundred dancers) was an honored female dancer, usually a princess, some other member of the royal family, or a village beauty chosen by her people. While lakalaka is a standing dance, another type of traditional genre is *ma'ulu'ulu*, a seated dance. Equally impressive when compared to lakalaka, but in a different way, ma'ulu'ulu is like a sea of heads, bobbing and swaying to the elaborate percussive sounds of a huge battery of membranophonic drums. One after another these huge groups performed for the king and guests, each dance sometimes lasting an hour.

A contrasting dance and musical form is *tau'alunga*, which features only one young and very beautiful female dancer to the accompaniment of singing, 'ukuleles, guitars, and banjos. Over and over, the music repeats itself until the audience finds itself singing along, so familiar does the tune become. All the while, the young dancer gracefully and almost humbly moves her arms, hands, head, and body, mimicking the text of the song. This, like the other dances, is dedicated to the king. During the dancing, hundreds of Tongans quietly come up to place money by the dancer, or stick it on her oily body. I'll never forget the beauty of that song (or the dancer).

Lullabies are songs usually sung by an adult to make a child go to sleep. They are usually soothing and quiet in Tonga, and in a similar quiet fashion, Tonga also has a type of music to gently awaken the king each morning—it is a melody played softly on the *fangu fangu* nose flute. Being a flutist myself, I wanted to own a fangu fangu and learn how to play it. Almost every day I asked the local people where I could buy one and how I could find someone to teach me how to play it. It wasn't until 10:30 PM on the evening before my wife and I were to leave Tonga for New Zealand, however, that my wishes were fulfilled. During the day I had met a young fangu fangu player and instrument maker at a museum, and he said he would bring me a flute to my hotel that night. I had almost given up hope, until late in the evening he finally arrived on his bicycle with a fangu fangu. I videotaped him by the glow of the street light as he performed for me and taught me how to play the nose flute. The only tune he knew was the traditional melody to awaken the king. I'm glad we were about a mile away from the palace where the king was asleep, because the sound of the Tongan nose flute doesn't carry very far.

Music Example

himeni

congregational singing from Tonga

Terms Define or identify the following terms, based on readings from text and/or other sources.

11. fasi

12. laulalo

13. dirge

14. nafa

15. ula

16. lakalaka

17. ma'ulu'ulu

18. kava

19. hiva kakala

20. tau'alunga

21. fangu fangu

22. panpipe

Music Example

fangu fangu

aerophone

nose flute from Tonga

Reading Comprehension Answer the following work questions (answers at end of this chapter):

11. Melodic rendering of poetry was often performed _____
    in two main parts called _____ and _____.

12. Dirges that were immediate expressions of grief at a wake were intoned essentially on one tone.   True or False.

13. Tongan lullabies were traditionally either accompanied by a _____ , were played by a solo _____or were played by an ensemble of _____.

14. An instrument that was used in Tonga, but disappeared when the Europeans came, was the _____.

15. Ceremonial dance songs are performed by the men, with dance paddles, to the accompaniment of the _____.

16. Traditional dances in Tonga were never performed by women. True or False.

17. How long were stamping tubes in Tonga? _____.

18. The music of Tonga is essentially _____ that has been elaborated with melody, rhythm, and dancing.

19. Narrative songs, describing famous places, past events and legends, are performed in a manner using _____ - _____, and may be accompanied by _____.

20. In Tonga, men and women never sing together. True or False.

West Polynesia—Other Islands (Text Pages 142–143)

Purpose To identify the basic cultural and musical characteristics of the west Polynesian islands of Samoa, Ellice Islands, Uvea, Futuna, Niue, Tokelau, and Fiji.

Guidance Hundreds of islands sit in the South Pacific within a certain proximity to the Kingdom of Tonga, which in itself covers a fairly large part of the Pacific Ocean. These are simply referred to in the text as "other islands" of West Polynesia. As the author rightly points out, however, they all show musical similarities with Tonga, which throughout history must have had great influence as sort of a cultural focal point. Only Fiji is somewhat of an exception because it is culturally and racially a part of Melanesia, yet much of its music bears such a resemblance to Tongan music that Fiji is classified musically as a part of West Polynesia.

During the several weeks my wife and I spent in Tonga for the king's eightieth birthday celebration, numerous music and dance performance groups came from other islands in West Polynesia (and elsewhere) to perform in honor of the king, including *sasa* dancers and musicians from Samoa and *kailao* dancers and musicians from Niue. Seeing the sasa dancers was great fun, because we (and the Tongan audience as well) thought it was humorous to see large nearly naked male dancers slap themselves on their

---

Music and Dance Examples

sasa, kailao, and soke

ensembles from Samoa and Niue

Music and Dance Example

vakamalolo

ensemble from Fiji

fleshy parts in rhythm to the drums. What we were watching and hearing were *corpophones* or body sounders, probably among the oldest types of musical instruments in the world. Part of the birthday celebration also included kailao stick or club dancers from Niue. To me, kailao resembled a type of warrior dance, as the male dancers banged their wooden weapons together to the rhythm of tin idiophones played by seated musicians. It was very noisy, and I was within just a few feet of the dancers during my videotaping of the event.

In Fiji, we attended a performance of *vakamalolo* music and dancing at a hotel on Taveuni, the "Garden Island." Taveuni is very rural, with just one dirt road that encircles about three-fourths of the island. Many traditional Melanesian villages are in the interior and at road's end in the south of the island, not too far from the hotel where the performance took place. This was not your usual tourist performance, as I soon realized, because practically an entire Melanesian village arrived to the hotel, sat down in a big circle, and prepared *kava* (a peppery narcotic drink) and drank it for about an hour before they started singing and swaying in the semi darkness of the hotel. It was evening, just after a rain, and the combination of heat, smell of the kava, and swaying of the singers soon gave way to some of the most beautiful part singing I had heard. This *was* similar to the singing I had heard in Tonga, but the atmosphere was different—not a celebration for a royal birthday, but a type of family gathering by an entire village (an extended family), complete with children, doing what they would normally do in the privacy of their own thatched huts on pilings. This was not religious music and dance, but yet I felt a particular solemnity and profundity about it. This was vakamalolo, a sitting dance, contextualized in a rather uncontextualized place—a tourist hotel!

Terms Define or identify the following terms or areas, based on readings from text and/or other sources.

23. kailao

24. sasa

25. meke

26. vakamalolo

Reading Comprehension Answer the following work questions (answers at end of this chapter):

21. One stylistic feature of Samoan game and children's songs includes melodies based on the interval of a _____.

22. The meter of the music is usually _____ .

23. Within a song, the tempo changes by _____ .

24. In traditional music, intensity or loudness is not varied for effect because this would inhibit understanding of the _____ .

25. Melodic consistency is most important in Polynesian music; therefore, change in pitch intervals is of little importance. True or False.

26. Melodic or polyphonic intervals were usually a major 2nd, a variable 3rd, or a 4th. True or False.

27. All Polynesian compositions can be divided into sections or movements. True or False.

28. Adult games are accompanied by songs that have erotic overtones. True or False.

29. Today in Uvea a dance is performed with clubs and accompanied by percussion instruments such as a _____ or an _____.

30. Fiji, included in either Polynesia or Melanesia, has music that is definitely Melanesian rather than Polynesian. True or False.

East Polynesia—Hawaii (Text Pages 144–150)

Purpose To identify the main components of Hawaiian music and musical instruments, within their cultural context. Some emphasis will be on Tahiti, also classified as east Polynesia.

Guidance Settled by Polynesians probably migrating from Tahiti, the Hawaiian Islands are located several thousand miles farther north than Tahiti, on the northern point of the Polynesian triangle. Western musical influences on Hawaiian music began soon after Hawaii's discovery by Captain Cook in 1778. Polyphonic or multipart music was introduced by the Protestant missionaries, and today this influence is called *himeni* (after hymn) by Hawaiians. Hawaii has become a land of many cultures, including Polynesian, Melanesian, East Asian, European, and, of course, American. Japanese immigrants (many from Okinawa) arrived over one hundred years ago to work in sugar cane plantations, and today Japanese culture is very prominent in Hawaii.

I was surprised by the amount of traditional Polynesian and traditional Hawaiian music we heard in Oahu during the summer of 1998. Right on the tourist strip of Waikiki Beach, less than a mile from our hotel and next to a statue of Hawaii's most famous surfer, was a performance of various types of hula, featuring live musicians and dancers. For the first time I heard live *hula pahu* (see Figure 8-5 in textbook, page 149) sung, drummed, and danced, plus many other types of standing hulas. It was an interesting experience, to have traditional Polynesian music and dance on one side of me and surfing on the other.

The next day in a large park between Waikiki Beach and Diamond Head was a *'ukulele* festival where hundreds of *'ukulele* players were on stage performing at the same time in one huge *'ukulele* orchestra. Now I had seen and heard everything, I said to myself. In Tonga we had seen and heard a blind Polynesian musician playing his 'ukulele with his teeth, and now we were enjoying several hundred musicians playing together in a massive orchestra. Was this the same instrument that was made popular in the continental United States by Arthur Godfrey and Tiny Tim, I asked myself? I felt that the uke had received a bum rap in the "states" during the past fifty years, and that it is much more of an instrument than those showmen made it out to be. How many musical stereotypes there are in our often make believe world! In Hawaii the 'ukulele has become a part of that culture's patrimony, and Hawaiians of many races take pride in performing it and perpetuating its artistic capabilities.

Terms Define or identify the following terms, based on readings from the text and/or other sources.

27. mele

28. oli

29. mele hula

30. 'ukeke

31. 'ukulele

32. nose flute

33. mouth bow

34. pahu

35. slit bamboo rattles

36. stone clappers

37. tabu

38. treadleboards

39. gourd rattles

40. himeni

Reading Comprehension Answer the following work questions (answers at end of this chapter):

31. Mele can be divided into two types: that which is *not* danced is called _____, and that which *is* danced is called _____.

32. The _____, a modern four-stringed chordophone considered "Hawaiian" to Westerners, is possibly a descen-

---

Music Examples

'ohe hano ihu

aerophone

nose flute from Hawaii

Music and Dance Examples

oli and hula

vocal with ensemble from Hawaii

Music Examples

'ukulele

chordophone

performers from Hawaii and Tonga

dant of the ancient _____.

33. Write the English descriptions of the four main types of Hawaiian music which are classified by the Hawaiians according to function:

   a. _____,

   b. _____,

   c. _____,

   d. _____.

34. Lovemaking songs were played on which two types of musical instruments:

   _____ and _____.

35. The large sharkskin-covered membranophone of Hawaii is the _____.

36. Another membranophone, often played at the same time as the sharkskin-covered membranophone, is made from _____ and covered with _____.

37. What was the first musical element to change when Western influence was felt?

   _____.

38. In the nineteenth century, many Hawaiian laments were based on what?

   _____.

39. Hawaiian vocal music, like other vocal music in Polynesia, is polyphonic. True or False.

40. Hawaii has some of the most acculturated music found in Polynesia and also some of the most traditional music. True or False.

Video Viewing

1. *Hawaiian Rainbow.* Directed and produced by Robert Mugge. Mug-Shot Productions.

2. *Kumu Hula: Keepers of a Culture.* Directed and produced by Robert Mugge. Mug-Shot Productions.

Sample Test Questions

Only one answer is correct.

1. The most important element in the study of Polynesian music is: a. rhythm, b. melody, c. visual expression, d. text.

2. Rhythm in Polynesian music is governed mainly by: a. dance, b. hand-clapping, c. instruments, d. text.

3. The variety of Polynesian music varies within the society and among: a. individual island regions, b. individuals, c. chiefs, d. island groups.

4. Evolved traditional music in Polynesia may be thought of as: a. continuation of pre-European times, b. incorporating Western pitch intervals and harmony, c. both a and b, d. neither a nor b.

5. Airport art music may include: a. danced pantomime, costume, fire, or knives, b. vocal dramatization, c. both a and b, d. neither a nor b.

6. The three major islands that are known for marking the points of the Polynesian triangle are: a. Hawaii, New Zealand, Easter Island, b. Micronesia, New Zealand, Hawaii, c. Easter Island, Micronesia, Tahiti, d. Hawaii, Easter Island, Micronesia.

7. Highly structured formal music is used to honor: a. gods and deities, b. gods and chiefs, c. gods and patron saints, d. none of the above.

8. Which songs were used in everyday Polynesian life: a. work songs, b. game songs, c. laments, d. all of the above.

9. Which is not a musical instrument from Tonga: a. mouth bow, b. nose flute, c. stamping tube, d. panpipe, e. skin drum.

10. A type of singing that consists of rhythmic-melodic speech is used in which context: a. lullaby, b. dance drama, c. sweet songs, d. narrative songs, e. love songs.

11. The *ula* is best described as what? a. sitting dance, b. standing dance, c. ceremonial dance, d. folk dance, e. children's game dance.

12. In Tonga the terms *fasi* and *laulalo* refer to what? a. musical instruments, b. dances, c. the two main parts in polyphonic singing, d. types of narrative songs, e. songs about the sun and the moon.

13. In Tongan traditional music or evolved traditional music, what are the two musical elements that have changed? a. pitch intervals and rhythm, b. Western harmonic decoration and the structure, c. the sentiment and the words, d. pitch intervals and Western harmonic decoration, e. musical instruments and speed of the music.

14. A dance from the island of Uvea is performed with what items as props? a. spears, b. fire torches, c. clubs, d. swords, e. leis.

15. Uvean implement dances and Samoan slap dances lack which element found in most other Polynesian dances? a. percussion accompani-

ment, b. poetry, c. traditional dress, d. striking of the body, e. hand movements.

16. Which is *not* a characteristic of Fijian music? a. use of the human voice, b. musical instruments used in conjunction with dance, c. melodic musical instruments, d. use of vocables, e. vocal polyphony.

17. In Fiji, vocal polyphony may nave as many as how many parts? a. 3, b. 7, c. 5, d. 2, e. 8.

18. Music in many of the Polynesian areas has been influenced by which European factor? a. church modes, b. invention of movable type, c. troubadours, d. minstrels, e. European scales.

19. In ancient Hawaii a special type of mele was composed that dealt with perpetuating the royal line. This was in honor of: a. the queen's grace, b. the princess' beauty, c. the prince's muscles, d. the chief's genitals.

20. In ancient Hawaii historical-genealogical epics and name songs were used to honor (not worship) the chiefs and to demonstrate: a. their ability to fight, b. their relationships to the gods and to nature, c. their long line of unbroken blood relationships, d. their ability to remember the ancestors in Dreamtime.

21. The Hawaiian classification of music by function distinguishes four main types. Which is *not* one of those types? a. religious chants used to call upon the gods, b. historical-genealogical epics and name songs, c. songs of a topical or endearing nature, d. dirges and laments, e. war songs that are group chanted and which excite the warriors.

22. The function of the mouth bow, the nose flute, and nose whistle in Hawaii was a. entertainment for lovers and to send messages, b. to provide dance music, c. placate the animals in the hunt, d. to while away the time for shepherds as they watch their flocks.

23. Hawaiian music is essentially poetry that has been decorated in various ways. Which is *not* one of those ways? a. harmony, b. melody, c. rhythm, d. movement, e. musical instruments.

Answers to Reading Comprehension Questions

1. text, melody, rhythm, movement
2. True
3. False: there is much variety, although certain characteristics make them related
4. traditional music, evolved traditional music, folk music, airport art music
5. False: folk music has changes in pitch intervals and harmony, and changes in structure that often incorporate aspects of Protestant hymns
6. True
7. indigenous, acculturate

8. True
9. Hawaii, Easter Island, New Zealand
10. religion
11. polyphonically, fasi, laulalo
12. True
13. nose flute, nose flute, nose flutes
14. panpipe
15. slit drum
16. False: they were performed by men and women
17. three to six feet
18. poetry
19. rhythmic-melodic speech, handclapping
20. False: men and women often sing together
21. perfect fourth
22. duple
23. acceleration
24. poetry
25. False: melodic consistency is relatively unimportant, and inconsistencies in pitch are widespread
26. True
27. False: structure is very elusive
28. True
29. sounding board, empty kerosene tin
30. False: it is related to Tonga, which is Polynesian
31. oli, mele hula
32. 'ukulele, 'ukeke
33. a. religious chants used to call upon the gods, b. historical-genealogical epics and name songs,
    c. songs of a topical or endearing nature, d. dirges and laments
34. nose flute, mouth bow
35. pahu
36. coconut shell, fish skin
37. pitch intervals
38. Protestant hymn tunes
39. False: there seems to be an absence of polyphony
40. True

Answers to Sample Test Questions

1. d
2. d
3. d
4. c
5. c

6. a
7. b
8. d
9. a
10. d
11. b
12. c
13. d
14. c
15. b
16. d
17. e
18. e
19. d
20. b
21. e
22. a
23. a

Listening Form

Student Name_____ I.D. Number_____
Course Name_____ Course Number_____
Date_____ Chapter Number_____ Listening Example Number _____
Record or Tape Number_____ Name of Culture and Location _____
Name of Performer(s)_____
Instructions: place an X, ✓, or • in appropriate boxes; give types; indicate native names.

performing elements (if vocal)	solo: M/F	duo: M/F	trio: M/F	quartet: M/F	group: M/F	other: M/F
performing elements (if instrumental)	corpophone	idiophone	membranophone	aerophone	chordophone	electrophone	other
texture	single melody	dense unison	heterophone	imitation	parallelism	disphony	other
more texture	with drone	with time indicator	chordal	polyphonic stratification	colotomy	combination	variable
melodic contour	static	ascending	descending	conjunct	disjunct	undulating	terraced
mode or scale	number of notes	vernacular	using cipher notation (numbers), indicate the mode or scale in ascending order
meter	free	duple	triple	compound	additive	poly	other
speed	very slow	slow	moderate	fast	very fast	variable	other
amplitude	very soft	soft	moderate	loud	very loud	variable	other
timbre (tone color)	clear	breathy	nasal	open	tight	masked	other
inflections	no vibrato	slow vibrato	fast vibrato	wide vibrato	falsetto	multiphonics	other
formal structure	vernacular name	expanding	reverting	strophic	theme and variations	other
structural or performance techniques	ostinato	responsorial	antiphonal	elastic rhythm	if vocal: syllabic or melismatic	non-synchronous parts	other

Chapter 9

Text Pages 154 – 171

The Traditional Music of the Australian Aborigines

Trevor A. Jones

Introduction to Chapter (Text Page 154)

Purpose To understand the migration and nomadic life style of the Aboriginal peoples of Australia.

Guidance The Australian Aborigines, racially classified as Australoid, are believed to have migrated from the present regions of Ceylon, Malaya, the East Indies, and New Guinea over a period of 40,000 years. As a nomadic food gathering and hunting people, they were probably urged on to richer lands by gathering and hunting the vast areas of the land (now ocean) created during the various ice ages. After first settling the present north coast of Australia (the Cape York Peninsula), they gradually spread across the continent where they developed distinctly different dialects and tribal customs. At one time there were as many as 500 tribes. The Aborigines first came into contact with Western society in 1788, and since then many of their traditional beliefs and musics have disappeared.

Terms Define or identify the following terms or areas, based on readings from text and/or other sources.

1. Australoid

2. Indonesia

3. Melanesia

4. Veddas of Ceylon

5. Malaysia

Reading Comprehension Answer the following work questions (answers at the end of the chapter):

1. The Australian Aborigines first came into contact with European settlers in the _____ century.

2. Aborigines were a _____ people who depended on _____ and _____ for subsistence.

3. Division of labor in Aboriginal society was equally divided between men and women, and women thus had an equal role in music and the arts. True or False.

4. Aboriginal traditional culture, including music, met with disastrous results when it first came into contact with European settlers. True or False.

5. All Aborigines speak the same language, and all their songs are understood throughout Australia. True or False.

Aboriginal Mythology (Text Pages 155–156)

Purpose To examine the basic principles of Aboriginal religious beliefs and practices and their relation to Aboriginal music.

Guidance The basis of Aboriginal religious belief is communication between the "powers" of The Dreaming and Aboriginal man. Music plays a major role in the Aboriginal religious and social system through ritual practices.

Terms Define the following terms, based on the reading from your text and/or other sources.

6. powers (as related to The Dreaming)

7. The Dreaming

8. Rainbow Serpent

9. totemism

10. rites of life

11. rites of death

12. increase rites

13. poison song

Reading Comprehension Answer the following work questions (answers at the end of the chapter):

6. The "powers" are portrayed by the Aboriginal people in _____ _____ and in _____, which are distorted in many ways.

7. Creativity and imagination is of utmost importance for expressing Aboriginal religious beliefs and practices, including music. True or False.

8. During the paranormal experiences of dream and trance, what four things may be received or acquired?

   a. _____,

   b. _____,

   c. _____,

   d. _____.

9. _____ powers are depicted in ground and rock art, and _____ powers are represented by human actors in ritual performances and body painting.

10. Two equally important types of ritual practices for which music plays a very important part are _____ and _____.

11. The rites of life in Aboriginal belief consist of initiatory and fertility rituals. True or False.

12. Death is often believed to be brought about by someone singing to the victim. True or False.

13. The songs associated with life and death are sung by the women because women give birth and are good at mourning. True or False.

Expressive Behavior and Music (Text Pages 157–158)

Purpose To examine the relationship between music and other expressive forms of behavior such as art and dancing, and to become familiar with Aboriginal musical instruments.

Guidance The author suggests that the most important factor to consider when examining Aboriginal music is the "basic principle of exchange." The outsider must recognize that music is a complex form in Aboriginal society.

All songs and music have specific functions in the culture. Aboriginal art and music are closely related, often being practiced together. Most Aboriginal music is vocal. Musical instruments are made and used in the culture, with most instruments being of a percussive nature. Body sounds, made with the hands or feet, plus other "unaided" sounds are also a part of Aboriginal musical repertory. Whistles and pipes are less common than percussive instruments, and the most distinctive Aboriginal musical instrument is the *didjeridu*. The bullroarer is another instrument that is occasionally found, and it consists of a small oval disk (like one blade of a propeller) attached to a string; it is swung over the head of the player and produces a whirring sound used originally to call supernatural entities.

Terms Define or identify the following terms or areas, based on readings from your text and/or other sources.

14. basic principle of "exchange"

15. rock art

16. body painting

17. bark painting

18. Wandjina cave paintings

19. Arnhem Land

20. wooden "gongs"

21. bullroarer

22. didjeridu

Reading Comprehension Answer the following work questions:

14. The most important concept to consider when examining Aboriginal music is the basic principle of "exchange." True or False.

15. Aboriginal music, even when considered purely as sound, has _____ and _____ significance to the culture.

16. Dance is closely linked with music in Aboriginal ceremonies. True or False.

17. Aboriginal music is primarily _____.

18. The _____ is a musical instrument which produces a buzz or whir when activated.

Didjeridu (Text Pages 158–161)

Purpose To acquaint the student with the didjeridu, its method of producing sound, and some elements of its musical style. Also, to acquaint the student with some aspects of polyvocality.

Guidance The *didjeridu* (did-jury-DOO) is an Aboriginal trumpet-type instrument found in the Northern coastal areas of Australia. It is most typically a tree branch hollowed out by termites, although other tubes are also used (bamboo, plastic, metal). The instrument is sounded by buzzing the lips into one end, while at times singing into it as well. When the player sings into the instrument while buzzing a low pitch (the fundamental tone), difference tones can be heard. These tones are the result of a physical phenomenon when two tones are heard together. The difference of their vibrations per second is heard as a distinct pitch (for example, a fundamental pitch of 500 vibrations per second, when subtracted from the sung pitch of 1200, equals a difference tone of 700 vibrations per second). The student is encouraged to read articles on combination frequencies and the harmonic series in the *Harvard Dictionary of Music* (1986 edition) for a fuller explanation of these acoustical and psycho-acoustical phenomena. It is sufficient to know that this is the explanation for the rich chordal effects that can be produced by the didjeridu player. The didjeridu player, sometimes referred to as the "puller," is often accompanied by the "songman" who beats a rhythm on his rhythm sticks.

In the section on polyvocality, reference is made to singers who cause their vocal cords to "divide." This refers to the singer producing the fundamental tone, as well as overtones. In the "Women's Chant" on Side 2 of the text record insert, this can be heard clearly (the fifth above the fundamental is audible).

>
> *Music Example*
>
> *didjeridu*
>
> *aerophone*
>
> *wooden trumpet*

Terms Define or identify the following terms, based on readings from your text and/or other sources.

23. didjeridu

24. clapping sticks or rhythm sticks

25. puller

26. songman

Reading Comprehension Answer the following work questions (answers at the end of the chapter):

19. Didjeridu playing is found among Aborigines mostly in the Great Victoria Desert. True or False.

20. The didjeridu's tone is produced by blowing through a double bamboo reed. True or False.

21. Didjeridu are made from tree branches that have been hollowed out by

termites. True or False.

22. The didjeridu is played by both _____ and _____ into it.

23. The very large didjeridu, which represents a _____, is used for which purpose: _____.

24. The very large didjeridu is played by using circular breathing. True or False.

25. The fundamental tone of the didjeridu functions as a _____.

26. Didjeridu are constructed only from indigenous materials. True or False

27. The employment of different vocal qualities that result in more than one pitch by a single singer is known as _____.

28. Aboriginal singers can sing chords by "croaking." True or False.

Aboriginal Music of South Australia
(Text Pages 161-163)

Purpose To describe the music of the Pitjantjatjara-speaking people of the western desert regions (between the Gibson Desert and the Great Victoria Desert) of southern Australia (in the southeastern part of Western Australia and the northwestern part of South Australia [the capitalized words are political divisions in Australia]).

Guidance Aboriginal songs in southern Australia are accompanied by percussion instruments only, rather than melodic ones. Therefore, rhythmical relationships are important for understanding the music. Most songs are attributed to supernatural power and are sung only in their proper context. These songs may be used to help members of the group, or they may be used to harm enemies. Only the elders may attempt such musical magic. The secret songs hold the most supernatural power, and the more power a song has the more complex is its inner melody and rhythmic makeup. Voice masking (which may include the technique described earlier as polyvocality) is often used when singing certain secret songs, a practice common to other peoples of the world when communicating with the supernatural. Other song types are children's songs, open or community songs that usually describe historical events, closed or secret songs that may describe antisocial behavior, and the "intoned story" or "history" songs, a succession of short songs which gradually unfold myths by alternating singing with the intoning of texts. Songs are, therefore, an essential part of the southern Australian Aborigine's existence, and the texts are largely syllabic.

Terms Define or identify the following terms or areas, based on readings from your text and/or other sources.

27. Pitjantjatjara

28. South Australia

29. Western Australia

30. Gibson Desert

31. Great Victoria Desert

32. Warbuton (a town and a range)

33. stick beating

34. history songs

Reading Comprehension Answer the following work questions:

29. Songs consist of an intensely elaborate encoding of information through interlocking layers of_____, _____ and _____ patterning.

30. Melody begins with a basic series of culturally accepted _____ _____ associated with a particular sacred being.

31. Songs including legal and moral codes serve to _____.

32. The most potent songs are known only by the _____, _____ _____ (_____).

33. Power through songs may be used for only good deeds. True or False.

34. Texts are often obscured by accent and rhythm to conceal secret meanings. True or False.

35. Deliberate grammatical ambiguities are never used to obscure or conceal secret meanings of songs. True or False.

36. The beating of sticks on the sand is often used to accompany sacred songs. True or False.

Aboriginal Music of Arnhem Land (Text Pages 163–168)

Purpose To describe the characteristic features of the music of the Arnhem Land Aborigines in the central north part of Australia.

Guidance The music of the northern Aborigines in Arnhem Land contrasts with the music of the southern Aborigines because it includes much use of melismatic texts and didjeridu accompaniment. In addition the north employs a large body of totemic song and dance materials (often referred to

> *Music Example*
>
> *wongga*
>
> *dance song*

as *corroboree* and/or *wongga*) that are secular (often referred to as camp music) with a sacred (but not secret) function as well. These performances border between being secular and sacred, showing the difficulty with making a distinction between sacred and secular music in northern Aboriginal culture (as in many non-Western cultures). Other songs are of "recent" origin (in quotes because they are often based on past song parts), that are said to be "found" or "dreamed" (a form of composition, often giving credit to the supernatural). These often have to do with contemporary life, and many are types of recreation songs for young men. In short, it seems that the Arnhem Land Aborigines have more songs for entertainment than in the southern part of Australia. Even within Arnhem Land, however, there are diverse musical areas that feature distinct types of music and performance styles. One of these styles is a highly syncopated performance style between the didjeridu, the vocal lines, and the rhythm sticks. Indeed, rhythmic complexity in the north is one of the main characteristics of Arnhem Land music.

Terms Define or identify the following terms or areas, based on readings from your text and/or other sources.

35. Arnhem Land

36. didjeridu

37. rhythm sticks

38. djedbangari

39. wongga (also wangga)

40. corroboree

Reading Comprehension Answer the following work questions:

37. Some Arnhem Land ceremonial chants make use of specific melodic _____that clearly identify them.

38. The Aborigines of northern Australia use the didjeridu extensively to accompany an immense body of traditional clan totemic songs of a sacred but not secret nature. True or False.

39. In the Wongga of western Arnhem Land, the elaborated melismatic songs are set to a rhymed verse. True or False.

40. The musical practice of the Tasmanian Island and Torres Strait is similar to that of the Australian mainland. True or False.

41. Torres Strait music is considered to belong more with Papua-New Guinea than with Australian Aboriginal culture. True or False.

42. In Aboriginal Australia, women have functional songs such as lullabies and ritual wailing at deaths and initiation. True or False.

Sample Test Questions

Only one answer is correct.

1. Nearly all Aboriginal rites for which there is music: a. exclude women, b. are for men and women in equal numbers, c. are family affairs, including children, d. include only men and the very old women.

2. Since the arrival of the Europeans, Aboriginal traditional music has: a. flourished, b. been taught in public schools throughout Australia, c. nearly become extinct, d. been played on radio stations throughout Australia.

3. Australian Aboriginal music, where it does exist, is in the hands of the: a. military, b. professional urban musicians, c. teenagers, d. the very old, e. women.

4. Which is *not* a "sign" of communication, for which there is music, between the "powers" and Aborigines? a. rainbows, b. dreams, c. trances, d. bountiful harvests, e. none of the above.

5. During paranormal experiences, which elements may be received or acquired? a. new songs, b. new dances, c. new rites, d. magical abilities, e. all of the above.

6. Aboriginal ritual practices, for which there is music, consist of which two main types? a. life and death, b. harvest and good fortune, c. magical gifts and predictions of the future, d. marriage and birth rituals, e. safe journey rituals.

7. Which is *not* an object in reference to the initiatory or fertility rites? a. body painting, b. headdresses, c. fasting, d. stone layouts, e. fires.

8. Women are: a. included in all the myths and rituals of the major cults, b. subservient only in the minor rituals, c. excluded from nearly all Aboriginal myths and rituals of major cults, d. the center and source of all rituals, e. equal to men in all rituals.

9. The accompanying chants to the Wandjina cave paintings in northwest Australia refer to: a. the quest for rain, b. the various parts of the spirit being's body, c. the recently dead relatives of the singer, d. magical help for the hunting of animals.

10. Which is *not* a context for music-making among the Aborigines? a. cave painting, b. bark painting, c. body painting, d. bone painting.

11. Very closely linked with music in Aboriginal ceremonies is: a. eating, b. drinking, c. fighting, d. dancing, e. fasting.

12. Aboriginal music is primarily: a. vocal, b. instrumental, c. produced by the body alone, d. mostly a dance form without musical accompaniment.

13. Aboriginal ceremonial dancing is composed of steps which suggest the observation of: a. religious beliefs, b. feelings for members of the cul-

ture, c. the animals found in their environment, d. their relationship to the universe.

14. The origin of the name didjeridu is perhaps: a. from an early British dialect, b. an onomatopoeic description of some of the instrument's sounds, c. from the tree of that name, d. from the name of the inventor of the instrument.

15. The didjeridu produces interesting sounds because a. it is coated inside with a special mixture of clay and blood, b. it has two fingerholes, c. it is both blown and sung into, d. the strings are made of vegetable fibers.

16. In its authentic context, how many didjeridu are used at one time? a. 1, b. 2, c. 3, d. 4, e. 5.

17. Didjeridu are made from a. plastic piping, b. bamboo, c. tree branches, d. metal piping, e. a through d.

18. An extremely large didjeridu, measuring up to three meters in length, is used for certain secret ceremonies in which it represents what? a. a large bird, b. a large kangaroo, c. a great snake, d. a giant lizard, e. the grandfather ancestor in Dreamtime.

19. Songs, if performed correctly, may draw on supernatural power left in the soil from: a. kangaroo droppings, b. the Dreaming, c. royal ancestors, d. slain enemies, e. evil spirits.

20. Songs about miscreants as well as talented hunters are used as a means of: a. social control, b. child education, c. teaching legal and moral codes, d. a and c only, e. a, b, and c.

21. Distorting the text of a song through accentuation, changing vowel sounds, and "turning" syllables is done to: a. create interesting tone colors, b. enhance rhythmical patterns, c. amuse the listener, d. obscure or conceal secret meanings, e. create a variation on a theme.

22. Totemic songs describe events in Aboriginal: a. socialization with whites, b. nature, c. love affairs, d. history, e. government.

23. Some Australian Aboriginal women sing lullabies and what other type of song form? a. wailing at deaths and initiations, b. juggling, c. planting, d. harvesting, e. shamanism.

24. A very prevalent rhythmical feature found in the didjeridu playing style and the vocal lines can be called: a. syncopation, b. hemiola, c. hocket, d. colotomy, e. heterophony.

25. A form of Aboriginal camp music and dance is known as: a. didjeridu, b. djedbangari, c. wongga, d. corroboree, e. c and d.

26. Scholars know virtually nothing about the music of the Tasmanian native peoples because: a. the Tasmanians have not allowed outsiders into their camps, b. the Tasmanians never sing, c. the Tasmanians have been extinct for more than a century, d. no outsider has ever dared to travel to Tasmanian camps, e. the Tasmanians are nomadic and

have always eluded outsiders.

27. One musical characteristic of the playing of didjeridu and rhythm sticks together during nonsecret music and dance performances is: a. precise unison playing, b. a constant changing of meters from triple to duple and back again, c. the simultaneous use of duple rhythm by the sticks against triple rhythm by the didjeridu, d. a complete lack of regularity.

Answers to Reading Comprehension Questions

1. 18th
2. nomadic, hunting, grazing
3. False: men were thought of as superior and were in charge of music and the other arts, while women did the menial tasks
4. True
5. False: there are hundreds of languages and songs are not mutually intelligible
6. sung stories, pictures
7. False: creativity is attributed to the powers only, and men simply receive and reproduce the songs
8. new songs, dances, rites, magical abilities
9. transcendental, totemic
10. rites of life, rites of death
11. True
12. True
13. False: women do not participate in ceremonials associated with life and death
14. True
15. social, spiritual
16. True
17. vocal
18. bullroarer
19. False: it is found across the northern part of Australia, but not inland
20. False: its sound is produced by buzzing the lips, like playing a trumpet
21. True
22. buzzing the lips, singing
23. great snake, secret ceremonies
24. False: it is so large that circular breathing cannot be employed
25. drone
26. False: plastic and metal tubing is also used
27. polyvocality
28. True
29. melodic, rhythmic, textural
30. intervals
31. educate children

32. old, wise men (tribal elders)
33. False: there are also power songs for killing
34. True
35. False: grammatical ambiguities are used to hide secret meanings
36. True
37. key figures or germinal motives
38. True
39. False: the songs are free and not effected by verbal meaning
40. False: the Tasmanians are extinct and their music unknown, while Torres Strait music is more similar to Papua-New Guinea than to the Australian Aborigines
41. True
42. True

Answers to Sample Test Questions

1. a
2. c
3. d
4. d
5. e
6. a
7. c
8. c
9. b
10. d
11. d
12. a
13. c
14. b
15. c
16. a
17. e
18. c
19. b
20. e
21. d
22. d
23. a
24. a
25. e
26. c
27. c

Listening Form

Student Name_____ I.D. Number_____
Course Name _____ Course Number_____
Date_____ Chapter Number_____ Listening Example Number _____
Record or Tape Number_____ Name of Culture and Location _____
Name of Performer(s)_____
Instructions: place an X, ✓, or • in appropriate boxes; give types; indicate native names.

performing elements (if vocal)	solo: M/F	duo: M/F	trio: M/F	quartet: M/F	group: M/F	other: M/F
performing elements (if instrumental)	corpophone	idiophone	membrano-phone	aerophone	chordophone	electrophone	other
texture	single melody	dense unison	heterophone	imitation	parallelism	disphony	other
more texture	with drone	with time indicator	chordal	polyphonic stratification	colotomy	combination	variable
melodic contour	static	ascending	descending	conjunct	disjunct	undulating	terraced
mode or scale	number of notes	vernacular	using cipher notation (numbers), indicate the mode or scale in ascending order
meter	free	duple	triple	compound	additive	poly	other
speed	very slow	slow	moderate	fast	very fast	variable	other
amplitude	very soft	soft	moderate	loud	very loud	variable	other
timbre (tone color)	clear	breathy	nasal	open	tight	masked	other
inflections	no vibrato	slow vibrato	fast vibrato	wide vibrato	falsetto	multiphonics	other
formal structure	vernacular name	expanding	reverting	strophic	theme and variations	other	
structural or performance techniques	ostinato	responsorial	antiphonal	elastic rhythm	if vocal: syllabic or melismatic	non-synchronous parts	other

Chapter 10

Text Pages 172 – 194

Music South of the Sahara

Atta Annan Mensah

Introduction to Chapter (Text Pages 172–173)

Purpose To introduce the basic musical influences in sub-Saharan Africa, and to become familiar with the importance of tradition in the musical practices of the region.

Guidance This chapter studies only the music south of the region known as the Maghreb, which is Arabic for "land of the setting sun." The Maghreb includes, then, the northern regions of the African continent, although sometimes Egypt is excluded. The map on page 173 of the text shows the countries found in the sub-Saharan region of Africa. With a continent as large, diverse, and dynamic as Africa, there are often changes in the names of countries (Rhodesia is now Zimbabwe). Consult a very recent atlas for current names. Taken as a whole, the continent of Africa is the second largest in the world (after Asia). Over 1000 different languages have been identified, although these have been classified within four large language families (see *Cultural Atlas of Africa,* Jocelyn Murray, ed., New York: Facts on File Publications [1982], text pages 24–30). There is also a great diversity of musical styles and traditions, including major differences between the many types of music south of the Sahara region alone.

During the twentieth century, European, American, Arabic, and Indian pop musics have been introduced into many parts of Africa. In addition, the phonograph, tape recorder, motion picture, and radio have given African people new ways of viewing their world. Yet, in spite of the influence of modern technology on African music and culture, the importance of traditional music and its function in African life are equally evident. In Africa south of the Sahara, music functions both as entertainment and ceremony for such activities as life passages, medical practices, and the continuation of belief systems.

The *New Grove Dictionary of Music and Musicians,* Volume I, pages 144–153, offers insights into the twentieth century influences on African music. This excellent resource for additional information about the sub-

Saharan region should be consulted because of its added perspectives.

Terms Define or identify the following terms or areas, based on readings from the text and/or other sources.

1. Locate Africa and the Sahara desert on a world globe, and notice their sizes.

2. Be able to identify the musical instruments in the pictures.

3. Maghreb

4. banjo

5. Nairobi

6. Accra

7. one-stringed violin

Reading Comprehension Answer the following work questions (answers at end of this chapter):

1. The _____-_____ _____ is a musical instrument whose presence throughout Africa, including the North, has been one unifying factor.

2. The most important twentieth century change in African music has resulted from the introduction of Western pop music. True or False.

3. Some of the change agents in twentieth century Africa are _____, _____, and modern _____.

4. Homemade toys among African children often include such musical instruments as _____, _____, _____ and _____.

5. The importance of new African music is often indicated by _____.

Traditional Music (Text Pages 173–186)

Purpose To show that the traditional music of Africa south of the Sahara has a variety of uses, functions, types, and components. The author divides this lengthy portion of his chapter into the following six subsections: *Instrumental Resources; Ensembles; Rhythm; Timbre; Pitch Combination;* and *Significance of Music*. The purpose of such divisions is to separate and study the principal elements that constitute sub-Saharan African music.

Guidance Traditional African music plays an important role in rituals of the human life cycle, also known as rites of passage. It is also used during religious ceremonies, preparations for and celebrations of war and the hunt, healing, divination, work, and entertainment. In Africa, as in many non-European cultures (and even in early Europe and in present rural Europe), a division between the sacred and the profane is not often found, or one blends into the other. Likewise, as in many non-European cultures, what non-Africans would call music is usually translated by the Africans themselves to mean something greater than just the sound.

> ♪
>
> *Music Examples*
>
> *African idiophones*

Instrumental Resources (text pages 174–176): The idiophone category is very large, including a great variety of instruments whose sounds are produced by objects rattling together. These can be container rattles made from gourds, calabashes, wicker, or other materials that contain seeds, stones, or other small objects that create sound when shaken. They can also be hard objects strung on fibers, such as strung bells, shells, husks, seeds, etc., which are wrapped around the legs, arms, or waists of dancers. Xylophones are struck wooden-keyed instruments ("xylon" is Greek for wood), and a common name for the xylophone in Africa (and the Americas) is marimba. Many African xylophones, such as the *chohun* of Ghana, are constructed in such a way that each pitch produces a sympathetic buzz. Called a mirlitone in English, the xylophone buzzer apparatus is made by the attachment of a thin membrane made from matted spider webbing over a hole in each gourd resonator. To make a connection between the African xylophone and the wooden or metal keyed instruments of Indonesia is known as diffusion theory, which is impossible to prove because of the great distance of ocean separating Africa and Indonesia. The common term "hand piano" is often used interchangeably with "finger piano" by English-speaking people to refer to the plucked idiophone. Another outsider term for the same type of instrument is the "lamellaphone." The principle of the plucked idiophone (pictured in Figure 10-2) is similar to the common American and European jewelry box or music box, except that the tongues in the Western music box are plucked by a mechanical device rather than with the fingers and thumbs. Friction drums are also common in South America (see Chapter 20), especially in Brazil. Indeed, many African musical instruments are associated with the Americas because they were constructed (not brought directly except in recent times) in the New World by African slaves, their descendants, or recent immigrants. The membranophone category in Africa includes dozens of skin drum types, both single- and double-headed. An important type from Nigeria is the *bata*, which is double-headed and shaped like a graceful hourglass. Bata drums, played in a set of three, are also fournd in Cuba and the United States, where decendents of the Yoruba people live and worship Shango, a West African deity who is evolked by the bata drums. Chordophones are subclassified as zithers, lyres, harps, and lutes (rather than fiddles). Bowed lutes (violins or fiddles, which are the same type of instrument) are the common one-stringed variety, and plucked lutes are similar to banjos (resonator covered with skin) and guitars (resonator not covered with skin). When the author refers to "shell" instruments (bowed fiddle and megaphones), he is referring to turtle or other animal shells, not sea or conch shells. Edge aerophones with fingerholes, or flutes,

Music Examples: African membranophones

Music Examples: African aerophones

Music Examples: African chordophones

may be without notch (like the Arabic nei), with notch (like the Chinese hsiao, Japanese shakuhachi, and Andean kena), with a plug (corked?) (like the recorder), whistle (like globular flutes or ocarinas; a whistle could also mean it is without fingerholes), and cross blown or transverse (like the European flute and Chinese ti). Trumpets (lip concussion aerophones) are made from animal horns, ivory, and/or wood.

Ensembles (text page 176): Musical instruments in sub-Saharan African are mostly played by men, although women play rattles, and on fewer occasions, drums during female initiation rituals where men are not allowed. Some chordophones are played by women as well as men. One of the most common musical instruments, played by everyone in ensemble, are the hands that are clapped together (corpophone).

Rhythm (text pages 176–180): One of the most important characteristics of African music is rhythmic complexity. Because of the diversity of African music and culture, one basic rhythmic characteristic should not be isolated. Study has shown there to be a number of characteristics that exist in a variety of combinations. Rhythmic and pulse interplay between several percussion instruments (and even melodic instruments, including voices) is very common. When various lines (multilinear texture) of music (each one may be performed by a particular drum or bell, for example) perform together, non-African analysts may use the terms divisive (e.g., 6/8 divided into 3+3 or 2+2+2), additive (e.g., 6/8 made up of 4+2 or 3+2+1), or hemiola (e.g., 6/8 stressing 2+2+2 while the underlying pulse is 3+3) to try to understand them better. African musicians, however, do not probably think in those terms. This entire section, in fact, is based on terms applied by non-Africans to explain African rhythm. The most widely used and accepted by analysts are "polyrhythm" and "metronome sense." Polyrhythm is when each line (as in an orchestra consisting of drums, rattles, and bells) is rhythmically independent in terms of its internal organization of strong and weak beats. Each line may also constitute a recurring rhythmic pattern, the principal beats of which may or may not coincide with the principal beats of the other lines in the texture. When these individual lines are being performed, the musician and/or the listener perceives a subjective pulse. This has been called the metronome sense, and it may differ from one person to the next. The author also refers to "burden text," which is a text of words or vocables, with or without definite meaning, employed as a memory aid to the sound and pattern of arhythmic or melodic fragment. Similar texts are employed in India and Japan as aids to the drummers.

Timbre (text page 180): Timbre is tone color or the unique and identifying sound characteristic of an instrument or a voice. For example, a flute and violin playing the exact same note are differentiated by their timbre or tone color. There are not, however, clear terms that describe such differences. When singers alter their voices, we often refer to the alteration as voice masking. Like its use among Native Americans and other indigenous people, voice masking in Africa often symbolizes the supernatural or royalty. The author refers to mirliton with reference to a gourd trumpet ensemble; a mirliton is a parchment over a hole that buzzes in sympathy with the voice or instrument. This membrane attachment is like a kazoo or a Chinese ti-tzu; in Africa, mirliton vibrators are used on xylophones and trumpets. The buzz effect is one of the most important African aesthetics.

Pitch Combination (text pages 180–184): When two or more pitches combine and sound together, European musicians call the phenomenon harmony. In Europe and other areas where European-derived music is found, this harmony is called tonal because certain chords (blocks of tones, usually a third apart) are more important than others, creating a hierarchy and a feeling of tension and rest. For that reason, many scholars do not choose to apply the term harmony to African music. Nevertheless, two or more notes are often combined to create a multipart texture that could be said to be harmonious, but not harmonic. The argument is not so much with the phenomenon of simultaneous tones as it is with the use of English (or European) terms to describe African (or other non-European) musics. For this reason the author chooses to use the term "pitch combination," meaning the manner in which various pitches are sounded together. Voices, as well as musical instruments, sometimes perform together in an interlocking fashon, creating a type of harmonious texture. The Mbuti Pygmies of the Ituri Rainforest sing as a large group, often celebrating a successful hunt.

Melody (text pages 184–185): A melody has shape or contour, ranging from static (very little movement up or down), upward, downward, or any combination of the above. African melodies, like many melodies of Native North and South Americans, often move downward. Melodies are constructed from conjunct (close or stepwise) or disjunct (far apart or skipwise) intervals. When a text is attached to a melody, the relationship is said to be melismatic (many notes to one syllable), syllabic (one note to each syllable), or a combination of the above. It is important to realize that musicians from most cultures strive to tune their instruments within the standard determined by the particular culture. The author points out a particular instance in which certain xylophones are tuned slightly apart on purpose so their simultaneously sounding similar pitches create a pulsation (interference waves or acoustic beats) similar to the bronze-keyed idiophones of Bali, Indonesia.

Significance of Music (text pages 185–186): It cannot be stressed enough how important music and dance are in traditional sub-Saharan cultures; music and dance work together to give meaning to life's existence.

Terms Define or identify the following terms, based on readings from the text and/or other sources.

8. spirit possession

9. sansa

10. mbira

11. kalimba

12. slit drum / slit gong

13. friction drum

14. xylophone

Music Examples

African vocal music

15. clash of rhythms

16. polymeter

17. metronome sense

18. gyamadudu

19. bata

20. master drummer

21. voice masking

22. mirliton

23. scale

24. story telling

Reading Comprehension Answer the following work questions (answers at end of this chapter):

6. Traditional African music occurs primarily during rites of _____ _____.

7. The importance of the functional role of music in African life has been the subject of research scholars. True or False.

8. Traditional African societies never view their music as entertainment. True or False.

9. The sansa is believed to have originated in which continent? _____.

10. African trumpets (lip concussion aerophones) may be made of _____, _____, and/or _____.

11. The friction drum's sound is produced by rubbing _____.

12. African music may be functional, for amusement, or a combination of both. True or False.

13. Idiophones are the most widely diffused instruments in sub-Saharan Africa. True or False.

14. African pot drums are classified as _____-phones.

15. African instruments are most often played by themselves. True or False.

16. African ensembles are usually restricted to three instruments. True or False.

17. In Akan (Ghana) drumming there is always one dominant _____ , but all other repeated rhythmic patterns may also be thought of as _____ _____.

18. Sub-Saharan music may be described in terms of one regulative principle. True or False.

19. Akan drumming should be described on a different set of principles from that of Ndebele or Zulu music. True or False.

20. In a multilinear rhythmic texture, the principal beats will never coincide. True or False.

21. The ability of a listener or player to maintain a subjective beat in order to orient himself/herself to changing rhythmic activity is known as _____ _____.

22. A line or phrase with a definite meaning employed as a memory aid to the sound and pattern of a rhythmic or melodic fragment is a _____.

23. In full drum orchestras, the main source of excitement is supplied by the _____.

24. The human voice is able to demonstrate the importance of sound quality when it changes from natural singing to _____ of a _____.

25. African drumming has a wide variety of tone colors. True or False.

26. In sub-Saharan African music, the aesthetic point of emphasis is rhythm. True or False.

27. The importance of sound quality in African music is always demonstrated by a musical instrument. True or False.

28. In sub-Saharan African music, _____ "voices" often act together and give rise to _____ effects.

29. Any simultaneous occurrence of two or more pitched sounds in African music may be regarded as a _____; the result may also be described as _____.

30. African cultures do not have names for their scales because they are chosen at random. True or False.

31. African instrumentalists are usually concerned about their instruments being in tune. True or False.

32. Among the Akan (Ghana), part singing is referred to as "organization." True or False.

33. During African story telling, audience members may stand up and act out portions of the story with _____ and _____.

34. Music in Africa is never organized just to please the ear. True or False.

Twentieth-Century Developments (Text Pages 186–187)

Purpose To identify several 20th century African popular music styles.

Guidance There are literally dozens of popular musical forms in sub-Saharan Africa, and as soon as something is written about any of them, new ones appear. This is true with popular music anywhere. By the time scholars write about popular forms, many will have already disappeared, will have crystallized into "classical" forms, or will have continued to develop and change into expressions differing from how they were originally described. Popular music forms not mentioned by the author are *juju*, *fuji*, Afro-beat, Yo-pop, and others in Nigeria; *soukous* in Zaire; *mbube* in South Africa; *makossa* in Cameroon; and many others (see *Popular Musics of the Non-Western World,* by Peter Manuel, New York: Oxford University Press, 1988). Additionally, European and American forms, such as jazz, rock, reggae, salsa, compas, and others, have had great popularity and acculturative influences on African popular forms.

Terms Define or identify the following terms or areas, based on readings from the text and/or other sources.

25. tarabu

26. kwela

27. soukous

28. highlife

29. juju

Reading Comprehension Answer the following work questions (answers at end of this chapter):

35. The popular music style called highlife from _____, probably originated with _____ that consisted of native soldiers and other musicians from the _____ _____.

36. Tarabu is a popular music from the _____ coast of Africa that shows _____ influence.

37. Kwela is often called "West African Jive." True or False.

38. Highlife has been performed by groups such as fife corps, brass bands, orchestras with strings, swing bands, and small combos. True or False.

Factors in the Spread of Pop Music
(Text Pages 187–188)

Purpose To explain why and how pop and other new musics developed in sub-Saharan Africa.

Guidance The author rightly explains that not all new music in Africa is pop music. Since Vatican II in the late 1950s, the Pope decreed that the Mass should be performed in the vernacular tongues of the people. "Missa Luba," a Catholic Mass sung in the Luba language and accompanied by traditional Luba drums and singers, was composed by a Belgian priest. Native composers, either working in the European tradition or incorporating African and European ideas in their music, have endeavored to create works of national flavor. Many countries have national dance and theater troupes that bring traditional and new works of art to foreign audiences as well as national urban centers.

Every country in Africa has its own unique types of pop music, usually consisting of varying degrees of traditional musical instrument usage. Few pop music groups make no use of traditional sounds, since native instruments are often an aspect of nationalism, cultural and ethnic pride, and originality. Pop musicians the world over are interested in originality, and cultural hegemony or patrimony are influential as nations and people struggle for political and economic equality. Pop music is a language for cultural communication as well as diversion, and many pop musicians have been imprisoned or exiled because of what their music communicates. Many others have become world famous, with lucrative recording contracts in Europe (particularly England and France) and America; this is almost always because African pop music is very danceable and because identification with African roots has become important for African-derived peoples in Europe, the Americas, and elsewhere. Because Africa is so large and varied, only three pop musical forms will be surveyed: *juju* (Nigeria), *soukous* (Congo and Zaire), *griot* "pop" (Gambia and Senegal [together referred to as Senegambia], Mali, and Guinea). Their musical roots and development can be seen in several excellent videos, especially *Born Musicians*, *West African Popular Music*, and *Konkombe: The Nigerian Pop Music Scene*.

Juju music today is essentially Yoroba (Nigeria) urban pop music that has evolved from its early development in Lagos in the1950s into many forms today. Such terms as *Yo-Pop* (*Yoruba pop*ular), *Afro-beat*, and *fuji* are related forms of Nigerian pop music. Before its urbanized form and variants, juju existed as a rural style known as "palm wine" music, featuring acoustic guitars and a variety of percussive instruments. Two historical events in particular caused urban juju to progress: World War II with consequent Western jazz band influences in Lagos, and the Nigerian Civil War in the late 1960s, which caused Ghanaian highlife musicians to move to Lagos. As an urbanized style, juju features electric guitars and vocals (often singing about Christian ideals), and several of the most important juju musicians are important guitarists and/or vocalists, such as Sunny Adé, Segun Adewale, and Ebenezer Obey. As an interest in originality and nationalism developed, many groups added traditional Nigerian drums to their highly amplified sound. Fuji developed in the 1980s as a Nigerian pop music that featured traditional drums more than guitars, and a continued vocal texture that took traditional and Islamic praise songs as its sources of inspiration. Sikiru Ayind Barrister, Wasui Barrister, and Ayinla Kollington are three of the most popular fuji singers and band leaders.

"Soukous" is a broad term used to categorize the urbanized pop/dance music (and the act of dancing itself) in the capital cities of Congo (Brazzaville) and Zaire (Kinshasa). Mensah (page 187) refers to this music as "Congolese" and "Congolese rhumba," the latter term suggests Cuban musical influences. Social unrest in Zaire has caused much of the recording of soukous to take place in Paris, and such stars as Kanda Bongo Man, Pepe Kalle, and Rigo Star recorded almost exclusively in France. Most of their music has featured guitars, some brass instruments, and, of course, vocals. Later groups, such as the funky Bobongo Stars, made considerable use of electric guitar as well as brass and saxophones. A more recent group known as Swede Swede has, like Nigerian fuji, dropped the heavy reliance on electric lead and rhythm guitars and included more traditional drums and marimba with their vocals (maintaining bass guitar, however).

For lack of a better term, I will use the words "griot pop" to refer to pop music fusion from Senegambia (Senegal and the Gambia), Mali, and Guinea; this is music based on the praise singing styles of the griot (*jali*) who is accompanied by the *kora* (harp lute). Great kora-playing griot artists have recorded in France, England, Germany, and the United States, and one in particular, Gambian Foday Musa Suso, has joined forces with Western musicians to develop a unique "griot pop" or "griot jazz" style. In 1978 he moved from the Gambia to the United States, where he began his ensemble known as the Mandingo Griot Society. Joining forces with trumpeter Don Cherry and pianist Herbie Hancock, he has produced several fusion albums that are unique. Another Gambian, a young kora master by the name of Soriba Kouyaté, has also fused his music with jazz and pop; he has also been featured with the famous Youssou N'Dour, Senegal's greatest pop singer who comes from a long line of well-known griots. Jali Musa Jawara from Guinea has also recorded contemporary music that includes griot singing, kora, balafon, guitar, and female chorus.

Terms   Define or identify the following terms, based on readings from the text and/or other sources.

30. "Missa Luba"

31. griot

Reading Comprehension
Answer the following work questions (answers at end of this chapter):

39. New African theater music makes use of traditional African choruses with drums and other traditional African instruments. True or False.

40. New African theater music also makes use of _____ part harmony and ensembles combining _____ and _____ instruments.

Video Viewing

1. Masked dance of the Dogon. Mali, the Dogon (17-10). *The JVC Video Anthology of World Music and Dance*, Middle East and Africa II (VTMV-47).

2. Sanza—finger piano performance. Cameroon, the Fulbe (17-12). *The JVC Video Anthology of World Music and Dance*, Middle East and Africa II (VTMV-47).

3. Balafon—xylophone performance. Cameroon, the Fulbe (17-13). *The JVC Video Anthology of World Music and Dance*, Middle East and Africa II (VTMV-47).

4. Dance of the Bambuti. Zaire, the Mbuti (17-21). *The JVC Video Anthology of World Music and Dance*, Middle East and Africa II (VTMV-47).

5. Orchestra of the Town of Mongo. Chad (18-1). *The JVC Video Anthology of World Music and Dance*, Middle East and Africa III (VTMV-48).

6. Sultan's orchestra of the town of Mao. Chad (18-2). *The JVC Video Anthology of World Music and Dance*, Middle East and Africa III (VTMV-48).

7. Festival orchestra. Chad, the Djonkor (18-3). *The JVC Video Anthology of World Music and Dance*, Middle East and Africa III (VTMV-48).

8. Hero praise song with kundinge [harp] accompaniment. Chad, the Djonkor (18-5). *The JVC Video Anthology of World Music and Dance*, Middle East and Africa III (VTMV-48).

9. Praise song with kukuma [one-string instrument] accompaniment. Chad, the Bulala (18-6). *The JVC Video Anthology of World Music and Dance*, Middle East and Africa III (VTMV-48).

10. Libo—transverse...[clarinet] performance. Chad, the Hausa (18-7). *The JVC Video Anthology of World Music and Dance*, Middle East and Africa III (VTMV-48).

11. Memorial ceremony for King Mkong Moteh. Cameroon, the Tikar (18-14). *The JVC Video Anthology of World Music and Dance*, Middle East and Africa III (VTMV-48).

12. Mourning music by a mask clan. Cameroon, the Tikar (18-15). *The JVC Video Anthology of World Music and Dance*, Middle East and Africa III

(VTMV-48).

13. Singing and performing on a bow harp. Ivory Coast (Cote d'Ivoire), the Baule (19-1). *The JVC Video Anthology of World Music and Dance*, Middle East and Africa IV (VTMV-49).
14. Drum language. Ivory Coast (Cote d'Ivoire), the Baule (19-2). *The JVC Video Anthology of World Music and Dance*, Middle East and Africa IV (VTMV-49).
15. Gbagba—masked dance of Asouakro. Ivory Coast (Cote d'Ivoire), the Baule (19-3). *The JVC Video Anthology of World Music and Dance*, Middle East and Africa IV (VTMV-49).
16. Goli—masked dance of Agubanjansou. Ivory Coast (Cote d'Ivoire), the Baule (19-4). *The JVC Video Anthology of World Music and Dance*, Middle East and Africa IV (VTMV-49).
17. Gegon mask dance: "The maple song." Ivory Coast (Cote d'Ivoire), the Dan (19-5). *The JVC Video Anthology of World Music and Dance*, Middle East and Africa IV (VTMV-49).
18. Stilt dance of the Kupegbouni. Ivory Coast (Cote d'Ivoire), the Dan (19-8). *The JVC Video Anthology of World Music and Dance*, Middle East and Africa IV (VTMV-49).
19. Acrobatic dance of the snake girl. Ivory Coast (Cote d'Ivoire), the Gere (19-10). *The JVC Video Anthology of World Music and Dance*, Middle East and Africa IV (VTMV-49).
20. Dance of Zorofla women: "Greagba." Ivory Coast (Cote d'Ivoire), the Guro (19-11). *The JVC Video Anthology of World Music and Dance*, Middle East and Africa IV (VTMV-49).
21. Musical bow performance. Botswana, the San [Bushmen] (19-14). *The JVC Video Anthology of World Music and Dance*, Middle East and Africa IV (VTMV-49).
22. Handelo—one-string instrument and song. Botswana, the San [Bushmen] (19-15). *The JVC Video Anthology of World Music and Dance*, Middle East and Africa IV (VTMV-49).
23. Dongo—hand piano and song. Botswana, the San [Bushmen] (19-16). *The JVC Video Anthology of World Music and Dance*, Middle East and Africa IV (VTMV-49).
24. Trance-dance treatment of sickness. Botswana, the San [Bushmen] (19-17). *The JVC Video Anthology of World Music and Dance*, Middle East and Africa IV (VTMV-49).
25. *Born Musicians: Traditional Music from the Gambia* (Program 1). Repercussions. A Celebration of African-American Music. Directed by Geoffrey Haydon and Dennis Marks. Home Vision VHS 833-9052.
26. *The Drums of Dagbon* (Program 5). Repercussions. A Celebration of African-American Music. Directed by Geoffrey Haydon and Dennis Marks. Home Vision VHS 833-9054.
27. *West African Popular Music* (Program 7). Repercussions. A Celebration of African-American Music. Directed by Geoffrey Haydon and Dennis Marks. Home Vision VHS 833-9056.
28. *Konkombé: The Nigerian Pop Music Scene*. Beats of the Heart series. Jeremy Marre, director and producer.

Sample Test Questions

Multiple choice questions. Only one answer is correct.

1. The occurrence of which African instrument type suggests a connection between the regions of North, East, West, and Central Africa: a. drum, b. one-string violin, c. xylophone, d. gourd rattle, e. flute.
2. A major force towards the introduction of change has been: a. traditional belief systems, b. urbanization, c. regional diversity, d. rites of passage.
3. New musical tastes have been introduced to African youth through: a. schools, b. churches, c. Western technology, d. a and b, e. all of the above.
4. One of the most common home-made musical instruments used as a child's toy is: a. guitar, b. whistle top, c. xylophone, d. flute, e. rattle.
5. Traditional African music can be heard in which context: a. spirit possession rites, b. rites of passage, c. divining, d. therapy, e. all the above.
6. The bell in drum ensembles from Ghana is used for what purpose? a. signaling, b. adding tonal clusters, c. maintaining a time line, d. calling the spirits, e. calling potential listeners to come.
7. A typical Ugandan third instrument in the xylophone and drum ensemble would be what? a. flute, b. panpipe, c. whistle, d. guitar, e. mbira.
8. Which is not an African chordophone type? a. musical bow, b. trough zither, c. lyre, d. tube harp, e. tube zither.
9. African membranophones are never played with which of the following: a. wet rag, b. sticks, c. hands, d. brush, e. a and d.
10. The bwola dance, incorporating over 200 drums, was performed for which president in 1971? a. Nixon, b. Amin, c. Sadat, d. Mobutu, e. Tubman.
11. The slit drum is constructed of which material: a. metal, b. bamboo, c. clay, d. gourd, e. wood.
12. Metronome sense refers to: a. the audible downbeats, b. the ability to orient oneself to changing rhythmic activity by a subjective beat, c. the ability to mark time with machine-like precision, d. b and c, e. none of the above.
13. The master drummer plays rhythmic units that are: a. endlessly repeated with minimal variation or elaboration, b. wide recurring cycles of consecutive rhythmic patterns, continuously reshuffled for variety, c. the rhythmic resultant of all other lines in the texture.
14. The principle of polymeter: a. is understood by every African musician, b. is a playing technique of the twentieth century, c. should only be regarded as an analyst's tool, d. is a solo flute technique.
15. Voice masking in sub-Saharan Africa often symbolizes: a. the supernatural, b. anger, c. royalty, d. happiness, e. a and c.
16. The provision of buzzer attachments to musical instruments, to an instrumentalist's wrist, or a dancer's calves or ankles, is one of the usual

devices: a. that serves as sacred amulets, providing supernatural power, b. that wards off evil spirits because they reflect evil, c. that functions as the voices of the spirits themselves, d. used to build up a background of tone color for aesthetic reasons.

17. Looking at sub-Saharan Africa as a whole, multipart musical traditions may include: a. up to 20 voice parts, b. from two to as many as six voices, c. two parts, but rarely more than that, d. side blown trumpets, drums, mbiras, guitars, and many other instruments performing together.

18. Concerning the tuning of musical instruments: a. only professional musicians know how to tune their instruments, b. tuning is not important, c. instrumentalists usually go to great lengths to insure that their own particular instruments or ensembles are well in tune, d. only aerophones and chordophones are tuned; the membranophones and idiophones do not require tuning.

19. As a technique of dramatic expression in Africa, music is important in: a. shamanistic curing, b. politics, c. divination, d. initiation rituals, e. story telling.

20. The themes of tarabu music are almost exclusively about: a. war, b. hunting, c. a good harvest, d. fertility, e. love.

21. Kwela was mostly popular in which African countries: a. Mali and Niger, b. Senegal, Guinea, and Sierra Leone, c. South Africa, Zambia, and Malawi, d. Cameroon and Chad, e. Togo and Ivory Coast.

22. Which is *not* typical of a kwela band: a. penny whistles, b. vocalists, c. guitar, d. trumpet.

23. Congolese pop music reflects which musical influences: a. Iranian and Arabic, b. Moroccan and Spanish, c. Japanese and Chinese, d. Latin American, e. Ukrainian.

24. Music for the theatrical stage is now being composed for: a. participating audiences only, b. listening audiences only, c. always a combination of both participating and listening audiences, d. only those who are very wealthy, e. tourists only.

25. "Missa Luba" was written by: a. a Belgian priest, b. a Luba chief, c. a Baptist missionary, d. a musicologist from Zaire, e. a French priest.

Answers to Reading Comprehension Questions

1. one-stringed violin
2. True
3. churches, schools, technology
4. banjo, guitar, snare drum, bass drum
5. press coverage
6. passage
7. True
8. False: it can be
9. Africa

10. wood, animal horn, animal tusks
11. with a wet cloth, a stick that is inserted into the drum and attached to the skin
12. True
13. False: membranophones are
14. aero-
15. False: also in ensembles or with voices
16. False: they range from two to many
17. rhythmic line, points of reference
18. False: there are a combination of regulative principles
19. True
20. False: they will eventually coincide
21. metronome sense
22. burden text
23. master drummer
24. imitation, musical instrument
25. True
26. False: tone color, interplay of pitch lines, and the exploitation of sheer beauty are also important
27. False: it also includes vocal sounds
28. pitched, chordal
29. chord, harmony
30. False: cultures usually have specific terms for their scales
31. True
32. False: it is "decoration"
33. song, dance
34. False: just the opposite is true
35. Ghana, marching bands, West Indies
36. East, Arabic
37. False: it is "South African Jive"
38. True
39. True
40. four, African, European

Answers to Sample Test Questions

1. b
2. b
3. e
4. a
5. e
6. c
7. a

8. d
9. d
10. b
11. e
12. b
13. b
14. c
15. e
16. d
17. b
18. c
19. e
20. e
21. c
22. d
23. d
24. b
25. a

Listening Form

Student Name_____ I.D. Number_____
Course Name _____ Course Number _____
Date_____Chapter Number_____Listening Example Number _____
Record or Tape Number_____Name of Culture and Location _____
Name of Performer(s)_____
Instructions: place an X, ✓, or • in appropriate boxes; give types; indicate native names.

performing elements (if vocal)	solo: M/F	duo: M/F	trio: M/F	quartet: M/F	group: M/F	other: M/F
performing elements (if instrumental)	corpophone	idiophone	membranophone	aerophone	chordophone	electrophone	other
texture	single melody	dense unison	heterophone	imitation	parallelism	disphony	other
more texture	with drone	with time indicator	chordal	polyphonic stratification	colotomy	combination	variable
melodic contour	static	ascending	descending	conjunct	disjunct	undulating	terraced
mode or scale	number of notes	vernacular	using cipher notation (numbers), indicate the mode or scale in ascending order
meter	free	duple	triple	compound	additive	poly	other
speed	very slow	slow	moderate	fast	very fast	variable	other
amplitude	very soft	soft	moderate	loud	very loud	variable	other
timbre (tone color)	clear	breathy	nasal	open	tight	masked	other
inflections	no vibrato	slow vibrato	fast vibrato	wide vibrato	falsetto	multiphonics	other
formal structure	vernacular name	expanding	reverting	strophic	theme and variations	other
structural or performance techniques	ostinato	responsorial	antiphonal	elastic rhythm	if vocal: syllabic or melismatic	non-synchronous parts	other

Chapter 11

Text Pages 195 – 215

Trends in the Black Music of South Africa, 1959 – 1969

John Blacking

Introduction to Chapter (Text Pages 195–198)

Purpose To introduce the sociocultural concepts that underlie the music of black South Africa, and to describe how it changes as the society changes.

Guidance The late John Blacking was a cultural anthropologist, a performing pianist, and an ethnomusicologist who had great insight in the study of music as social behavior. In his introduction he makes several important statements that are important to remember. First he defines music as "a special mode of nonverbal communication," a relatively simple definition that opens the door for discussion. In order to understand the music of a culture, he stresses the need to understand the social system (and more broadly, the sociopolitical context) that produces the music. Then we as outsiders should also be able to learn how to listen to the music as the insiders (music makers and native perceivers) do. This is a lesson that we should adhere to for each chapter in this book and for every music culture that we study.

One important part of the lesson is that outsiders often tend to "dilute" another culture's music and try to make it fit within the outsider's own aesthetic framework. His story about the German Lutheran minister's African church choir is an example. Blacking gives examples of music groups that developed along the lines of the changes that took place in South Africa's social system. In addition to the influence of music from the United States and Europe in the 1960s, the idea of "Black Power" infused South African music with a self-conscious African idiom. Foremost was the collaborative production by whites and blacks of the musical *King Kong* in 1959, which was financially successful, and both composer and performers were black. Thereafter, politics in South Africa became more oppressive to blacks, and music became an agent of political expression partially because of the economic successes of many urban music groups.

Terms Define or identify the following terms or areas, based on readings from the text and/or other sources.

1. Locate South Africa and Mozambique on a recent African map. Pinpoint the major urban areas and the black townships; be aware of recent changes of political boundaries.

2. apartheid

3. Johannesburg

4. Bantu homelands

5. Zulu

6. Xhosa

7. Black power

8. Miriam Makeba

Reading Comprehension Answer the following work questions (answers at end of this chapter):

1. The decade in which Black Power came into prominence in South Africa was the _____.

2. The most obvious change in South African music in the 1960s was the infusion of the _____ _____.

3. *King Kong* was a _____ which provided a starring role for _____ _____ and helped to establish her career.

4. South African Freedom Songs came into existence in the _____.

5. Blacking defines music as "a special _____-_____.

6. LeRoi Jones wrote that music is "the result of certain _____ _____, certain specific ways of _____ about the _____, and only ultimately about the _____ in which music can be made."

The Social and Political Background
(Text Pages 198–202)

Purpose To understand the social and political changes of the 1960s in South Africa and the resulting affects on black South Africans and their music.

Guidance Musical activity in South African cities during the 1960s was affected by political changes in several ways. Throughout the country, African people had to be careful not to express political ideas in their song texts. As a result, the music itself became a vehicle for protest, and certain musical elements became unifying factors of the oppressed people. One dance, the Venda pipe dance, is so called because each dancer (Figure 11-5) plays a single-tubed pipe (edge aerophone, like blowing across a soda bottle) made from a piece of steel tubing. The many dancers-musicians interlock their individual notes to create a rhythmical melodic fabric. This communal music making, where the whole is dependent on the parts, is symbolic of the South African native people striving for unity within their diversity.

Terms Define or identify the following terms or areas, based on readings from the text and/or other sources.

9. Venda

10. Chopi

11. township

12. pipe dance

13. mine dance

14. Witwatersrand Gold Mines

Reading Comprehension Answer the following work questions (answers at end of this chapter):

7. Political changes of the 1960s forced blacks in South Africa to express political sentiments in the _____ of their music.

8. The disappearance of the social conditions when certain kinds of music were performed meant that the music was eliminated. True or False.

9. _____ _____ are performed by workers of the Witwatersrand Gold Mines during leisure hours and Sunday mornings.

10. Teams of dancers have a _____, a _____, a _____, and assistants.

11. In most of the mine dances, the _____

are usually played by men, although there are exceptions.

12. Changes in social and political life have often created some of the best performances of traditional South African communal music. True or False.

13. In South Africa, the traditional music is never as politically significant as the event that it accompanies. True or False.

14. List at least five uses for music and dancing in South Africa.

    a._____,

    b._____,

    c._____,

    d._____,

    e._____.

15. Managers of dance teams always take part in the dancing themselves. True or False.

16. The dance team director of music is responsible for _____ and _____ each dance.

17. In traditional South Africa, dances are never performed by men and women together. True or False.

18. The dance team director of dance blows a _____ to _____ a change of step and calls out the name of the new _____.

19. In South Africa, everything that sounds like music to us is regarded as music by them. True or False.

20. Some men wear costumes to look like women in South African mine dances, because traditionally these dances were danced by both sexes. True or False.

21. All musical instruments, except for the drums, have their tuning checked by the director of music of the dance team before each performance. True or False.

22. The manager of a dance team is responsible for ensuring that there is beer to drink. True or False.

Some Common Elements of the Musical Systems
(Text Pages 202–212)

Purpose To identify, describe, and examine various aspects of South African music and relate them to the various cultures that make them.

Guidance The dynamics of culture, or the "folk" process, affects how all music develops, grows, changes, and even disappears. South Africa provides an interesting case study for change because of the situations discussed in earlier sections of this chapter. Change also took place before the advent of European colonization, although there are no written records to prove it. Today there are new compositions written for Chopi xylophone orchestras each year.

In this section of the chapter, the author uses a number of terms from European music to explain the traditional music of South Africa. The technique of individual, single-pitched instruments interlocking their single notes (referred to as hocket technique on text page 205), discussed in the beginning of the chapter, is also used with voices. While the human voice is not limited to a single note, the technique is employed by other African cultures (Pygmies of the Ituri Forest, for example) and perhaps symbolizes the aspect of communalism or collectivity in living. Blacking defines "scale" as "fixed stores of notes" (text page 206), which is the same as an arbitrary arrangement of notes in descending or ascending order. Pentatonic (five-tone), hexatonic (six-tone), and heptatonic (seven-tone) scales are used by the Venda, and these are not exactly the same as five-, six-, and seven-tone scales in European music, as is obvious when heard. He also uses the terms "harmony" and "tonality" (text page 209), but as in Chapter 10, they do not usually mean European harmony and tonality, except in the case of vocal polyphony where one of the present techniques includes parallel motion and tonic-dominant progressions. All multipart music creates a type of harmony when sounded, and all music has a tonality, meaning it has a note or pitch that functions as a central point of relaxation. Even blocks of notes (chords) create points of tension and/or relaxation, as the author's diagram in Example 11–4 explains.

South African pop music flourished within that country from 1969 until the release from prison of Nelson Mandela in 1991 and his election as president of South Africa in 1993. South African pop music was an important voice for political and social change, and since the demise of apartheid, it has become increasingly more popular outside that country than within it. A style called township jive was very popular in South Africa in the 1970s, made famous by the Boyoyo Boys. Township jazz was another popular style in the 1970s.

The 1990s have seen important popular musical changes in South Africa. Miriam Mekeba, for example, who was exiled in 1962, returned in 1993. Likewise, Hugh Masekela also returned from exile; they and other jazz-pop artists developed new sounds, such as *mbaqanga*, a type of jazz fusion. After Paul Simon's release of *Graceland*, Joseph Shabala and Ladysmith Black Mambazo became very popular with their style of *mbube*, which is also

---

♪

Music Examples

South African musical instruments

♪

Music Examples

South African vocal music

vocal ensembles

found in Zimbabwe. Since their first recording in 1973, the group has recorded many albums, including "Shaka Zulu," which won a Grammy award in the World Music category in 1988. Newer pop music styles have been created by the following artists, to name just a few: The Mahotella Queens, a female vocal group employing a contemporary idiom while wearing traditional Zulu clothing as a symbol of identity; Simon "Mahlatini" Nkabinde, whose deep, growling voice is popular; Bubblegum, with singer Chaka Chaka, a group which relies heavily on synthesizers and drum machines for its pop sound; and Busi Mhlongo who has an eclectic style ranging from jazz to Zulu elements.

Terms Define or identify the following terms, based on readings from the text and/or other sources.

15. musical bow

16. mbira

17. lamellaphone

18. interlocking technique

19. "folk" tradition

20. tshikona

Reading Comprehension Answer the following work questions (answers at end of this chapter):

23. Southern African music remained static for several centuries until European influences affected it. True or False.

24. In South Africa, orally transmitted music is performed less accurately than that which is written down. True or False.

25. In the case of ritual music, every performance may be almost identical. True or False.

26. As a system of socially accepted concepts and conventions, Venda music is a _____ experience.

27. Among the Venda, most music is composed by individuals whose names are not known. True or False.

28. In African music, musical structures are correctly performed when each individual _____ himself or herself and at the same time _____ to the "invisible conductor" of the collective.

29. Communal instrumental and communal vocal musics are found in South Africa. True or False.

30. During the pipe dance of the Venda, the men play the _____ and the women and girls play the _____.

31. In African music, successful musical performance depends on the mutual interaction of all the players. True or False.

32. The South African Venda do not recognize the interval of the octave. True or False.

33. In South African traditional cultures, hoeing, threshing, grinding, or pounding maize (corn) have no affect on the metrical patterns of the music that accompanies it. True or False.

34. The musical rules of the Venda are so abstract that children cannot distinguish between the correct and incorrect ways of singing a particular melody. True or False.

35. Because regular _____ is the basic criterion of music, in song the rhythms of _____ are ignored.

36. In South Africa, categories of music are distinguished by their _____.

Video Viewing

1. Lullaby accompanied by musical bow. Republic of South Africa, the Zulu (19-18). *The JVC Video Anthology of World Music and Dance*, Middle East and Africa IV (VTMV-49).
2. Wedding ceremony. Republic of South Africa, the Zulu (19-19). *The JVC Video Anthology of World Music and Dance*, Middle East and Africa IV (VTMV-49).
3. *Graceland: The African Concert*. Paul Simon, Miriam Makeba, Hugh Masekela, Ladysmith Black Mambazo. Directed by Michael Lindsay-Hogg, produced by Ian Hoblyn. Warner Reprise Video 38136-3.
4. *Rhythm of Resistance: The Black Music of South Africa*. Beats of the Heart series. Jeremy Marre, director and producer.
5. *Voices of Sarafina! Songs of Hope and Freedom*. Directed by Nigel Noble. Music by Mbongeni Ngema and Hugh Masekela, with Miriam Makeba. Lincoln Center Theater/Noble Enterprises (1988).

Sample Test Questions

Multiple choice questions. Only one answer is correct.

1. Apartheid means: a. equality, b. separateness, c. affirmative action for minorities, d. all of the above.

2. A musical play produced in South Africa in 1959 as the result of collaboration between whites and blacks is titled: a. *A Streetcar Named Hope*, b. *King Kong*, c. *The Zulu Wars*, d. *Apartheid*, e. *Man of the Mines*.

3. The name of the singer who got her career start in the above musical play is: a. Shirley Bassey, b. Abia Akita, c. Miriam Makeba, d. Sade, e. Winnie Mandela.

4. Blacking defines music as a special mode of what kind of communication? a. verbal, b. nonverbal, c. music, d. instrumental, e. speech.

5. The success of the drama *King Kong* made South African musicians and composers realize that a source of strength was in: a. America, not Africa, b. Europe, not America, c. Africa, not America, d. Africa, not Europe, e. Hollywood.

6. Because of oppression, South African blacks realized they had to express political ideas in: a. instrumental sounds, b. words of songs, c. theater, d. poetry, e. film.

7. Unity of South African musical expression came from: a. a single European tradition, b. American jazz, c. Cuban salsa, d. commonalities among South African ethnic groups, e. a composite of European and American popular traditions.

8. The duties of the director of music on a mine dance team include: a. choosing and leading the songs, b. checking the tuning of the instruments, c. supervising the coordination of music and dance, d. all of the above, e. a and c.

9. The duties of the director of dance on a mine dance team include: a. blowing a whistle to signal a change of step, b. calling out the name of a new step, c. demonstrating new dance steps, d. all of the above, e. a and c.

10. Which is *not* a responsibility of the dance team manager: a. to arrange the rehearsals, b. making sure people attend regularly, c. ensure that there is beer, d. to dance with the team, e. to choose the dance costumes.

11. Which is *not* a responsibility of the dance team director of music: a. choosing the songs, b. leading the songs, c. overseeing the correct performance of the songs, d. making sure the drums are tuned, e. blow whistle to signal dance steps.

12. Among the Venda, vocal polyphony is *not* produced by: a. four-part canonic imitation (a round), b. the overlap of solo and chorus parts in responsorial singing, c. the addition of various parts in counterpoint to the basic melody, d. harmonization with a blend of parallel motion and tonic-dominant progressions, e. the use of voices to produce a total pattern of sound from very short phrases.

13. The *mbira* is a: a. reed flute, b. wooden drum, c. hand piano, d. rat-

tle, e. lute.

14. The Venda national dance, *tshikona*, is played on how many sets of stopped pipes? a. 5 to 7, b. 20 to 24, c. 50 to 60, d. 200, e. 500 or more.

15. One type of South African quasi-percussive polyphonic vocal technique provides accompaniment for the: a. stamping dance, b. girls' initiations, c. gold mining, d. a and b, e. a and c.

16. Chopi xylophone orchestras: a. play newly composed compositions, b. play at mine dances, c. were reported in the sixteenth century, d. a and c, e. all the above.

17. The musical instrument that is most commonly used for the tshikona dance is constructed from what? a. wooden slabs over a frame, b. gourd, c. steel tube, d. cedar wood, e. metal tongues in a frame.

18. A lamellaphone is also classified as what? a. aerophone, b. membranophone, c. chordophone, d. idiophone, e. corpophone.

19. During Venda children's games played at night, someone in disguise comes out while a song is sung and: a. scares the children, b. tells a story, c. plays the drum, d. dances, e. chases the children home.

20. During the *domba*, the dance of the Venda premarital initiation school: a. women and girls play the drums, b. men and boys play the drums, c. women and girls dance without instrumental accompaniment, d. men and boys dance without instrumental accompaniment, d. a Catholic priest presides.

Answers to Reading Comprehension

1. 1960s
2. African idiom
3. jazz opera, Miriam Makeba
4. 1950s
5. mode of non-verbal communication
6. attitudes, thinking, world, ways
7. sound
8. False: the music acted as a catalyst for new kinds of social activity
9. Mine dances
10. manager, director of music, director of dance
11. drums
12. True
13. False: the music may become more political than the event
14. used to lighten the load of communal labor, for weddings, funerals, initiations, ceremonies, religious rites, to ease the harshness of life, to provide entertainment at a beer party
15. False: they do not usually take part, but stand next to their teams

16. starting, stopping
17. False: several dances are performed by men and women together
18. whistle, signal, step
19. False: just the opposite is true
20. True
21. False: drums also have to be in tune
22. True
23. False: this is inconceivable
24. False: it is supposed to be just as accurate
25. True
26. shared
27. True
28. conducts, submits
29. True
30. pipes, drums
31. True
32. False: the Venda system does recognize it
33. False: they do impose metric patterns on music
34. False: children do distinguish between them
35. meter, speech
36. social function

Answers to Sample Test Questions

1. b
2. b
3. c
4. b
5. d
6. a
7. d
8. d
9. d
10. d
11. e
12. a
13. c
14. b
15. d
16. e
17. c
18. d
19. d
20. a

Listening Form

Student Name_____I.D. Number_____
Course Name _____Course Number_____
Date_____Chapter Number_____Listening Example Number _____
Record or Tape Number_____Name of Culture and Location _____
Name of Performer(s)_____
Instructions: place an X, ✓, or • in appropriate boxes; give types; indicate native names.

performing elements (if vocal)	solo: M/F	duo: M/F	trio: M/F	quartet: M/F	group: M/F	other: M/F
performing elements (if instrumental)	corpophone	idiophone	membrano-phone	aerophone	chordophone	electrophone	other
texture	single melody	dense unison	heterophone	imitation	parallelism	disphony	other
more texture	with drone	with time indicator	chordal	polyphonic stratification	colotomy	combination	variable
melodic contour	static	ascending	descending	conjunct	disjunct	undulating	terraced
mode or scale	number of notes	vernacular	using cipher notation (numbers), indicate the mode or scale in ascending order
meter	free	duple	triple	compound	additive	poly	other
speed	very slow	slow	moderate	fast	very fast	variable	other
amplitude	very soft	soft	moderate	loud	very loud	variable	other
timbre (tone color)	clear	breathy	nasal	open	tight	masked	other
inflections	no vibrato	slow vibrato	fast vibrato	wide vibrato	falsetto	multiphonics	other
formal structure	vernacular name	expanding	reverting	strophic	theme and variations	other
structural or performance techniques	ostinato	responsorial	antiphonal	elastic rhythm	if vocal: syllabic or melismatic	non-synchronous parts	other

Chapter 12

Text Pages 216 – 231

Anlo Ewe Music in Anyako, Volta Region, Ghana

Alfred Kwashie Ladzekpo

and Kobla Ladzekpo

Introduction to Chapter (Text Pages 216–219)

Purpose To describe the geographical location of the Anlo Ewe people, survey the history of Ewe migration, discuss the occupations of the Ewe people, and examine the Afã and Yewe religious cults and their music.

Guidance The authors are from the very region they write about. Their insights into their own culture are very personal and detailed. Such an approach is often called "emic," or an insider approach. In ethnomusicology it is not uncommon for nationals to conduct research in their own cultures; we as outsiders are fortunate to have such scholarship available to us. Many cultural facts are presented in the introduction. Music is shown to be a part of the mythology of the Anlo Ewe. Indeed, many cultures frequently transmit musical information through mythology, folklore (legends, epics, songs), and oral history.

Terms Define or identify the following terms or areas, based on readings from the text and/or other sources.

1. Look at a recent map of Africa, or a recent world globe or atlas. Determine the exact location of Ghana in West Africa, and observe the many countries that are nearby. You will notice that the present name for the neighboring country called Dahomey on the map on page 217 is now Republic of Benin.

2. Afã

3. Yewe

4. Yoruba

5. Fon

6. Nigeria

Reading Comprehension Answer the following work questions (answers at end of this chapter):

1. Afã is the god of _____ and Yewe is the god of _____ and _____, and the religious cults centered around them preserve the oldest and most traditional music among the Anlo Ewe. True or False.

2. Most traditional Ewe communities begin their _____ and _____ performances with Afã _____.

3. After initiation into the Yewe cult, the novices are presented to the townspeople with _____ and _____ in a performance known as _____.

4. At a performance of Afã drumming, nonmembers dance with the full members of the cult. True or False.

5. Why do the Ewe in Anlo use Afã drumming in a great number of secular dance clubs?
   _____
   _____
   _____
   _____
   _____

6. Yewe music is considered to be one of the most _____ forms of _____ music in Anlo.

7. In the Yewe cult of the Ewe, drums do not connote the physical instruments but rather mean different _____, _____, _____, and _____.

8. Yewe festivals are open to the public. True or False.

9. The cult house of the Yewe is the center of activities. True or False.

10. A special Yewe ritual called "counting the drums" means that the women count the number of drums used in the daily ceremony. True or False.

The Dance Clubs (Text Pages 219–227)

Purpose To examine the membership and types of musical styles of the Ewe dance clubs.

Terms Define or identify the following terms, based on readings from the text and/or other sources.

7. axatsewu

8. akpewu

9. gahu

10. kete

Music and Dance Examples

Ghanaian dances

membranophone ensemble

Reading Comprehension Answer the following work questions (answers at end of this chapter):

11. Drumming and dancing in Anlo are organized in _____ _____ which function as a _____ in the communities.

12. Music making among the Ewe in Anlo is a daily activity. True or False.

13. Membership in the Ewe dance clubs is for men only. True or False.

14. Each Ewe dance club has its own distinctive _____, but certain clubs share the same _____ music.

15. The chief organizer and leader of the Ewe dance clubs is the _____ / _____.

16. In Anlo music, _____, _____, _____, and _____ are a single whole, and if any part changes, the whole is changed.

17. Among the Ewe of Anlo, two or three dance clubs with different names may perform the same style of music. True or False.

18. In Anlo communities, a funeral without music is referred to as "_____."

19. With music, Anlo Ewe mourners can take out their grief on the _____.

162   Musics of Many Cultures: Study Guide and Workbook

20. What two things are signified by good music at a funeral among the Anlo Ewe?

   a._____

   b._____

21. Recreational dance music among the Ewe in Anyako is classified into three groups. List them and define each one.

   a._____

   b._____

   c._____

Instrumental Music (Text Pages 227–229)

Music Examples

Ghanaian drum ensemble music

membranophone ensemble

Purpose   To identify important idiophones, membranophones, and aerophones used by the Anlo Ewe.

Guidance   One of the most important idiophones to remember is the gourd rattle with a net of beads around it. This common West African rattle is also found in the Caribbean, especially among the people of African heritage in Cuba and Florida (Miami), where it is used in religious ritual music. There are various names for this instrument, depending on the culture using it. Another common West African instrument is the hourglass-shaped pressure drum. The performer on this instrument can increase the pitch by hitting a drum head and squeezing the leather thongs that are attached from one drum head to the other at the same time (it is usually placed under the performer's arm and squeezed). This way the musician can speak with the tones of the drum, employing the same three levels of tones used in the speech language.

Terms   Describe and be able to identify the drawings of the instruments listed below.

11. gankogui

12. atoke

13. axatse

14. adodo

15. brekete

Anlo Ewe Music in Anyako, Volta Region, Ghana   163

Reading Comprehension Answer the following work questions (answers at end of this chapter):

22. Anlo Ewe idiophones are divided into three classes that include _____, _____, and _____.

24. Anlo Ewe membranophones are carved from a _____ or made of _____ _____.

25. All the Anlo Ewe membranophones are played either by _____, with _____ _____, with _____ _____, or _____-and-_____ technique.

26. Anlo Ewe aerophones include flutes carved out of _____ and trumpets made from_____or _____.

27. Anlo Ewe trumpets are used in club dances. True or False.

Vocal Music (Text Page 229)

Purpose To examine the structure and uses of vocal music.

Reading Comprehension Answer the following work questions (answers at end of this chapter):

28. There is no difference between the music of the northern and southern Ewe in Ghana. True or False.

29. Vocal music as practiced by the Ewe dance clubs in the south consists of three kinds of songs, including _____, _____, and _____.

30. Northern Ewe employ the _____-tone scale, and harmonize with the interval of a _____.

31. The Anlo Ewe use the _____ scale in their vocal music.

Conclusion (Text Page 229)

Purpose To very briefly summarize and broadly discuss the relevance of musical study among the Anlo Ewe.

Guidance It is certainly true that some African music south of the Sahara is influenced by the music of Islam and by the tenets of Islam. However, as the authors point out, the music of the Anlo Ewe has not apparently been affected by Islamic culture.

Terms Define or identify the following terms or areas, based on readings from the text and/or other sources.

16. Locate the Near East on a world globe, and notice the great size of north Africa and the Sahara desert.

17. Islam

Reading Comprehension Answer the following work questions (answers at end of this chapter):

32. Some scholars think that all African music south of the Sahara is influenced by Islam. True or False.

33. Some elements of Anlo Ewe music have not been found elsewhere. True or False.

Sample Test Questions

Multiple choice questions. Only one answer is correct.

1. The fast circle dance with a game quality among the Ewe of Ghana is called: a. gahu, b. kete, c. atoke, d. gankogui, e. axatse.

2. In Anlo, Ghana, drumming and dancing are organized in: a. school teams, b. church groups, c. family groups, d. gender and age groups, e. dance clubs.

3. Music making among the Ewe of Ghana: a. is a daily event, b. occurs only at night, c. takes place only on Sundays, d. is occasional, e. is seasonal.

4. Dance movements and music are passed down from one Ewe generation to the next via: a. notation, b. participant observation, c. teacher-student relationships, d. classroom situations, e. cassette tapes.

5. The vocal music of the Anlo Ewe is based on the: a. chromatic scale, b. minor scale, c. pentatonic scale, d. major scale, e. scale that happens to come to mind.

6. Aerophones of the Anlo Ewe include: a. whistles and bugles, b. elephant tusk trumpets, c. wooden flutes, d. bull horn trumpets, e. all the above.

7. Instrumental music of the Anlo Ewe is dominated by which types of instruments? a. aerophones and membranophones, b. membranophones, c. idiophones and membranophones, d. idiophones, e. idiophones and aerophones.

8. Vocal music of the Anlo Ewe is used in the following three occasions:

a. church services, civic meetings, political rallies, b. processions, dances, interludes, c. work, home celebrations, athletic events, d. dances, curing ceremonies, life cycle events, e. elections, funerals, births.

9. Carved drums are becoming extinct among the Ewe due to: a. the lack of time to carve, b. the scarcity of wood, c. the lack of teachers to teach carving, d. religious taboos, e. scarcity of knives.

10. The instrument used for Ewe royal functions is the: a. ivory trumpet, b. pressure drum, c. wooden flute, d. double bell, e. one-stringed fiddle.

11. The Ewe axatsewo is a rattle containing: a. seeds, b. stones, c. shells, d. pellets, e. none of the above.

12. Among the Ewe, the opening in the bottom of the large barrel drum is used for what purpose? a. to let the spirits in and out, b. to allow the sound to go out, c. to put water into, d. to put stones into, e. to put a membrane over.

13. Among the Anlo Ewe in Ghana, drums are: a. not only the physical elements of the instruments, but also the rhythms, songs, clapping, and dance steps, b. most often made from logs with tacked-on heads, c. not used except on the concert stage, d. found only in the interior jungle regions because the city people consider them too old-fashioned.

14. Which drum among the Anlo is a version of an importation from northern Ghana? a. adodo, b. gankogui, c. brekete, d. axatse, e. atoke.

15. In Anlo Ewe music from Ghana, drumming, dancing, singing, and handclapping: a. are a single whole, and if any part changes, the whole is changed, b. are separate entities that can exist alone, and one is not dependent upon the other, c. were older forms of expression that are today replaced by dance bands, d. were learned from Yoruba tribes to the south.

16. Since death is a sorrowful event among the people in Anyako, and in other Ewe communities in Ghana: a. music is never performed at funerals, b. only dirges are performed during funerals, c. the mourners can take out their grief on the dance floor through music, d. sitting around with little or nothing to do makes both the bereaved family and the mourners feel their grief less.

17. Membranophones in Ghana are played: a. by hand, b. with one stick, c. with two sticks, d. with one stick and one hand, e. all the above.

18. Side blown flutes made from elephant tusks or bull's horns: a. are associated with the royal houses, b. are used in club dances, c. are performed for marriage dances, d. are performed by shepherds, e. do not exist.

19. The popular hourglass-shaped drum known as *adodo* among the Ewe in Ghana and *dundun* among the Yoruba in Nigeria is subclassified as: a. a friction drum, b. a pegged drum, c. a kettle drum, d. a goblet drum,

e. a pressure drum.

20. Which is *not* one of the functions of the dance clubs among the Ewe in Anlo, Ghana?   a. to make money, b. to entertain, c. to provide recreation, d. to be a venue for ceremonial activity, e. to be a social outlet.

Answers to Reading Comprehension Questions

1. divination, thunder, lighting. True
2. drumming, dancing, music
3. drumming, dancing, outdooring
4. True
5. to propitiate the Afã god in order to invoke its blessing for the success of the performance
6. developed, sacred
7. rhythms, songs, clapping, dance steps
8. False: they are forbidden to nonmembers
9. True
10. False: it means playing the seven different styles of drumming that belong to the cult
11. dance clubs, social outlet
12. False: it is occasional
13. False: it is open to both sexes
14. songs, drumming
15. poet / composer
16. drumming, dancing, singing, handclapping
17. True
18. what a sad thing
19. dance floor
20. a. the deepest expression of the loss of the beloved one, b. it is a way of sharing with the deceased member of a group the music he had once enjoyed
21. a. axatsewu — a style of music dominated by rattles, b. akpewu — a style of music dominated by handclapping or wooden clappers, c. specific style — a style of music that consists of distinctive styles of drumming and dancing different from those of the first two groups
22. bells, rattles, clappers
23. True
24. solid tree, wooden slats
25. hand, one stick, two sticks, stick-and-hand
26. wood, elephant tusks, bull's horns
27. False: they are associated with the royal houses
28. False: there are major differences
29. processional, dance, interlude
30. seven, third

31. pentatonic
32. False: some, not all
33. True

Answers to Sample Test Questions

1. b
2. e
3. d
4. b
5. c
6. e
7. c
8. b
9. b
10. a
11. e
12. c
13. a
14. c
15. a
16. c
17. e
18. e
19. e
20. a

Listening Form

Student Name_____ I.D. Number_____
Course Name _____ Course Number _____
Date_____ Chapter Number_____ Listening Example Number _____
Record or Tape Number_____ Name of Culture and Location _____
Name of Performer(s)_____
Instructions: place an X, ✓, or • in appropriate boxes; give types; indicate native names.

performing elements (if vocal)	solo: M/F	duo: M/F	trio: M/F	quartet: M/F	group: M/F	other: M/F
performing elements (if instrumental)	corpophone	idiophone	membranophone	aerophone	chordophone	electrophone	other
texture	single melody	dense unison	heterophone	imitation	parallelism	disphony	other
more texture	with drone	with time indicator	chordal	polyphonic stratification	colotomy	combination	variable
melodic contour	static	ascending	descending	conjunct	disjunct	undulating	terraced
mode or scale	number of notes	vernacular	using cipher notation (numbers), indicate the mode or scale in ascending order
meter	free	duple	triple	compound	additive	poly	other
speed	very slow	slow	moderate	fast	very fast	variable	other
amplitude	very soft	soft	moderate	loud	very loud	variable	other
timbre (tone color)	clear	breathy	nasal	open	tight	masked	other
inflections	no vibrato	slow vibrato	fast vibrato	wide vibrato	falsetto	multiphonics	other
formal structure	vernacular name	expanding	reverting	strophic	theme and variations	other	
structural or performance techniques	ostinato	responsorial	antiphonal	elastic rhythm	if vocal: syllabic or melismatic	non-synchronous parts	other

Chapter 13

Text Pages 232 – 252

The Music of Ethiopia

Cynthia Tse Kimberlin

Introduction to Chapter (Text Pages 232–234)

Purpose   To briefly introduce the student to demographic and historical foundations for the study of Ethiopian music.

Guidance   The location of Ethiopia in northeastern Africa is important to an understanding of its musical and cultural history. Ethiopia is located in an area known as the "East Horn" of Africa. When you look at a map of the African continent, you will clearly see how the region bordering on the Red Sea and the Gulf of Aden projects eastward like a horn. Although not at the tip of the horn, Ethiopia constitutes a part of that peninsula. As of May 24, 1993, Eritrea is no longer a part of Ethiopia, but is now an independent country.

Terms   Define or identify the following terms or areas, based on readings from the text and/or other sources.

1. Find Ethiopia on a modern map of Africa and on a globe of the world. Notice its proximity to both north Africa and Africa south of the Sahara. Compare Ethiopia's size with other African countries and the United States of America.

2. Amharic

3. East Horn

4. Islam

Reading Comprehension   Answer the following work questions (answers at end of this chapter):

1. Ethiopia's bravery and past exploits have been celebrated in song. True or False.

2. One of the musical characteristics one hears when listening to Ethiopian music is infinite _____.

3. The music of the Amharic people is representative of the entire country of Ethiopia. True or False.

Status of the Musician (Text Pages 234–236)

Purpose To explain the various statuses of musicians in Ethiopia, to briefly introduce how certain musicians learn songs, and to discuss some of the common ways that Ethiopian musicians perform their duties.

Guidance The student is advised to read the third section on musical instruments before reading this section, because several instruments are mentioned even though they have not yet been discussed.

Terms Define or identify the following terms or areas, based on readings from the text and/or other sources.

5. azmari

6. Addis Ababa

7. Ethiopian Christian Orthodox Church

8. däbtära

9. krar

10. masinqo

11. bäganna

Reading Comprehension Answer the following work questions (answers at end of this chapter):

4. Although the azmari was originally known as one who would _____ _____ his patron, he later became one who _____ and then one who _____.

5. All Ethiopians make music during _____ festivities.

6. The krar is thought of as the instrument of _____ and _____.

7. The usual purpose of the krar is the accompaniment of contemporary religious songs. True or False.

8. Both males and females can become azmari musicians. True or False.

9. To be an Ethiopian azmari is to be in the _____ occupational status, along with _____ who have jobs

requiring use of the _____.

10. The most common method of repertory building includes _____ _____ the songs of other azmari.

11. Many Azmari know several texts that are set to one melody. True or False.

12. What are the three ways an azmari can gain popularity and wealth:

   a. _____

   b. _____

   c. _____

13. The Ethiopian musician who plays a Western instrument is considered to be a very low-status person. True or False.

14. The Ethiopian who plays Western instruments becomes _____ _____ and a member of the emerging _____ class.

15. The traditional musical instrument of the Ethiopian nobles and upper class is the krar. True or False.

16. The Ethiopian bägänna is a concert instrument that is played on stage in front of large audiences. True or False.

Musical Instruments (Text Pages 236–238)

Purpose To identify several of the most important musical instruments in Ethiopia.

Guidance The author uses the phonetic alphabet common in linguistics to spell the musical instruments in this section. For some of the most common instruments, you will also find the following spellings (they are presented here according to their numbers in the textbook; the following spellings are from *Roots of Black Music* by Ahenafi Kebede): 3. *tsenatsil*, known as a sistrum in Latin, 8. *begena*, 10. *masinKo* (the K means that it is pronounced with an explosive sound according to Kebede, p. 79), 11. *washint* (a ductless flute similar to the Arabic *nay*), and 12. *embilta*. The drawing of the masinqo on page 238 (Figure 13-4) is somewhat misleading because the instrument's bridge is collapsed and the bow is stuck under the end string. This is how the instrument is stored and obviously not played. During a performance, the musician passes the bow across the single string like any bowed lute. The raised bridge transmits the vibrations of the string onto the skin and into the resonator. The musician touches the string with his fingers at the points required to change the pitches (he does not press his fingers all the way to the fingerboard).

♪

Music Example

masinqo and male singer

chordophone

♪

Music Example

embilta ensemble

aerohones

> ♪
> *Music Example*
> *vocal duet*

Terms Define or identify the following terms based on readings from the text and/or other sources, and be able to identify the musical instrument types in the drawings.

12. tsenatsil or sistrum

13. begena or bägänna

14. masinKo or masinqo

15. krar

16. washint

17. embilta

Reading Comprehension Answer the following work questions (answers at end of this chapter):

17. Instruments of a particular Ethiopian ethnic group are partially _____ determined. Give one example of this: _____.

18. Instruments of a particular Ethiopian ethnic group can also be _____ determined. Give one example of this: _____.

19. Bowls are common shapes for parts of musical instruments in Ethiopia. True or False.

20. Some Ethiopian membranophones are made from old one gallon or five gallon metal containers. True or False.

21. The sound box of the bägänna is covered with _____, and the strings are made from _____ _____.

22. The sound box of the krar may be _____ or _____ shaped.

23. The sound box of the krar is covered with _____, and the strings are made from _____, _____, or _____.

Music Examples (Text Pages 239–250)

Purpose To examine five types of Ethiopian musical genres.

Guidance Although the musical notations are highly technical, the explanations contain valuable descriptive information about cultural contexts for Ethiopian music, musical instrument performance practices, and music theory. The author explains how the embilta flutes are played

The Music of Ethiopia 175

together in a hocket technique. This is an interlocking method whereby each instrument is played in a manner similar to how bells are played in an American ensemble of bell ringers.

Reading Comprehension Answer the following work questions (answers at end of this chapter):

24. When performed by an Ethiopian priest, the staff has a movement that imitates the movement of _____ blown gently by the _____.

25. Drumming is not as predominant in Ethiopia as in other parts of Africa. True or False.

26. Women rarely play drums in Ethiopia. True or False.

27. Sometimes accented beating accompanies drumming in Ethiopia. True or False.

28. Washint flutes are made by special artisans and then purchased by flutists. True or False.

29. Embilta flutes are made from _____, _____, or _____, depending on the province where they are made and used.

30. Sometimes embilta flute players _____ in a _____ while playing.

31. The meter employed by the embilta players in Example 13-3 is _____.

32. Embilta are primarily used for _____ gatherings and _____, and are not usually _____ by other instruments.

33. When a bäganna player tunes his instrument there is no precise _____ range; the player's _____ range determines the _____ range.

34. It is not always necessary for a bäganna player to tune all the strings on his instrument. True or False.

35. Ethiopian music mirrors Ethiopian society and its people. True or False.

Conclusion (Text Page 250)

Purpose To make several conclusions of a comparative nature.

Guidance The author concludes by pointing out similarities between

Ethiopian music and that of other cultures. It must be emphasized that these similarities are purely coincidental and do not indicate any type of cultural borrowing.

Ethiopian pop music has flourished more among the exiled Ethiopians, especially in the United States, than among the people living in Ethiopia. Since the restoration of democracy in 1991, however, pop music has been revived in the motherland, and new groups have emerged. Probably foremost among them is Ethio Stars, which joins saxophone and brass with electric bass, keyboards, guitar, and drum set, resulting in a funky style—somewhat like a combination of reggae (Jamaica) and soukous (Zaire). Although it is referred to as "Amharic music" by the band members, only the song texts sung in Amharic define many of the songs as Ethiopian. Some of the instrumental compositions, however, are based on Ethiopian scales, such as the ambassel mode mentioned by Kimberlin (pp. 246–247 and 250). An experimental fusion group is the Tukul Band, which uses only traditional Ethiopian musical instruments that have been electronically enhanced (electric lead krar, electric bass krar, electric masinko, washint, and traditional drums). In addition, the band's musical style is a fusion of traditional ostinatos, improvised solos, heavy bass, and traditional tunings and scales.

One of Ethiopia's leading female singers is Aster Aweke, who records in England and the United States. Her style, accompanied by a driving band of electric keyboards, bass, guitar, trumpet, saxophone, and drums, fluctuates between an almost Caribbean salsa sound to a florid improvisatory solo style derived from traditional Amharic singing. Sometimes she performs with only krar accompaniment, and at other times her band provides a very funky rhythm and blues foundation. Aster Ameke's accompaniment styles are quite varied, while her own vocal work is very florid and traditionally based---therein lies her uniqueness in Ethiopian pop music. This is perhaps only possible because she makes her home outside of Ethiopia (in the United States since 1981). More of a fusion artist is Alemayehu Eshete, one of Ethiopia's leading male vocalists who has recorded in Paris. While the style of his band (trumpet, saxophones, keyboards, bass, drums) can also be funky, with heavy bass and many ostinatos, his keyboardist often plays in a florid style that is a nearly perfect imitation of the krar.

Sample Test Questions

Multiple choice questions. Only one answer is correct.

1. According to the scholar Alan Merriam, the music of the East Horn region of Africa is distinguishable from most of the other music in East Africa by the intensity of which influence: a. Jewish, b. Christian, c. Islamic, d. Shamanistic, e. Buddhist.

2. Ethiopia is susceptible to many musical influences because of: a. location, b. religion, c. ethnic divisions, d. slavery, e. colonialism.

3. Through the years the term *azmari* for the Ethiopian musician has come to mean: a. one who defames, b. one who has loose morals, c. heav-

enly musician, d. in the king's grace, e. entertainer.

4. An Ethiopian musician will: a. play his music in whichever mode comes mind, b. choose one of the two modes for his music and then seldom change to another mode, c. modulate freely from one mode to another, d. not base his music on a mode.

5. How does the masinqo player learn his instrument? a. from a method book, b. by trial and error, c. from cassette tapes, d. from his father or uncle, e. from a teacher.

6. Which is *not* a method that the masinqo player uses to build his musical repertory? a. to compose his own songs, b. to learn from song books, c. to imitate songs of other musicians as they work, d. to imitate songs played on the radio, e. to imitate songs from recordings.

7. The traditional musical instrument of the Ethiopian nobles and upper class is the: a. tsenatsil or sistrum, b. begena or bäganna, c. masinKo or masinqo, d. krar, e. washint.

8. The traditional musical instrument of Ethiopian pimps and prostitutes is the: a. tsenatsil or sistrum, b. begena or bäganna, c. masinKo or masinqo, d. krar, e. washint.

9. The traditional musical instrument of Ethiopian priests is the: a. tsenatsil or sistrum, b. begena or bäganna, c. masinKo or masinqo, d. krar, e. washint.

10. The traditional musical instrument of Ethiopian shepherds and cowherds is the: a. tsenatsil or sistrum, b. begena or bäganna, c. masinKo or masinqo, d. krar, e. washint.

11. Strings of the Ethiopian krar are never made from: a. metal, b. gut, c. nylon, d. silk.

12. The sound box of the Ethiopian krar: a. can be made from a wooden bowl, b. can be made from a metal bowl, c. is covered with goat skin, d. a and c of the above, e. all of the above.

13. In Ethiopia, Adari women sometimes play the drums during: a. weddings, b. funerals, c. births, d. dinner, e. camel caravans.

14. Which material is never used in manufacturing an Ethiopian embilta? a. plastic, b. wood, c. metal, d. bamboo, e. a and c of the above.

15. The musicians who play which instrument dance in a circle while they play: a. tsenatsil or sistrum, b. embilta, c. masinKo or masinqo, d. krar, e. washint.

Answers to Reading Comprehension Questions

1. True
2. melodic variation
3. False: there is not one kind of music that could represent Ethiopia

because there are so many ethnic groups that live there
4. praise, criticizes, defames
5. life cycle
6. pimps, prostitutes
7. False: popular songs only
8. False: it is strictly a male profession
9. lowest, illiterates, hands
10. imitating
11. True
12. a. to cut a record and hope it sells, b. to join a performance group and hope it succeeds, c. to leave traditional instruments and take up Western ones
13. False: just the opposite—he is not thought of as low-status
14. sophisticated, middle
15. False: bägänna
16. False: it is seldom played for an audience
17. geographically, no bamboo flutes where there is no bamboo
18. culturally, Moslems do not play stringed instruments
19. True
20. True
21. cowhide, sheep's gut
22. trapezoidal, bowl
23. goatskin, gut, metal, nylon
24. grass, wind
25. True
26. False: among some Ethiopian cultures women play drums during wedding celebrations
27. True
28. False: the owner is usually the maker
29. metal, wood, bamboo
30. dance, circle
31. triple
32. social, weddings, accompanied
33. pitch, vocal, instrumental
34. True
35. True

Answers to Sample Test Questions

1. c
2. a
3. a
4. b
5. e

6. b
7. b
8. d
9. a
10. e
11. d
12. e
13. a
14. a
15. b

Listening Form

Student Name_____ I.D. Number _____
Course Name _____ Course Number _____
Date_____Chapter Number_____Listening Example Number _____
Record or Tape Number_____Name of Culture and Location _____
Name of Performer(s)_____
Instructions: place an X, ✓, or • in appropriate boxes; give types; indicate native names.

performing elements (if vocal)	solo: M/F	duo: M/F	trio: M/F	quartet: M/F	group: M/F	other: M/F
performing elements (if instrumental)	corpophone	idiophone	membranophone	aerophone	chordophone	electrophone	other
texture	single melody	dense unison	heterophone	imitation	parallelism	disphony	other
more texture	with drone	with time indicator	chordal	polyphonic stratification	colotomy	combination	variable
melodic contour	static	ascending	descending	conjunct	disjunct	undulating	terraced
mode or scale	number of notes	vernacular	using cipher notation (numbers), indicate the mode or scale in ascending order
meter	free	duple	triple	compound	additive	poly	other
speed	very slow	slow	moderate	fast	very fast	variable	other
amplitude	very soft	soft	moderate	loud	very loud	variable	other
timbre (tone color)	clear	breathy	nasal	open	tight	masked	other
inflections	no vibrato	slow vibrato	fast vibrato	wide vibrato	falsetto	multiphonics	other
formal structure	vernacular name	expanding	reverting	strophic	theme and variations	other
structural or performance techniques	ostinato	responsorial	antiphonal	elastic rhythm	if vocal: syllabic or melismatic	non-synchronous parts	other

Chapter 14

Text Pages 253 – 268

Secular Classical Music in the Arabic Near East

Jozef M. Pacholczyk

Introduction to Chapter (Text Page 253)

Purpose To establish the geographic, linguistic, and cultural settings for the classical music of the Arabic Near East.

Guidance The Arabic Near East, or Middle East, includes large portions of northern Africa and western Asia, but does not include Turkey and Iran. The most important unifying characteristic of this area, and many others, including Turkey, Iran, and many countries that are in the outer fringes of the Near East, is Islam. An excellent map titled "An Ethnic Mosaic of Islam's Heartland" was published as a supplement to the September, 1980, issue of *National Geographic*, Vol. 158, No. 3. It is valuable for helping to understand the history of the Middle East as well as the population percentages in each country of the followers of Islam.

Terms Define or identify the following areas, based on readings from the text and/or other sources.

1. Find the Near East on a world globe. Notice the sizes of the countries compared to European countries.

Reading Comprehension Answer the following work questions (answers at end of this chapter):

1. List the three different language families of the Near East, and give the name of the people who speak them:

   a._____ (_____).
   b._____ (_____).
   c._____ (_____).

2. List the four great civilizations from this large area:

   a._____, b. _____,
   c._____, d. _____,

3. Name the three capitals of the caliphates during the historical period of the Islamic empire:

   a._____, b. _____,
   c._____.

4. The _____ music of the Near East developed in those capitals; it was rooted in the _____-_____ Arabic traditions, and enriched by the musical traditions of the countries that the Arabs conquered.

5. Present Near Eastern artistic music is rooted in the folk music of the ancient Islamic empire. True or False.

History (Text Pages 253–256)

Music Examples

Arabic musical instruments

Purpose To explain the historical periods of the Near East, and to show how Arabic music developed.

Guidance Understanding the historical periods within which Arabic music began, developed, and exists today is simplified by the author as he places them into four basic periods. These may also be thought of as the pre-Islamic period, period of Islamic conquests, period of waning Islamic influence, and period of Western contact. While entire books are devoted to any portion of these periods, the author's survey provides an accurate glimpse of the historical framework for Arabic musical development. The study of the music of ancient Egypt alone, however, occupies the lifeworks of many scholars, so extensive are the research possibilities. A number of the instruments mentioned by the author for the Jahiliya period are depicted on the walls of ancient Egyptian tombs, especially the long-necked lute, double reed pipes (probably double oboes), the harp, and various instruments of percussion.

Terms Define or identify the following terms or areas, based on readings from the text and/or other sources.

2. duff

3. 'ud

4. forbidden pleasures

5. Qur'an

6. Andalusian

Reading Comprehension Answer the following work questions (answers at end of this chapter):

6. The two continents in which the Arabic Near East lie, as seen in the map on text page 254, are _____ and _____.

7. During the pre-Islamic period of Arabic history, music was primarily _____ and closely related to _____.

8. The oldest form of vocal music is the _____ song, whose rhythm was inspired by the _____'s gait.

9. Islam had no influence on the development of Arabic music. True or False.

10. During the Umayyad Empire (661–750), _____ music became popular.

11. The period of the 'Abbasid dynasty (750–1258 A.D.) is called the _____ of Islamic culture, when many branches of scholarship flourished. List the six important types of learning that developed during that time.

    a._____, b._____,
    c._____, d._____,
    e._____, f._____

12. Beginning in Spain in 822 A.D., a new Arabic style developed called _____.

13. In 1492, to which countries of North Africa did the Spanish-Arabic musical style known as the Andalusian move? _____, _____, and _____.

14. Today, many musicians continue to perform traditional Arabic musical forms in the traditional manner. True or False.

History of Theory (Text Pages 256–260)

Purpose To identify the historical trends in Arabic music theory.

Guidance All music cultures have music theory—some are transmitted orally and others are written down in treatises or books. Within the Near East there are four basic music theory systems—the Arabic and the Andalusian discussed in this chapter, the Persian discussed in Chapter 15, and the Turkish, which is not included in this book. While this section of the chapter is very clear, several terms and concepts will be explained. The term "tetrachord" is often referred to with reference to Arabic and Persian musical scales. "Tetra" means "four," and "chord" means "notes"—tetrachord refers to the four uppermost notes of the scale (upper tetrachord) or the four lowermost notes of the scale (lower tetrachord). Many of the intervals or spaces between the notes are smaller or larger than the intervals used in European music. The cents system first used by John Alexander Ellis, a British mathematician, divides the European chromatic scale into 1200 equal parts whereby each half step gets 100 cents. Therefore, when the author discusses a quarter tone interval as having 50 cents (text page 259), this is not perceived in traditional European music (the Arabic scale was divided into 24 intervals of approximately 50 cents each). He mentions the neutral third interval which is approximately halfway between a minor and major third in European music. This interval is also not easily perceived by European musicians, although the "blues" third in African American music is somewhat similar to the Near Eastern neutral third. The author also mentions the *taqsim* and *layali*, which are instrumental and vocal improvisatory forms respectively. The taqsim is somewhat similar to the Persian *daramad* discussed in Chapter 15 and the Indian *alap* discussed in Chapter 6. On text page 260 the author introduces the English word "realizing," which means "interpreting." The drummer makes a "realization" of the rhythmic mode (i.e., he interprets and applies the rhythmic mode to the musical performance).

Terms Define or identify the following terms or people, based on readings from the text and/or other sources.

7. al-Kindi

8. al-Farabi

9. taqsim

10. maqam / maqamat

11. mode

12. intermodal scale

13. finger modes

14. iqa'a / iqa'at

Reading Comprehension Answer the following work questions (answers at end of this chapter):

15. The development of Arabic musical theory was stimulated by translations of _____ musical theory.

16. A cycle of beats repeated throughout a section of Arabic music is a ____ _____ mode.

17. Influenced by the Greeks, the Arab theorists considered the doctrine of ethos, or the effect of music on people. True or False.

18. Although systems of notation have been developed in the Arabic Near East, the primary way of teaching is by rote. True or False.

19. Because Islam frowned on music, from the eighth century on there was no verbalization of music and organization into systems. True or False.

20. The musical scholars or carriers of the culture in the early period of Near Eastern music theory were _____, _____, and _____.

21. The two periods of Near Eastern music theory cover the _____ to the end of the _____ century for the first, and the end of the _____ to the _____ for the second.

22. The favorite instrument among Near Eastern musicians was the _____.

23. The iqa'at presented by al-Kindi consist of how many rhythmic modes? _____.

24. The intermodal scale is a concept similar to that of the Western chromatic scale. True or False.

25. The oldest Arabic musical notation comes from the _____ century.

26. The scale of the maqam usually consists of _____ pitches to the octave.

27. In Arabic vocal pieces, the words are usually divided and written in reverse order because the notation is written in one direction while the language is written in the other direction. True or False.

28. In the Arabic Near East, drummers supply the _____ _____ of a piece, and they realize the _____.

Forms (Text Pages 260–266)

Purpose To examine the musical structures, instruments, and regional features and variations of the traditional music of the Near East.

Guidance Monophony (single line music) and heterophony (variegated unison, i.e. variation and unison sounding together) are the two most important elements of musical texture in the Near East, as they are in China and

> **Music Example**
>
> *Arabic vocal music*

Japan as well. The author (text page 265) explains, however, that sometimes Near Eastern heterophony becomes so complex that it is almost polyphony (quasi-polyphony). At other times the monophony is accompanied by a membranophone such as the darabukka, duff, or tar. These types of musical textures were also the norm in medieval Europe, and still exist in many rural musics around the world. Monophony is the result of a single instrument playing a taqsim, or a single voice performing a layali—both are based on improvisation and are in free rhythm, without meter. Heterophony results when two or more instruments play together in a suite—the most common type of ensemble playing in the Near East. The suite is characterized by using the same musical mode or maqam throughout and having slight acceleration towards final movements. The Near Eastern suite is probably the prototype of the European Renaissance and Baroque suite because of structural similarities (such as maintaining the same key throughout). The principal instrument in Near Eastern suites is the 'ud, which is the prototype of not only the European lute (called la 'ud or laud in Spain) but also of the Chinese p'i-p'a and the Japanese biwa.

> **Music Examples**
>
> *Arabic ensemble music*

Terms Define or identify the following terms, based on readings from the text and/or other sources.

15. be able to identify the musical instruments in the pictures

16. nawba

17. layali

18. qanun

19. darabukka

20. nay

21. rebab

Reading Comprehension Answer the following work questions (answers at end of this chapter):

29. The main characteristics of the music of the Arabic Near East are _____ and _____, a highly developed _____, the use of _____ and _____ modes, an association with the Arabic language and _____, and the use of particular _____.

30. The two present musical styles are the _____ and _____.

31. Oriental Near Eastern music is cultivated mainly in Egypt, Lebanon, Syria, Iraq, Afghanistan, and Malaysia. True or False.

32. Occidental Near Eastern music is cultivated mainly in Morocco, Algeria, and Tunisia. True or False.

33. Oriental Near Eastern music is mainly _____ and with _____ character.

34. The use of microtones is more frequent in Occidental than in Oriental Near Eastern music. True or False.

35. The nawba is a _____ of pieces organized in a particular _____ and centered around a single _____.

36. There are four different kinds of nawba, _____ belonging to the Oriental tradition and _____ to the Occidental tradition

37. The nawba belonging to the Occidental tradition are from _____, _____, and _____.

38. Traditionally, training of classical musicians in the Arabic Near East was done with notation. True or False.

39. Today, some Near Eastern schools offer training in European and Near Eastern music. True or False.

40. Traditionally, the Near Eastern musical suite is associated with complex mystical and healing concepts. True or False.

Video Viewing

1. Azan—Islamic call to worship (Turkey) (16-1). *The JVC Video Anthology of World Music and Dance*, The Middle East and Africa I (VTMV-16).
2. Saz—plucked lute solo (Turkey) (16-7). *The JVC Video Anthology of World Music and Dance*, The Middle East and Africa I (VTMV-16).
3. Asik performance [vocal and saz] (Turkey) (16-9). *The JVC Video Anthology of World Music and Dance*, The Middle East and Africa I (VTMV-16).
4. Bedouin Dance (Iraq) (16-12). *The JVC Video Anthology of World Music and Dance*, The Middle East and Africa I (VTMV-16).
5. Contemporary Iraqi song: "Ya zahrat al-madiyin" (Iraq) (16-13. *The JVC Video Anthology of World Music and Dance*, The Middle East and Africa I (VTMV-16).
6. Egyptian popular song: "Ana gambak ya kol Iraqi" (Egypt) (17-1). *The JVC Video Anthology of World Music and Dance*, The Middle East and Africa II (VTMV-17).

7. Bedouin dance [qanun, darabukka, flute, violin] (Tunisia) (17-2). *The JVC Video Anthology of World Music and Dance*, The Middle East and Africa I (VTMV-16).

8. Ma'luf—classical music [ud, nai, darabukka, tar, naqqara, violin, cello] (Tunisia) (17-3). *The JVC Video Anthology of World Music and Dance*, The Middle East and Africa I (VTMV-16).

9. Nawba—classical music selection: prelude to "Sunset" (Morocco) (17-5). *The JVC Video Anthology of World Music and Dance*, The Middle East and Africa I (VTMV-16).

Sample Test Questions

Multiple choice questions. Only one answer is correct.

1. The music of the pre-Islamic period in the Near East was: a. mostly vocal, b. related to poetry, c. accompanied by instruments, d. all of the above, e. a and b only.

2. The pre-Islamic period in the Near East is called Jahiliya which means: a. nothingness, b. way of the gods, c. ignorance, d. beginning, e. chaos.

3. The oldest form of chant in the Near East is the: a. caravan song, b. praise song, c. dance song, d. death song, e. drinking song.

4. Persian songs and instruments were imported into the Arabic Near East by: a. traders, b. merchants, c. slaves, d. missionaries, e. soldiers.

5. When the Arabs entered Spain in 822 A.D., a new Arabic musical style developed called what? a. Andalusian, b. Cordoban, c. Moziarabic, d. Moorish, e. Hispanic.

6. The first opera house in the Arabic world was opened in 1869 in which city? a. Alexandria, b. Cairo, c. Baghdad, d. Mecca, e. Tunis.

7. The Islamic attitude towards music is: a. negative, b. positive, c. indifferent, d. none of the above, e. all of the above.

8. Cultural and intellectual stagnation in the Arabic Near East began in 1258 with the fall of: a. Madrid, b. Baghdad, c. Mecca, d. Jerusalem, e. Cairo.

9. Which was *not* a problem addressed by Arabic music theorists? a. tonal material, b. melodic modes, c. rhythmic modes, d. harmony.

10. The earliest system of describing Arabic modes used "finger modes" based on: a. a sign language system based on the fingers of the left hand, b. the fingering of the 'ud, c. the names of the fingers in Arabic, d. ten frets on the 'ud because there are ten fingers.

11. The maqamat, or modes as used in the Arabic Near East, contain how many notes to the octave? a. 7, b. 17, c. 27, d. 43, e. 72.

12. In the second period of Arabic music theory, which was *not* one of the

three principal kinds of writings? a. by Islamic clerics, b. by musicians and scholars educated in the East, c. by musicians and scholars educated in the West, d. by non-Arabs, mostly Europeans.

13. The Arabic music theorist al-Kindi was influenced by the music theories of which culture? a. European, b. Persian, c. Indian, d. American, e. Greek.

14. Which Near Eastern musical instrument was the most used in developing Arabic music theory? a. 'ud, b. duff, c. taqsim, d. nay, e. maqam.

15. The most common method of transmitting the Arabic musical repertoire is: a. listening to recordings, b. teaching by rote, c. using Arabic notation, d. using European notation, e. singing.

16. In Morocco, the individual nawbat are associated with: a. deities, b. spirits of ancestors, c. times of the day suitable for performance, d. seasons of the year.

17. A musical suite of pieces in the Near East is called: a. darabukka, b. qanun, c. layali, d. nawba, e. maqam.

18. Stylistic differences between Occidental and Oriental Near Eastern music can be explained as: a. the result of different degrees of political stability, b. the preference of Oriental musicians for complex, microtonal modes, c. the desire of Occidental musicians to appeal to popular audiences in preference to elite courts, d. a and c, e. all the above.

19. Occidental Near Eastern music is principally for: a. dance, b. solo performance, c. ensemble, d. religion, e. royal courts.

20. The Christian reconquest of Spain caused Moslems to migrate to: a. North Africa, b. Egypt, c. Saudi Arabia, d. Portugal, e. Iraq.

21. The usual context for a Moroccan nawba performance may be a: a. funeral, b. birth, c. wedding, d. religious service, e. parade.

22. Which instrument would not be found in a Moroccan nawba performance? a. violin, b. viola, c. 'ud, d. rebab, e. nay.

23. The darabukka is a Near Eastern: a. idiophone, b. membranophone, c. aerophone, d. chordophone.

24. The rebab is a Near Eastern: a. idiophone, b. membranophone, c. aerophone, d. chordophone.

25. The qanun is a Near Eastern: a. idiophone, b. membranophone, c. aerophone, d. chordophone.

Answers to Reading Comprehension Questions

1. a. Indo-European (Persians), b. Semito-Chamitic (Arabs), c. Uralo-Altaic (Turks)
2. a. Mesopotamian, b. Egyptian, c. Persian, d. Islamic

3. a. Damascus, b. Baghdad, c. Cordoba
4. classical, pre-Islamic
5. False: in the court music of the medieval Islamic empire
6. Africa, Asia
7. vocal, poetry
8. caravan, camel
9. False: it had a profound influence on music
10. Persian
11. Golden Age, a. medicine, b. astronomy, c. alchemy, d. geography, e. mathematics, f. music theory
12. Andalusian
13. Morocco, Algeria, Tunisia
14. False: few musicians perform it
15. Greek
16. rhythmic
17. True
18. True
19. False: there was a continuous effort by a number of scholars and musicians
20. Arabs, Persians, Turks
21. eighth, eighteenth, eighteenth, present
22. 'ud
23. eight
24. True
25. thirteenth
26. seven
27. True
28. rhythmic skeleton, rhythmic mode
29. monophony, heterophony, melodic line, melodic, rhythmic, poetry, instruments
30. Oriental, Occidental
31. False: not in Afghanistan and Malaysia
32. True
33. improvised, virtuoso
34. False: less rather than more frequent
35. suite, order, maqam
36. one, three
37. Morocco, Algeria, Tunisia
38. False: it was done by rote
39. True
40. True

Answers to Sample Test Questions

1. d
2. c
3. a
4. c
5. a
6. b
7. a
8. b
9. d
10. b
11. a
12. a
13. e
14. a
15. b
16. c
17. d
18. e
19. c
20. a
21. c
22. e
23. b
24. d
25. d

Listening Form

Student Name_____ I.D. Number _____
Course Name _____ Course Number _____
Date_____Chapter Number_____Listening Example Number _____
Record or Tape Number_____Name of Culture and Location _____
Name of Performer(s)_____
Instructions: place an X, ✓, or • in appropriate boxes; give types; indicate native names.

performing elements (if vocal)	solo: M/F	duo: M/F	trio: M/F	quartet: M/F	group: M/F	other: M/F
performing elements (if instrumental)	corpophone	idiophone	membrano-phone	aerophone	chordophone	electrophone	other
texture	single melody	dense unison	heterophone	imitation	parallelism	disphony	other
more texture	with drone	with time indicator	chordal	polyphonic stratification	colotomy	combination	variable
melodic contour	static	ascending	descending	conjunct	disjunct	undulating	terraced
mode or scale	number of notes	vernacular	using cipher notation (numbers), indicate the mode or scale in ascending order
meter	free	duple	triple	compound	additive	poly	other
speed	very slow	slow	moderate	fast	very fast	variable	other
amplitude	very soft	soft	moderate	loud	very loud	variable	other
timbre (tone color)	clear	breathy	nasal	open	tight	masked	other
inflections	no vibrato	slow vibrato	fast vibrato	wide vibrato	falsetto	multiphonics	other
formal structure	vernacular name	expanding	reverting	strophic	theme and variations	other
structural or performance techniques	ostinato	responsorial	antiphonal	elastic rhythm	if vocal: syllabic or melismatic	non-synchronous parts	other

Chapter 15

Text Pages 269 – 283

Classical Iranian Music

Ella Zonis

Introduction To Chapter (Text Page 269)

Purpose To introduce several sociocultural ideas that have helped to shape the classical music of Iran (Persia).

Guidance This chapter is concerned with the classical musical types of Persian music that are no longer a part of Iranian daily life since the revolution that overthrew the Shah (Pahlavi Empire) in 1979 and established the present orthodox Shiite Islamic government. Since the revolution, Iranian classical music is mostly found outside Iran, in cities where Iranian culture lives in exile, such as Paris, Los Angeles, New York, and elsewhere in the West. Today, this music may seem sad because of the political and cultural changes in Iran; in a traditional sense, however, it is best to consider it pensive and mystical rather than sad. As the author points out, it *is* religious in a sense, although it is not used in worship. Here the line between sacred and secular is not clear cut, and the performance of classical Iranian music *is* often a religiously inspired philosophical expression. It is a music that often moves its traditional listeners to tears because of its profundity and deep Persian cultural ties, which includes religion as inseparable from life itself. Neither the chanting of texts from the Koran nor the Islamic call to prayer are considered to be music by Moslems. Although an Islamic country, Iran is not Arabic. Its history, music, language, and culture are quite different from other countries in the Middle East.

Terms Define or identify the following terms or areas, based on readings from the text and/or other sources.

1. Find Iran on a world globe and on a map of the Middle East. Notice its geographic location at the most easterly part of the Middle East, bordering Afghanistan and Central Asia.

2. Locate Teheran, the capital of Iran.

3. Islam

198 Musics of Many Cultures: Study Guide and Workbook

4. Mohammed

5. Persia

6. Farsi

7. dastgah

8. Sufi

9. Koran

10. Omar Khayam

Reading Comprehension Answer the following work questions (answers at end of this chapter):

1. Name the five types of non-Western music found in Iran today, and briefly explain each one.

    a. _____
    _____,

    b. _____
    _____,

    c. _____
    _____,

    d. _____
    _____,

    e. _____
    _____.

2. In Iran, among strict Moslems, the rise and fall of a voice chanting the Koran is not considered to be music. True or False.

3. Dastgah, which means _____, is religious to traditional Iranians. True or False.

4. The founder of Islam, _____, frowned upon "wine, woman, and song," as written in _____ _____.

History (Text Pages 269–271)

Purpose To examine the history of Iran and relate it to the classical Persian musical traditions.

Guidance The author again stresses the sadness of Persian music, and uses history to try to explain it. To present another point of view, however, the following passage, written by an Iranian musicologist, should be considered:

> It is a common tendency to label Persian music...as extremely melancholy. Although such judgments are based entirely on personal impressions, it is this writer's belief that if a single adjective describes the emotional quality of Persian music, it is not *melancholy*. To one who is able to understand the subtleties of this refined art, its spiritual effects seem to transcend such common worldly experiences as sadness or joy. Just as much of the poetry and other fine arts of Persia convey a profound feeling in which all human emotions and thoughts are blended into one, Persian music, as a whole, appears unconcerned with isolated expressions. Perhaps the not altogether lucid adjective *mystic* is best suited to describe the essence of Persian music. (Homaz Farhat, "Persian Classical Music" in *Festival of Oriental Music and the Related Arts*, University of California, Los Angeles, 1960, p. 64)

The same type of careful, emic (from within the culture) scrutiny should also be applied to the Iranian people, as to any culture. To do otherwise is to view a culture, its music and its people, from our own point of view (this is ethnocentrism). Certainly, however, historical events have caused ups and downs in most civilizations, and musical expressions in Iran have been greatly affected by events in Iran's history. Some of these events include foreign domination, as indicated in the author's chronological chart. Many changes, however, have occurred during regimes that have been Iranian. The author's words (not her chart) make it clear, for example, that traditional Persian music was encouraged during the Safavid Kingdom (1501–1736), was discouraged during the rise of the orthodox Shiite (Shi'a) sect of Islam (until 1900), was encouraged during the Pahlavi Empire (1925–1979), and is discouraged today because of orthodox Shiite beliefs. However, during the Iranian Pahlavi Empire, Western musical influences were very strong, with European popular and classical musical forms and performances nearly replacing traditional Iranian music. Today, classical Iranian music is mostly continued outside of Iran. Thus, history and culture (including music) are very dynamic; that is, they are constantly changing.

Terms Define or identify the following terms or people, based on readings from the text and/or other sources.

11. Know the historical periods on text pages 269–270.

12. Ibn Sina (Avicenna)

13. Safi al-Din

Reading Comprehension Answer the following work questions (answers at end of this chapter):

5. The first known major influence on Persian music came from the ancient _____ civilization, dating from about the fourth century B.C. until the second century A.D.

6. During the time of the great Persian theorists Ibn Sina and Safi al-Din, the religious atmosphere was relaxed and allowed for the practice of music to flourish. True or False.

7. The adoption of the Shiite sect of Islam lead to a flourishing state of music-making. True or False.

8. Persian music theory is Arabic in origin. True or False.

9. While the author says that Iranian music is _____, an Iranian musicologist says it is _____. One can also think of Iranian music as _____.

10. Generally, the historical periods in Iranian history were very short. True or False.

Classical Iranian Music (Text Pages 271–279)

Purpose To identify the basic principles of Iranian music—specifically theory, rhythm, and improvisation.

Guidance Persian music is organized into dastgah-ha (the *ha* is the plural form in Farsi), or modes, and each has a name of its own. A performer may play in one dastgah from five minutes to one hour. All of the dastgah-ha have unifying elements, such as special notes and specific ending patterns. Classical Iranian music today is basically unmeasured and performed in a free style (rubato), relying on the poetry of the text in vocal performances to give some kind of rhythmic structure. Persian music relies heavily on the performers' skill to improvise, within an elaborate scheme that must be followed. In order to better understand diagram 15-1 on page 272, pencil or color in each of the six rectangles, showing how the gusheh-ha #1-5 rise, returning to the original level with gusheh #6 (#1).

Terms Define or identify the following terms, based on readings from the text and/or other sources.

14. dastgah

15. gusheh

16. maqam

17. koron

18. sori

19. daramad

20. radif

21. iqa'at

22. mode

23. zarbi

25. avaz

Reading Comprehension Answer the following work questions (answers at end of this chapter):

11. In the classical art music of Iran, the audience, or group of people listening to music in a traditional setting, are totally passive and leave all improvisatory ideas to the performer. True or False.

12. An Iranian musician never modulates from one dastgah to another during the duration of a single piece. True or False.

13. List four English words that may be used to mean dastgah.

    a. _____, b. _____,

    c. _____, d. _____.

14. The term for the total of all the gusheh-ha in all twelve dastgah-ha is called what?

    _____.

15. In classical Iranian vocal music, generally one poetic verse (couplet) is set to a single gusheh. True or False.

16. Though most Iranian classical music is improvisatory, there is a definite scheme for performance ranging from a definite melody or tune, to a section of purely melodic contour, to a section of melodic patterns or motives. True or False.

Instruments (Text Pages 279–280)

Purpose To introduce the variety and uses of the musical instruments found in classical Persian music.

Guidance The term "sehtar" means three strings, although today the instrument has four because of Western violin influence. It is plucked with finger nails. The tar is a larger lute with a double-chambered body covered with skin. It is plucked with a plectrum. The sehtar and the Arabic 'ud are comparable (as the author states) only in so far as they are plucked lutes (the former has a long neck, and the latter has a short neck). The santur is a 72-stringed zither that is very similar to the hammered dulcimer popular in the folk music of the United States. Indeed, the hammered dulcimer principle traveled eastward into China (yang ch'in or foreign zither) and northward into Europe. The European piano developed from the Persian santur—the piano is basically a large hammered dulcimer that has mechanical hammers (one for each course of strings, however) attached to a keyboard. The santur and its relative, the Arabic qanun, are both zithers (psaltery is another name for zither), but the former is struck with light-weight hammers, and the latter is plucked. The nay is an end-blown flute without an air duct. The nay musician produces a stream of air in two different ways: for the lower notes he places the edge of the mouthpiece between his two front teeth and blows, and for the upper notes he puckers his lips and blows. The former technique is like whistling between the teeth, and the latter is like whistling with the mouth formed into a pucker. The kamanchay, meaning "little bow," is a bowed lute whose neck pierces the body. Lutes constructed in that fashion are called "spike" or "spiked" when the fingerboard goes straight through the resonating body, from top to bottom, and comes out the bottom as if it were a long spike. The kamanchay, like the sehtar, originally had three strings but today has four. The traditional Iranian membranophone is known by two names, zarb and tombak—the latter term is a good example of onomatopoeia (the name for the instrument is derived from the sound it makes; for example, hitting the drumhead in the center produces "tom" and hitting it on the edge produces "bak").

European musical instruments have found their way into classical Iranian music particularly during this century. The violin, in particular, lends itself well to the music of Iran; it is so popular, in fact, that it is no longer considered a foreign instrument. Also found, particularly in ensembles with traditional instruments, are the clarinet, oboe, flute, trumpet, and the piano (often retuned to one of the Iranian scales).

Terms Define or identify the following terms, based on readings from the text and/or other sources.

26. Be able to identify the musical instruments in the pictures

27. sehtar

28. tar

29. santur

30. nay

31. kamanchay

32. zarb

33. tombak

Reading Comprehension Answer the following work questions (answers at end of this chapter):

17. The Persian tar has triple resonator chambers that are interconnected with a skin membrane. True or False.

18. In ethnomusicology the Persian _____ can be classified as a struck chordophone. It is also called a _____ in English.

19. The kamanchay is called a _____ in English.

20. Which instrument derives its name from the sounds it produces? _____ .

Classical Persian Music Today (Text Pages 280–281)

Purpose To examine the state of classical Persian music today.

Guidance The author discusses certain limitations of Persian music. It must always be kept in mind, however, that Persian music is not European music—it never has been, never will be, and does not need to be. Additionally, Persian music should not be discussed in terms of European music. The fact that it does not have measured rhythm (which it does sometimes), harmony (sometimes it has multipart texture, especially the santur), or counterpoint is not a limitation; lacking those elements as they exist in Western music simply shows that Persian music is different from Western music. It stands on its own merits, and will continue to do so. It exists, however, in exile.

None of the major sources on world music pop even mentions Iran. Perhaps because of the musically oppressive Islamic government since the fall of the Pallavi regime, anything approaching rock or fusion music may be frowned upon. Some pop musicians, however, have remained in Iran, and their styles are conservative yet danceable. Most famous in Iran is Gogoush, a female vocalist who continues to be very popular. Many traditional and pop musicians left Iran during the revolution and scattered throughout Europe and America.

In the United States among Iranian exiles, pop music flourishes on recordings and is performed live during dances, especially in Los Angeles, New York, and other metropolitan areas. Many of the pop musicians live in Los Angeles, where their desires to become recording stars are often unfulfilled. The Iranian pop music cassette industry, however, was big in southern California (replaced now by CDs), and many of the immigrant Iranian singers copy the styles of the more famous musicians. The top male Iranian pop singers in Los Angeles today are Moin, Sattar, and Shahram (pop stars mainly go by a single name), and Shahram even has his own television show. Female Iranian pop singers include Fataneh, Haideh, Ebie, and Deleram. Particularly unique in Iranian pop is the use of electronic keyboards with a variety of stops that can imitate such traditional Persian instruments as the santur, tar, dombak, and others. Depending on the song, keyboard solos that follow verses by the lead singer often produce a traditional instrument timbre, complete with ornamentations such as a tremolo that is reminiscent of the *tahrir* or voice warble. One of the best known Iranian keyboardists is Siavash Ghomeishi (goes by his complete name), who is famous for his interesting piano style and original songs.

Video Viewing

1. Santur—hammered dulcimer solo: "Nagme-ye karevan" (Iran) (16-11). *The JVC Video Anthology of World Music and Dance*, The Middle East and Africa I (VTMV-16).

Sample Test Questions

Multiple choice questions. Only one answer is correct.

1. The idea in Iran that Mohammed, the founder of Islam, was against wine, women, and song is found in: a. the Bible,   b. the Koran,   c. Omar Khayam,   d. Zur Khaneh,   e. the Torah.

2. Which words best characterize Persian classical music?   a. light and carefree,   b. slow and majestic,   c. gay and boisterous,   d. pensive and mystic,   e. frenzied.

3. In the seventh through tenth centuries A.D., there was thorough blending of music, instruments, and musical terminology between the Persian culture and the: a. Arabic,   b. Eastern Orthodox,   c. Turkish,   d. Mongolian,   e. European.

4. During which Iranian period were musicians publicly respected and public concerts permitted?   a. Safavid Kingdom,   b. Sassanian Empire,   c. Achaemenid Empire,   d. Pahlavi Empire,   e. Khomeini Regime.

5. At the height of Persian classical culture, music was played only for: a. friends and away from the public,   b. the Shah and his court,   c. the religious leaders,   d. the public in town squares.

6. Iranian music is presently organized into twelve systems called: a. raga,   b. dastgah,   c. makam,   d. koron,   e. rasa.

7. In Persian music, the strongest rhythmic factor in music of the radif comes from: a. marching,   b. human pulse,   c. dance,   d. poetry,   e. swinging clubs laced with chains.

8. Persian music uses a great deal of: a. measured rhythm, b. harmony, c. counterpoint, d. heterophony, e. improvisation.

9. Which was *not* an effect of Western music in Iran? a. Iranian composers and performers were attracted to Western music rather than to traditional Persian music, b. Iranian composers often grafted features of Western music onto Persian music, c. Iranian composers developed a modern style of composing contemporary music for Persian instruments.

10. For centuries in Iran, musical performance: a. was a family affair, b. was a part of religious worship, c. was performed in towers, d. was written down in notation.

11. Persian music is organized into how many dastgah-ha? a. 2, b. 5, c. 12, d. 25, e. unlimited number.

12. The Persian kamanchay is: a. held close to the musician's body and plucked, b. rested on the ground and bowed, c. rested on the player's knee and bowed, d. rested on a table or stand in front of the player and struck, e. placed under the player's chin and bowed.

13. The Persian nay is played how? a. between the teeth, b. against the puckered lips, c. by buzzing the lips, d. a and b, e. b and c.

14. The sehtar is related to which other Persian instrument? a. tar, b. santur, c. tombak, d. nay, e. kamanchay.

15. Which Persian instrument's name is derived from the sound it produces? a. tar, b. santur, c. tombak, d. nay, e. kamanchay.

Answers to Reading Comprehension Questions

1. a. folk music, found outside of Teheran, that belongs to tribal and non-Moslem people
    b. popular music that uses traditional scales and the Farsi language, but Western instruments and rhythms
    c. the music from *Zur Khaneh*, or House of Strength, and *Nagarah Khanah*, or Tower Music
    d. Iranian classical music
    e. "music" that is the chanting of the Koran
2. True
3. melody type, True
4. Mohammed, Omar Khayam
5. Greek
6. False: Islam disapproved of music
7. False: the Shiite sect discouraged music
8. False: it is Greek in origin
9. sad, mystic, pensive
10. False: they generally lasted very long

11. False: they verbally and visually influence the performer
12. True
13. apparatus, mechanism, scheme, framework
14. radif
15. True
16. True
17. False: it has double chambers
18. santur, hammered dulcimer
19. spiked fiddle
20. tombak

Answers to Sample Test Questions

1. c
2. d
3. a
4. d
5. a
6. b
7. d
8. e
9. c
10. a
11. c
12. c
13. d
14. a
15. c

Listening Form

Student Name_____ I.D. Number_____
Course Name _____ Course Number_____
Date_____Chapter Number_____Listening Example Number _____
Record or Tape Number_____Name of Culture and Location _____
Name of Performer(s)_____
Instructions: place an X, ✓, or • in appropriate boxes; give types; indicate native names.

performing elements (if vocal)	solo: M/F	duo: M/F	trio: M/F	quartet: M/F	group: M/F	other: M/F
performing elements (if instrumental)	corpophone	idiophone	membranophone	aerophone	chordophone	electrophone	other
texture	single melody	dense unison	heterophone	imitation	parallelism	disphony	other
more texture	with drone	with time indicator	chordal	polyphonic stratification	colotomy	combination	variable
melodic contour	static	ascending	descending	conjunct	disjunct	undulating	terraced
mode or scale	number of notes	vernacular	using cipher notation (numbers), indicate the mode or scale in ascending order
meter	free	duple	triple	compound	additive	poly	other
speed	very slow	slow	moderate	fast	very fast	variable	other
amplitude	very soft	soft	moderate	loud	very loud	variable	other
timbre (tone color)	clear	breathy	nasal	open	tight	masked	other
inflections	no vibrato	slow vibrato	fast vibrato	wide vibrato	falsetto	multiphonics	other
formal structure	vernacular name	expanding	reverting	strophic	theme and variations	other	
structural or performance techniques	ostinato	responsorial	antiphonal	elastic rhythm	if vocal: syllabic or melismatic	non-synchronous parts	other

Chapter 16   Text Pages 284 – 306

On Jewish Music

Abraham A. Schwadron

Introduction to Chapter (Text Pages 284–285)

Purpose To define the parameters of what being a Jew is, using the concepts of tradition and compromise.

Terms Define or identify the following terms, people, or areas, based on readings from the text and/or other sources.

1. Locate Israel on a world globe or map. On a detailed map of the Near East, locate the Tigris and Euphrates Rivers. Be able to locate the various countries mentioned in this chapter.

2. Torah

3. Pentateuch

4. Idelsohn

Reading Comprehension Answer the following work questions (answers at end of this chapter):

1. Jews have maintained their individuality because Judaism is _____ _____, _____, and _____.

2. A common statement is that the Jews are a people of _____ _____.

3. In Jewish tradition there is a common Semitic-Oriental origin, a basically common set of sacred beliefs, history, books, language, and music. True or False.

4. Differences in Hebrew folk as well as in synagogue music are notable. True or False.

5. The ethnomusicologist can study the music of Israel and know every-

thing there is to know about Jewish music. True or False.

6. The music of the Jews in Peru has been studied in depth. True or False.

7. The traditional sacred language of the Jews is _____.

8. Three postures or tenets that characterize contemporary Judaism are _____, _____, and _____.

9. In considering what a Jew is, the key terms are _____ and _____.

History and Development of Jewish Music
(Text Pages 286–290)

Purpose To study both traditional and compromised Jewish music by surveying its history as well as its sociocultural contexts.

Guidance There were many musical instruments used in biblical times. The musical instruments referred to by the author as woodwinds were probably bamboo-winds. The *shalishim* and *menaanim*, as they are described, are sistrums (compare with the Ethiopian sistrum on page 236, Figure 13-1). The ancient areas of the Mediterranean, North Africa, and the Near East share many musical instrument similarities.

Terms Define or identify the following terms, based on readings from the text and/or other sources.

5. kinnor

6. shofar

7. Diaspora

8. Sephardim or Sephardic Jews

9. Ashkenazim or Ashkenazic Jews

10. piyutim movement

11. Spanish-Arabic school

12. chazzanic movement

13. chassidic movement

14. Society for Jewish Folk Music

15. klezmorim (klesmorim)

Reading Comprehension
Answer the following work questions (answers at end of this chapter):

10. The most important musical contribution of the ancient Hebrews was the elevation of the status of _____ music in union with _____ / _____.

11. From descriptive accounts of _____, we learn that 24 choral groups consisting of 288 musicians were utilized in some 21 weekly services.

12. The Law of Moses provided precise instructions for music making. True or False.

13. Throughout history, the Hebrews never accepted features from other cultures that were compatible with their own religious institutions. True or False.

14. Because of the Diaspora, instrumental music—sacred and secular—was banned and lost. True or False.

15. In the Jewish vocal tradition, remnants of the _____ still prevail from ancient times.

16. The Diaspora has been studied from the following two broad classifications:

    _____ / _____
    and _____.

17. The music of the Yemenite Jews is not considered highly representative of ancient practices. True or False.

18. In general, European Jews have been classified either as _____ _____ or _____.

19. Piyutim are _____, religious _____ that climaxed during the tenth to twelfth centuries in the _____ _____-_____ school.

20. The Jewish Renaissance movement took place in Florence, Italy. True or False.

21. The Jewish Reform movement sought to introduce the _____ _____ (_____) and to discard what remained of Semitic-Oriental _____ _____.

22. The Haskalah movement was a philosophical struggle between

_____ and _____
that led to the development of the Society for _____
_____ _____.

23. Klesmorim are professional Jewish orchestral musicians. True or False.

24. The Renaissance movement in Jewish history is noted for its reforms in _____ music.

25. Text is the most important element of chassidic song. True or False.

Jewish Music after 1948: Israeli and American Trends (Text Pages 290–291)

Music Examples

religious songs

Purpose To introduce Jewish musical trends in Israel and the United States since 1948, including the genres of composed, folk, pop, and theatrical music.

Guidance Since the population of the modern state of Israel (established in 1948) includes a diverse mixture of Jews (and non-Jews) from all over the world, music has played an important role in fostering a sense of Jewish national unity. The wide variety of genuinely "Jewish" music makes a precise and incontestable definition unlikely. Nevertheless, the author suggests the concept of Yiddishkeit as a unifier. This is a rather subjectively conceived idea, and the further Jews are from Israel (except in America), the less "Jewish" it may sound (the Jewish music from Bukhara in Central Asia is one example).

Terms Define or identify the following terms, based on readings from the text and/or other sources.

16. Yiddishkeit

17. cantillation

18. melodicles

Reading Comprehension Answer the following work questions (answers at end of this chapter):

26. The music of the Israeli Composers' League is a blend of the _____ and the _____, of _____ and _____ themes, resulting in an eclecticism that includes _____ melody and rhythms with Western _____.

27. Israeli music has benefited from well-organized and well-supported musical institutions. True or False.

28. Professional liturgical singers are known as _____.

29. Biblical chant is traditionally a written tradition. True or False.

Jewish Musical Characteristics (Text Pages 291–294)

Purpose To explain the most important musical characteristics of today's Jewish musical traditions.

Guidance Among Jews, klezmer music has always been a type of popular music, and has always been associated with dancing and festive occasions. The Klezmatics have fused that traditional popular music with jazz/rock elements (e.g., heavy electric bass, electronic effects, sophisticated drumming, improvisation) and Middle Eastern musical characteristics (which also include sophisticated drumming and improvisation).

Terms Define or identify the following terms, based on readings from the text and/or other sources.

19. freilach

20. zemirot

21. klezmorim (a second definition is on text page 297)

Music Example
klezmer ensemble

Reading Comprehension Answer the following work questions (answers at end of this chapter):

30. The oldest surviving Jewish musical remnant is _____ _____, usually referred to as _____.

31. Hebrew vocal cantillations are structured on _____.

32. The chanting of _____ both by laymen and professional _____ constitutes a genre of existing Jewish music.

33. The music for the liturgical and semiliturgical poems was often borrowed and adapted from the popular melodies of the peoples in whose midst the Jews lived. True or False.

34. The tonal (pitch) systems between Oriental and Occidental Jews resulted respectively in _____ and _____ practices.

35. Sometimes Oriental Jewish music is out of tune. True or False.

36. Jewish folk song is not important as a category of existing Jewish music because it is too varied. True or False.

37. Jewish biblical cantillations are purely _____, while folk songs are generally _____

by _____-_____, simple improvised or complex _____ _____, _____, small vocal or instrumental _____, or even full _____.

38. Many Jewish folk songs are in minor modes because they are sad. True or False.

39. Zemirot or _____ songs are sung for the _____ and _____ occasions.

40. Most Jewish folk songs are in a major mode. True or False.

41. Some Jewish folk song melodies are sung on textless syllables. True or False.

42. The Yiddish _____ often performs for festive occasions such as weddings.

43. To understand Jewish music, one must have a grasp of both historical roots and the _____ _____.

Video Viewing

1. *Jewish Soul Music. The Art of Giora Feidman.* Produced by Ludi Boeken and Ben Elkenbout, directed by Uri Barbash. Ergo Medio 760.

Sample Test Questions

Multiple choice questions. Only one answer is correct.

1. Which Jewish musical instrument is held in the Jewish subconscious with symbolic messianic significance? a. halib, b. kinnor, c. shofar, d. shalishim.

2. In Jewish music, piyutim are recognized as: a. poetic religious prayers, b. folk songs, c. folk dances, d. musical collections.

3. During the Jewish Renaissance movement, reforms were attempted in: a. folk music, b. vernacular musical expression, c. synagogue music, d. secular melodies.

4. One characteristic of the Jewish chassidic movement was the lack of: a. rhythm, b. melody, c. accompanying instruments, d. texts.

5. Klesmorim are: a. itinerant folk musicians, b. dance tunes, c. religious

expressions, d. musical instruments, e. professional orchestral musicians.

6. Modern Israeli music includes: a. composed folk-songs, b. avant-garde music, c. cantillation, d. orchestral compositions, e. all of the above.

7. Yiddishkeit is a term roughly analogous to: a. American jazz, b. African-American soul, c. Tin Pan Alley's hit parade, d. nationalism, e. oral tradition.

8. Which interval is most characteristic of the Jewish folk song? a. the octave, b. augmented second, c. major third, d. fifth, e. none of the above.

9. The Jewish quote "How shall we sing the Lord's song in a foreign land?" comes from: a. *Fiddler on the Roof*, b. the exiled Babylonian psalmist, c. Proverbs, d. Haskalah.

10. Who wrote a massive study and compilation of Hebrew-Oriental melodies that constitutes a prime musicological contribution? a. Idelsohn, b. Mendelssohn, c. Ohlson, d. Schwadron, e. Falasha.

11. Which is *not* an ancient Jewish aerophone? a. silver trumpets, b. woodwinds or bamboo-winds, c. ivory trumpets, d. ram's horn.

12. The music of ancient Israel represents about how many centuries of change? a. 5, b. 14, c. 25, d. 100.

13. In Jewish musical history, restrictions on instrumental music were gradually lifted for joyous occasions like: a. weddings, b. births, c. harvests, d. plantings, e. saints' days.

14. Which Israeli organization fosters creativity toward a unified Jewish musical identity? a. Zionist Musicians of Israel, b. Jewish Composers' and Performers' Society, c. Unified Jewish Musicians Association of Israel, d. Brotherhood of Israeli Composers, e. Israeli Composers' League.

15. One of the most important musicals that uses Jewish music is: a. *South Pacific*, b. *West Side Story*, c. *Peter Pan*, d. *Sound of Music*, e. *Fiddler on the Roof*.

16. Which is *not* one of the instruments mentioned in the Old Testament of the Bible? a. lyre, b. harp, c. ram's horn, d. metal cymbals, e. lute.

17. In order to understand Jewish music today, one must understand: a. the Spanish Inquisition, b. the Diaspora, c. the music of Persia, d. the Torah, e. the Bible.

18. In Judaism, the oldest surviving musical remnant is: a. biblical chant, b. the harp of Solomon, c. silver trumpets, d. reciting of the Koran.

19. In Jewish music, differentiation in tonal (pitch) systems developed culturally between: a. Oriental and Occidental practices, b. northern and southern practices, c. Hindustani and Karnatak traditions, d. sacred and secular ideologies.

20. Probably the most important musical contribution of the ancient Hebrews was: a. the elevation of the status of liturgical music in union with ritual ceremonies, b. the introduction of the use of the drone in the Near East, c. vocal music, d. to introduce improvisation into the Near East.

21. Of the musical cultures in the Middle Eastern-Central Asian regions, which music is probably most commonly heard in the United States of America? a. Turkish, b. Indian, c. Iranian, d. Jewish, e. Arabic.

22. Jewish textless dance tunes are known as: a. zemirot, b. klezmorim, c. freilachs, d. shofars.

23. Jewish domestic songs are known as: a. zemirot, b. klezmorim, c. freilachs, d. shofars.

24. Yiddish musical bands are known as: a. zemirots, b. klezmorim, c. freilachs, d. shofars.

25. Jewish ram's horn trumpets are known as: a. zemirots, b. klezmorim, c. freilachs, d. shofars.

Answers to Reading Comprehension Questions

1. reflective, adaptive, unifying
2. books
3. False: music is diverse
4. True
5. False: because of diversity, there are no geographic limitations
6. False: it has not been studied
7. Hebrew
8. Orthodox, Conservative, Reform
9. tradition, compromise
10. liturgical, ritual ceremonies
11. Solomon's Temple
12. False: there is a lack of precise information
13. False: they have been quick to accept new features
14. True
15. biblical cantillations
16. Oriental / Middle East, Occidental
17. False: it is highly representative because of their isolation
18. Sephardim, Ashkenazim
19. poetic, prayers, Spanish-Arabic
20. False: in Mantua, Italy
21. vernacular (German), song
22. rationalism, mysticism, Jewish Folk Music
23. False: they are itinerant folk musicians
24. synagogue

25. False: lack of text
26. old, new, religious, biblical, Middle Eastern, harmonies
27. True
28. cantors
29. False: it is an oral tradition
30. biblical chant, cantillation
31. melodicles
32. prayers, cantors
33. True
34. microtonal, semitonal
35. False: the microtones make it different than Western tuning, but not out of tune—to call it out of tune would be ethnocentric
36. False: it is very important
37. vocal, accompanied, stamping-clapping, folk instruments, piano, ensembles, orchestra
38. False: sadness cannot be presumed to be associated with minor modes
39. Sabbath, special
40. False: although many are in minor, others are major, and many are modal
41. True
42. klezmorim
43. Jewish Diaspora

Answers to Sample Test Questions

1.	c	2.	a
3.	c	4.	d
5.	a	6.	e
7.	b	8.	b
9.	b	10.	a
11.	c	12.	b
13.	a	14.	e
15.	e	16.	e
17.	b	18.	a
19.	a	20.	a
21.	d	22.	c
23.	a	24.	b
25.	d		

Listening Form

Student Name_____ I.D. Number_____
Course Name _____ Course Number_____
Date_____ Chapter Number_____ Listening Example Number _____
Record or Tape Number_____ Name of Culture and Location _____
Name of Performer(s)_____
Instructions: place an X, ✓, or • in appropriate boxes; give types; indicate native names.

performing elements (if vocal)	solo: M/F	duo: M/F	trio: M/F	quartet: M/F	group: M/F	other: M/F
performing elements (if instrumental)	corpophone	idiophone	membranophone	aerophone	chordophone	electrophone	other
texture	single melody	dense unison	heterophone	imitation	parallelism	disphony	other
more texture	with drone	with time indicator	chordal	polyphonic stratification	colotomy	combination	variable
melodic contour	static	ascending	descending	conjunct	disjunct	undulating	terraced
mode or scale	number of notes	vernacular	using cipher notation (numbers), indicate the mode or scale in ascending order
meter	free	duple	triple	compound	additive	poly	other
speed	very slow	slow	moderate	fast	very fast	variable	other
amplitude	very soft	soft	moderate	loud	very loud	variable	other
timbre (tone color)	clear	breathy	nasal	open	tight	masked	other
inflections	no vibrato	slow vibrato	fast vibrato	wide vibrato	falsetto	multiphonics	other
formal structure	vernacular name	expanding	reverting	strophic	theme and variations	other	
structural or performance techniques	ostinato	responsorial	antiphonal	elastic rhythm	if vocal: syllabic or melismatic	non-synchronous parts	other

Chapter 17

Text Pages 307 – 331

North American Native Music

David P. McAllester

Introduction to Chapter (Text Page 307)

Purpose To introduce the basic musical styles of six Native American cultural areas, and to show how the traditions have developed because of inside and outside pressures and influences.

Guidance It would be worth while to look carefully at a world globe to see the possible migration routes of Native Americans from East Asia to the Western Hemisphere. The following two routes stand out: (1) across the land bridge formed when the Bering Strait was exposed during the Ice Age, and (2) across the Aleutian Islands to Alaska.

The map on text page 308 gives approximate locations of the geographic/cultural zones of the Native Americans of North America, and only the names of selected cultures are included. For a more complete map consult the *National Geographic* (December 1972) insert entitled "Indians of North America." The National Geographic Society map is also useful for Native American prehistory because its other side includes a physical and archaeological map entitled "North America Before Columbus." Also added to both sides of the publication are informative paragraphs about particular cultures, geographic areas, archaeological sites, and history. This National Geographic Society map is an excellent study guide for Native America in itself. Consult any recent *National Geographic* for the address of the Society.

The Eastern Woodlands (Text Pages 307–311)

Purpose To identify the native cultures of the Eastern Woodlands region, define the musical traditions found in that area, and describe the cultural contexts for the music of the people from that part of North America.

222 Musics of Many Cultures: Study Guide and Workbook

Music and Dance Examples

stomp dance

Creek from Southeast

Guidance At the time of the Europeans' arrival to the Atlantic seaboard of the land represented by the present United States of America, numerous indigenous nations existed. Collectively called Eastern Woodlands Native Americans by anthropologists, they included such cultures as the Cherokee, Choctaw, Chickasaw, Natchez, Creek, and Seminole in the south, and the Delaware, Iroquois, Mohican, Pequot, Powhatan, Fox, Illinois, Menominee, Miami, Winnebago, Ojibway, Cree (who are also found in the Plains region), and a few others in the north. Some of these cultures were huge powerful nations, like the Iroquois and Delaware, while others were smaller.

Terms Define or identify the following terms or areas, based on the reading from text.

1. Eastern Woodlands cultural area

2. "Three life-giving sisters"

3. vocables

4. stomp dance

5. drum dance

Reading Comprehension Answer the following work questions (answers at end of this chapter):

1. The greatest development of the Eastern Woodlands culture region was in which area of the United States of America? _____.

2. The Woodlands cultures were noted for their agricultural development. True or False.

3. The Woodlands cultures were totally based on hunting skills. True or False.

4. The religions of the Woodlands cultures gave thanks to _____ _____ and _____.

5. The "three life-giving sisters" of the Iroquois Native Americans are _____ _____, _____, and _____.

6. The music of Woodlands singers is similar, with its open relaxed style, to that of the ballad singers of northern Europe. True or False.

7. Vocables are almost never used in the texts of Woodlands music. True or False.

8. In the stomp dance one leader conducts the dance and another leader the song. True or False.

9. Some ceremonial songs of the Woodlands region focus on ritual texts and do not include dances. True or False.

10. The forces of nature are often conveyed in some Midewiwen Native American songs. True or False.

The Plains (Text Pages 311–314)

Purpose To identify the native cultures of the Plains region, define the musical traditions found in that area, and describe the cultural contexts for the music of the people from that part of North America.

Guidance The region known as the Plains can be described as west of the Mississippi River to the Rocky Mountains. Plains Indians were nomadic people who lived in portable *tipis,* traveled by horseback, and hunted the bison, their source of food and clothing. Many cultures lived in the Plains region, including the Dakota, Crow, Blackfoot, Arapaho, Kiowa, and Cheyenne. The 49 dance is a typical song and dance that is often performed late into the evening by young men after a powwow. It is a social dance song, performed for fun, with texts about women, social events, and concerns.

Terms Define the following terms, based on the reading from text.

6. 49 dance

7. rabbit dance

8. sun dance

9. war dance

10. fancy dance

11. powwow

12. giveaway

13. Medicine Society and Soldier Society

Reading Comprehension Answer the following work questions (answers at end of this chapter):

11. When compared or contrasted to the music of the Woodlands peoples, Plains music is _____ and more _____; it is often sung in a powerful _____ and the songs tend to start at the _____ of the _____.

12. Plains music is characterized by choral singing in which there is no group leader. True or False.

Music and Dance Examples

powwow music and dance

membranophone and singers

powwow music from Plains

Music Examples

courting flute

aerophone

vertical flute from Plains

13. Many individual songs are given in dreams or visions. Who gives these? _____; and why are they given? They will _____ the _____ at the _____ _____ in his _____.

14. List three prototypes of the powwow. _____ in the _____, _____ and _____ of _____.

15. The favorite exhibition dance at powwows, Indian fairs, Indian shows, and even Boy Scout Jamborees is the _____.

16. The modern day marching band instrument often used by Plains Indians is a _____.

17. Unlike the Woodland peoples, Native Americans of the Plains use no vocables. True or False.

18. Texts of Plains Indians songs are often long and in an epic style. True or False.

19. In performing a war dance, the dancer needs little knowledge of the music being played. True or False.

20. Native Americans of the Plains have a culture based on agriculture for which there is no music. True or False.

The Southwest (Text Pages 314–324)

Music Examples

songs

Navajo from Southwest

Purpose To identify the native cultures of the Southwest region, define the musical traditions found in that area, and describe the cultural contexts for the music of the people from that part of North America.

Guidance In the Southwest region two main contrasting Native American cultures are found: the Pueblos, who are predominantly an agricultural society, and the Apaches and Navajos, who combine raising livestock with farming. The musical styles, history, and general social characteristics of these two main groups should be considered individually.

The Pueblos of present New Mexico were living in villages and farming corn, beans, and squash as early as 300 B.C. From ancient times they developed their distinctive multistoried apartment dwellings built of adobe or sandstone, and used sophisticated flood-farming methods to irrigate their crops. Pueblo religion and mythology are complex with many variations of deities, mythological characters, and myths from one village to another. Much of Pueblo traditional religion and mythology is centered on agricultural needs, such as sufficient rain and a bountiful harvest. In the myth of the Corn Maidens, for example, the perpetual flight of the maidens and their return symbolize the constant annual cycle of replanting and harvesting the corn. When the Corn Maidens return as "matrons," they symbolize the plump, healthy kernels at harvest time. The Pueblos believed that since they ate corn, they were made of corn and shared a corn "essence" with the Corn Maidens. They were the "children," and the Corn Maidens their "mothers." If the people displeased the Corn Maidens, they would go away. Therefore, the Corn Dance was one of the many ways in which the Pueblos tried to appease the Corn Maidens. With the Spanish encounter of the 1600s, the Pueblos were forced to adopt Catholicism, but they continued to practice their traditional religion in secret. An unsuccessful Pueblo revolt in 1680 led to a softening of Spanish repression and greater tolerance for native religion. With the coming of American rule, repressive attitudes were reintroduced, and Indian children were made to attend American schools in an effort to acculturate the Pueblos and wipe out the remaining traces of their culture. More recently, court battles have enabled the Pueblos to retain more autonomy and religious freedom.

The Navajos and Apaches (who are being considered together) were originally nomadic hunters who later adopted much of the Pueblo's agricultural lifestyle when they migrated to the Southwest ca. 1200–1300 A.D. Today they inhabit parts of Arizona, New Mexico, Colorado, and Utah. The Navajos and Apaches, unlike the Pueblos, became horsemen after the Spanish encounter. The Navajos were more greatly influenced by the Pueblos and learned weaving, sand painting, and Pueblo ceremonials, while the Apaches became expert raiders and traders. The Navajos and Apaches both practice a shamanistic religion with a rich mythology. Medicine men, or shamans, conduct cures, ceremonies, and séances.

While both the Pueblo and the Navajos/Apaches use heavy pulsations and tension in their vocal styles, there are several musical differences between them. The Pueblo (and also the Hopi), for example, employ long developments of musical ideas, complex rhythms, and yelps or shouts; the Navajo and Apache use a very wide vocal range, falsetto, and the soft background accompaniment of a water drum.

Terms Define the following terms, based on the reading from text.

14. Enemyway

15. Corn People and Gatzina song

16. circle dance

17. Blessingway

18. Mountainway

19. Zuni harvest song

20. Apache fiddle

21. Shootingway

22. water drum

Reading Comprehension Answer the following work questions (answers at end of this chapter):

21. The Pueblo Indians migrated to the Southwest long after the Navajos and Apaches had established farming communities there. True or False.

22. Ceremonies of the Pueblo Indians are largely focused on agricultural needs. True or False.

23. The use of vocables in the "Corn People Gatzina Song" is a characteristic unique to Pueblo Indian music. True or False.

24. Pueblo songs feature long developments of musical ideas, and may include a dozen or more different phrases. True or False.

25. Ceremonies of the Navajo and Apache are often devoted to healing the sick. True or False.

26. Apache social singing is high, tense, and nasal, with subtle, ornamental inflections of the melody. True or False.

27. The Apache fiddle is made from what? _____.

28. The Apache water-drum uses what type of drum stick? _____.

29. The Apache water-drum is covered with what type of skin? _____.

The Plateau and Great Basin Area
(Text Pages 321–324)

Purpose To identify the native cultures of the Plateau and Great Basin region, define the musical traditions found in that area, and describe the cultural contexts for the music of the people from that part of North America.

Guidance The Native Americans of this area were comprised mainly of small, nomadic hunting and gathering bands. Their religion was based primarily on dreams that led to healing powers or special leadership in the hunt. The music of these peoples is open and relaxed in vocal style. Melodies are usually brief and paired phrases are often employed. Some of the cultures included in this area are the Paiute, Modoc, Klamath, and Northern Ute. The bear dance is one of the most common expressions of the Ute.

Terms Define or identify the following terms or areas, based on the reading from text.

23. Plateau Area

24. Great Basin

25. ghost dance

26. Native American Church

27. rasp

28. Water drum

29. "He ne yo wa"

30. Wovoka

Reading Comprehension Answer the following work questions (answers at end of this chapter):

30. The religion of the Plateau and Great Basin area is based on _____ _____ that led to healing powers or special leadership in the hunt.

31. Melodies of the Plateau and Great Basin Native Americans are _____ in duration and _____ in compass.

32. The Ghost Dance religion originated among the _____ Native Americans of _____.

33. A prophet named _____ dreamed that dance and prayer would cause the European invaders to disappear.

34. The basis of the Native American Church included _____ visions, all-night _____, prayer, and singing.

35. The sacred dwelling in which the Peyote Church ceremony ideally takes place is the Plains style _____.

36. Peyote songs have a relatively narrow range and are restricted to only _____ and _____ European-derived note values.

37. The texts of the songs of the Peyote Native American church consist largely of _____.

38. A padded drumstick is used to beat the head of a water drum in Peyote ceremonies. True or False.

39. Peyote Native American church musical performance includes whistling and yelping. True or False.

The Northwest Coast (Text Pages 324–326)

Purpose To identify the native cultures of the Northwest Coast region, define the musical traditions found in that area, and describe the cultural contexts for the music of the people from that part of North America.

Guidance This region includes a number of cultures among which the Tlingit, Tsimshian, Haida, Kwakiutl, Bella Coola, and the Nootka are the best known. The Northwest Coast area is generally known for its wooden objects of decorative artistry, such as the ornate totem poles that tell of historic events and/or signify family heraldry and hierarchy. Songs of the Native Americans in this area are owned by certain families who pass them on to their descendants. Among other functions, music is used in courtship, for honoring nature spirits, and in "potlatches," ceremonies in which gifts are exchanged between families to bolster prestige, honor ancestors, or celebrate the memory of the dead.

Terms Define the following terms based on the reading from text.

31. dream song

32. personal song

33. spirit dance

34. Shaker church

35. potlatch

36. Raven Song

Reading Comprehension Answer the following work questions (answers at end of this chapter):

40. Songs and supernatural power are acquired from the _____ _____.

41. The spirit dance is an appeal to _____ spirits.

42. Which dance is a part of a new religion which combines old and new beliefs?

   _____.

43. The melody of the Raven Song generally and uncharacteristically moves in which direction?

   _____.

44. There is a tendency in Northwest Coast music to _____ in pitch as much as the interval of a third.

45. The Native Americans of the Northwest Coast are the only indigenous people in North America to have a double-reed aerophone. True or False.

46. The Native Americans of the Northwest Coast are the only indigenous people in North America to teach their songs traditionally by using a type of musical notation. True or False.

47. The vocal style of the Northwest Coast is reminiscent of the Plains style. True or False.

48. More than any other Native American culture, those of the Northwest Coast carve their rattles in shapes of birds. True or False.

49. Religion is not often a subject of the songs of the Northwest Coast Native Americans. True or False.

New Native Music and Musical Instruments
(Text Pages 326–328)

Purpose To identify many of the styles of new music prevailing today on the reservations and in Native American communities in large cities of the United States.

Guidance As the Native Americans began to be integrated into Western society, they began to assimilate Western musical elements. Country and western music, especially, became their favored form because of their closeness to nature. It is perhaps because many Native Americans identify with the outdoors, the excitement of the roundup and the rodeo, and the cowboy (according to McAllester in *Worlds of Music*), that there are numerous southwestern Indian country and western bands. As with popular music nearly everywhere, bands come and go. The once popular groups like the Fenders, the Sundowners, Redbone, and XIT (pronounced ex-it, meaning "intertribal crossing") are now defunct.

Native American pop music develops much like other pop musics in the United States. Bands, vocal groups, solo singers, instrumentalists and other performers come and go; styles discontinue and others take their places. While the well-known rock band of the 1980s, XIT, for example, has disbanded, its lead singer, Tom Bee, continues to record. In 1994 he began to perform with actor Russell Means, the two of them creating a narrative style they call "Rap-ajo." In order to see the big picture, it is perhaps most useful to place Native American pop music loosely into the following categories: rap, rock, rhythm and blues, country, and new age.

In addition to Tom Bee and Russell Means and their "Rap-ajo," another Native American singer, John Trudell, has also developed a narrative style. While not rap in the style of American hip-hop artists, his music relies heavily on text over melody. These musical styles are imbued with protest themes, as many of Trudell's song titles suggest: "Baby Boom Ché," "Bombs over Baghdad," and "Rich Man's War" (from the CD *AKA Grafitti Man*). The former piece incorporates a 1950s rock beat ala Elvis, the middle is contemporary rock, and the latter is the most fusion-style of all of Trudell's compositions on this CD—the narrative of "Rich Man's War" is accompanied by a heavy heart beat, Native American drum beat, and a traditional-based powwow melody that is enhanced electronically.

Native American rock styles vary, following typical pop music trends. In the 1980s Buddy Red Bow (who tragically died in the late 80s) made his recording entitled *Journey to the Spirit World* (1983), which was eclectic in that it incorporated traditional Lakota singing with rhythm and blues and synthesizer styles of the times. Like other singers, Buddy Red Bow always used his music as a means of teaching others about Indian ways, and protest was often a part of that teaching. Mitch Walking Elk (Cheyenne-Arapaho) also recorded in an eclectic style that was imbued with protest and Native American pride. More recently, in the 1990s, Keith Secola (Ojibway) recorded a Native American hit with "NDN Kars," a humorous song about a young man (himself) going to a powwow in his car held together with bumper stickers. In south Florida, a Miccosukee duo known as Tiger Tiger incorporates Indian themes into their rock 'n' roll style. Their biggest hit is entitled "Space Age Indian."

Cherokee Rose recorded a number of her compositions in a rhythm and blues / country style in 1993. Her "Black Irish Indian" is based on her own words about her ethnicity. As a sensitive poet and skilled songwriter, she has a powerfully personal style. Joanne Shenandoah and A. Paul Ortega have also recorded in a popular country music style. More recently (1995) Shenandoah has joined forces with Peter Kater on piano and synthesizer in a recording based on traditional Haudenosaunee-Iroquois songs with an easy listening, light jazz backup. On one of her songs (Fish Dance), she features Kazu Matsui on Japanese shakuhachi flute (one wonders why Native American flute was not used instead). Another basically country singer, (former) Chief Jim Billy (Seminole), has incorporated humor in his song "Big Alligator."

The undisputed leader of Native American new age music is traditional flutist R. Carlos Nakai. His many albums range from light jazz styles in *Jackalope* (1986) to new age with *Carry the Gift* (1988), in which he collaborates with William Eaton on guitar. Many other groups have entered into the Native American new age musical market, including the Native Flute Ensemble, which uses traditional flutes, synthesizer, and drums to create meditative sounds that have become the trademark of Native American new age music.

Three women (Jennifer, Pura Fe, and Soni) make up a contemporary vocal ensemble called Ulali. They write the following about themselves as a musical ensemble (cited from *Mahk Jchi*, Original Vision Records, 1997): "We are a First Nations women acapella trio that sings in the many languages and styles of our people. We do not call ourselves 'Native American' because our blood and people were here long before this land was called the Americas. We are older than America can ever be and do not give recognition to the borders. Our brothers and sisters run from North to South and into and under the waters for miles and years back. We are the people, we are the land...." The term they use for their ensemble, "ulali," means "wood thrush" [a song bird] in the Tuscaroran language. They explain that "in ancient times a Tuscorora woman carried the name ulali for her beautiful voice."

Contemporary Native American popular music, through its meaningful and sometimes forceful song texts, reveals that Native American music has the power to incite and inspire other Native Americans and express feelings of anger, social awareness, laughter, folkways, ethnic pride, history, love, heritage, and togetherness. In this way, perhaps, music is universal, but to realize this fact is a step toward understanding Native American culture as a living phenomenon rather than a museum artifact.

Terms Define or identify the following terms, based on outside reading.

37. Gospel music

38. Mormon church

39. country and western music

40. Nashville style

41. The Fenders

42. The Sundowners

43. Redbone

44. XIT

Reading Comprehension Answer the following work questions (answers at end of this chapter):

50. Country and western music, prevailing today on the reservations and in other Native American communities, illustrates some features that could be called traditionally Native American. True or False.

51. The lyrics used by Navajo Gospel groups include vocables. True or False.

52. The lyrics used by Navajo Gospel groups are in English. True or False.

53. The most favorite new music with Native American people today is Enemyway music. True or False.

54. Inspirational Native American music from the Mormon church does not include Native American elements. True or False.

55. The guitar is one of the least popular instruments in the new Native American music. True or False.

56. Among many Native American cultures in the United States, which has been the most successful at assimilating Western musical elements into its popular music? _____.

57. List two once popular Native American country and Western groups. _____ and _____.

58. List two once popular Native American rock bands. _____ and _____.

59. There are thousands of radio stations that devote air time to Native American listeners. True or False.

Video Viewing

1. *Discovering American Indian Music.* BFA.
2. Haida potlatch (Canada) (27-10). *The JVC Video Anthology of World Music and Dance*, The Americas I, North American Indians and Inuit (Eskimos) (VTMV-27).
3. Ceremonial song (Nez Perce) (27-15). *The JVC Video Anthology of World Music and Dance*, The Americas I, North American Indians and Inuit (Eskimos) (VTMV-27).

Sample Test Questions

Only one answer is correct.

1. Which is *not* one of the three elements of religious practice among the Woodlands Native Americans? a. dance, b. fire, c. prayer, d. music.

2. One feature of Woodlands' music is: a. microtonal melodies, b. short, abrupt melodic phrases, c. long, complex melodic phrases, d. chromatic melodies.

3. Which is *not* a genre or type of Woodlands' music? a. popular songs, b. social dance songs, c. sacred songs and dances, d. genealogical songs.

4. Examples of religious society songs of the Ojibway people are: a. epic poems, b. 49 songs, c. war dance songs, d. lyric ballads.

5. In the singing of North American Native peoples, nonsense syllables should be more precisely referred to as: a. meaningless syllables b. words of an original language, c. vocables, d. imitation of animals, e. war whoops.

6. Which dance has now become the favorite exhibition dance at North American Indian powwows? a. the stomp dance, b. the potlatch, c. the Hopi eagle Dance, d. the Plains war dance, e. the sun dance.

7. Regular events at a powwow are interrupted for a. Enemyway, b. Red

Antway, c. Giveaway, d. Peyote Ceremony, e. Safeway.

8. Which of the following is *not* a Plains Indian social dance? a. grass dance, b. fancy dance, c. ghost dance, d. 49 dance, e. war dance.

9. Most Plains Indian songs begin with: a. women and children singing in harmony, b. drum and rattle introduction, c. male chorus singing in fifths, d. extended flute solo, e. one man using falsetto voice and singing a descending melodic line.

10. A traditional religious society of Native Americans of the Plains is: a. Medicine Society, b. Ghost Society, c. Native American Church, d. Powwow Society, e. High Society.

11. The long chants of the Navajo and Apache, sung during healing ceremonies lasting as long as nine days and nights, in which art, theater, and music are brought together to bring supernatural power to the aid of some person in need of help, invoke deities such as Changing Woman, Talking God, and: a. Turtle Man, b. Spider Man, c. Deer Slayer, d. Enemy Slayer, e. Fire Walker.

12. The Navajo Enemyway ceremony, which includes song and dance, commemorates what? a. the time when the European invaders will disappear, b. Christian worship using peyote as a sacrament, c. elaborate gift exchanges, d. return of warriors from a mythical war party.

13. Apache social dance songs are accompanied by: a. Apache flute, b. water drum, c. ceremonial chanting by a priest, d. hand clapping, e. anklet rattles.

14. The social songs of the Navajos often include: a. vocables only, b. texts dealing with famine, c. text and vocables, d. yelps, e. growls.

15. Pueblo singing characteristically employs: a. high, nasal sounds, b. deep pitches, c. precision of choral singing, d. b and c, e. a and c.

16. The Paiute Indian Ghost Dance religion commemorates what? a. the time when the European invaders will disappear, b. Christian worship using peyote as a sacrament, c. elaborate gift exchanges, d. return of warriors from a mythical war party.

17. The music of the Plateau and Great Basin Native American is: a. closed and tense, b. long and drawn out, c. open and relaxed, d. responsorial.

18. The name of the Native American prophet who originated the Ghost Dance religion is: a. Wovoka, b. Jehovah, c. Chief Standing Bear, d. Geronimo, e. Waliwomka.

19. Peyote songs are usually: a. slow, with an ascending melody line, b. moderately fast with a downward melodic line, c. alternating between slow and fast with no real melodic tendency, d. recitations on one note, e. frenzied.

20. Most Peyote songs end with which musical characteristic? a. "He ne

yo wa," b. an extended water drum finale, c. rhythmic hand clapping, d. high falsetto yell.

Answers to Reading Comprehension Questions

1. south
2. True
3. False: they also used agriculture
4. plants, animals
5. corn, beans, squash
6. True
7. False: vocables are commonly used in much Native American music
8. False: the same person does both
9. True
10. True
11. higher, piercing, falsetto, upper limit, singer's range
12. False: many singers sing the melody together, with the women an octave higher; there is a leader
13. spirit helper, aid, dreamer, difficult points, life
14. social gatherings, past, tribal fairs, rodeos, recent times
15. Plains war dance
16. bass drum
17. False: vocables are used
18. False: the texts are brief
19. False: the dancer must know the music perfectly well so he knows when to stop
20. False: all cultures have music, and the Plains Native Americans were warriors and hunters
21. False: it is the other way around because the Navajos and Apaches migrated to the Southwest hundreds of years after the Pueblo were there
22. True
23. True
24. True
25. True
26. True
27. hollowed-out century plant stalk
28. looped stick
29. buckskin
30. dreams
31. brief, narrow
32. Paiute, Nevada
33. Wovoka
34. sacred, worship
35. tipi

36. quarter, eighth
37. vocables
38. False: it is unpadded
39. False: it includes only singing
40. family
41. ancestral
42. Shaker Dance
43. downward
44. rise
45. True
46. False: nowhere in traditional usage have Native Americans used musical notation
47. False: it is stepwise and even chromatic, whereas Plains music moves downward in successive lower arcs
48. True
49. False: it was a common subject
50. False: little or nothing is native about it
51. False: the Mormon songs do
52. False: the Mormon songs are
53. False: new music is a mixture of many things, some Native American and some Western
54. False: it does, such as native languages and vocables
55. False: it is probably the most popular
56. Navajo
57. The Fenders and The Sundowners
58. Redbone and XIT
59. False: there are between 20 and 30

Answers to Sample Test Questions

1.	b	2.	c
3.	d	4.	a
5.	c	6.	d
7.	c	8.	c
9.	e	10.	a
11.	d	12.	d
13.	b	14.	c
15.	d	16.	a
17.	c	18.	a
19.	b	20.	a

Listening Form

Student Name_____ I.D. Number_____
Course Name_____ Course Number_____
Date_____ Chapter Number_____ Listening Example Number _____
Record or Tape Number_____ Name of Culture and Location _____
Name of Performer(s)_____
Instructions: place an X, ✓, or • in appropriate boxes; give types; indicate native names.

performing elements (if vocal)	solo: M/F	duo: M/F	trio: M/F	quartet: M/F	group: M/F	other: M/F
performing elements (if instrumental)	corpophone	idiophone	membranophone	aerophone	chordophone	electrophone	other
texture	single melody	dense unison	heterophone	imitation	parallelism	disphony	other
more texture	with drone	with time indicator	chordal	polyphonic stratification	colotomy	combination	variable
melodic contour	static	ascending	descending	conjunct	disjunct	undulating	terraced
mode or scale	number of notes	vernacular	using cipher notation (numbers), indicate the mode or scale in ascending order
meter	free	duple	triple	compound	additive	poly	other
speed	very slow	slow	moderate	fast	very fast	variable	other
amplitude	very soft	soft	moderate	loud	very loud	variable	other
timbre (tone color)	clear	breathy	nasal	open	tight	masked	other
inflections	no vibrato	slow vibrato	fast vibrato	wide vibrato	falsetto	multiphonics	other
formal structure	vernacular name	expanding	reverting	strophic	theme and variations	other
structural or performance techniques	ostinato	responsorial	antiphonal	elastic rhythm	if vocal: syllabic or melismatic	non-synchronous parts	other

Chapter 18

Text Pages 332 – 362

Music of the Alaskan Eskimos

Lorraine D. Koranda

Introduction to Chapter (Text Page 332)

Purpose To introduce the basic musical styles of the Eskimos of Alaska, discuss music's relation to Eskimo culture, and to specifically point out the location of Eskimos.

Guidance There are two basic Eskimo language groups in North America—the Inupiaq who inhabit the Arctic and Sub-Arctic regions of Canada and Greenland, and the Yupik who live in Alaska and Siberia. This chapter concerns the latter group. It would again be worthwhile to look carefully at a world globe to see the migration routes of the Eskimos from East Asia to the Western Hemisphere. Since their migration came after the Ice Age, only one route stands out: across the Aleutian Islands to Alaska. While the map on page 333 gives exact locations of some important Alaskan Eskimo areas, the map on page 308 gives approximate locations of the other Eskimo groups in North America. Once again, for a more thorough map consult the National Geographic, December 1972, insert map entitled "Indians of North America."

The author points out that the shaman (angakok) functions as an intermediary between man and the supernatural. The term "shaman" in fact is derived from a Siberian term, and this points to the connection with Asia. A shaman, in order to be an intermediary, must go into a trance state for purposes of communication with the supernatural. This trance state, when the shaman's soul leaves the body, is often referred to as a flight of ecstasy by anthropologists; the shaman almost always uses song for achieving or maintaining his trance state.

Terms Define, identify, or locate the following terms or areas, based on the reading from text and/or a map.

1. Inupiaq

2. Yupik

3. Arctic

4. Alaska

5. Canada

6. Greenland

7. Siberia

8. Aleutian Islands

Power Songs (Text Pages 333–336)

Music Examples — songs from Alaska

Purpose To investigate the socio-cultural context of hunting and other power songs of the Eskimos.

Guidance Since hunting is the most important activity for the Eskimo's survival, there are many hunting songs composed by the hunter himself or by an angakok to assure success in the hunt. These songs specifically relate to particular purposes that are essential for success. For example, if a whale does become weak after it has been harpooned, it could pull the hunter out to sea; thus, the power of the song makes sure the whale weakens. There are also songs that give praise to the spirits of the animals that are to be hunted. Animals are believed to have souls, and they are also believed to exist to feed humans. Therefore, it is proper to honor them before killing them. Other shamanic power songs are used during the shaman's flight of ecstasy, to transport his soul to the cosmos. Many song types, such as those for certain games, festivals, feasts, and fortunes, are also types of power songs. Here it is impossible to separate the sacred from the secular, since the two are so closely related.

Terms Define or identify the following terms or areas, based on the reading from text.

9. shaman

10. angakok

Reading Comprehension Answer the following work questions (answers at end of this chapter):

1. The angakok's hunting power songs include songs for stitching the open skin boat. True or False.

2. Hunting songs for good fortune belong to the shaman's hunting power songs. True or False.

3. Many power songs were composed to honor the spirits of the _____ and the spirits _____.

4. If a son were to sing his father's seal-hunting power song for enjoyment or any other purpose than what it was intended for, it may never again have power. True or False.

5. The old angakok power songs were learned by relatively few singers, but they were sung very often. True or False.

6. A ritual game song composed for the whale hunt celebration is known as the _____ song.

7. Some of the most popular power songs are polar bear and walrus songs. True or False.

8. List six activities that took place during rituals and festivals to honor the spirits:

   a._____, b._____,
   c._____, d._____,
   e._____, f._____.

9. Power songs can be purchased. True or False.

10. How are Eskimo songs performed? _____.

Game Songs (Text Pages 336–340)

Purpose To identify several types of Eskimo songs that can be referred to as game songs.

Guidance Blanket toss, juggling, and string game songs are used for particular Eskimo rituals. The blanket toss and its song, for example, are a part of the whale hunt celebration. The game, involving tossing a person on a blanket made from walrus hide, is played outside. Juggling songs accompany a women's game of juggling beach rocks, a style found along the coast in northern Alaska. String games are also the activities of women, and the songs that accompany them are, like other games, songs, very old, with song texts that are not completely understood by the singers themselves. Often the song texts have to do with sexual matters.

Terms Define the following terms, based on the reading from text.

11. blanket toss

12. string games

13. juggling

Reading Comprehension Answer the following work questions:

11. The texts of _____ songs sung by _____ treated the subject of a woman's lack of physical attraction for her husband.

12. According to a legend and suggested in the text of a song, the _____ was said to have given the blanket toss to the Eskimos.

13. The music for the blanket toss is composed by an angakok. True or False.

14. Christianized Eskimo women, especially, enjoy singing juggling songs in a family context. True or False.

15. Each juggling song is different, and the texts are never related. True or False.

16. Why were rude insults sung to the contestant during the blanket toss? __ _____.

17. The texts of string game songs often contain _____ or _____ words.

Ritual Songs (Text Pages 340–345)

Purpose To investigate the sociocultural context of certain ritual and ceremonial songs of the Eskimos.

Guidance An explanation of the political organization of Eskimo societies may help clarify the importance of the ridicule song form as a ritualistic medium of social control. Eskimos are typically organized in small nomadic groups called bands, led by a headman who holds no permanent authority or power to punish. In such a society, however, the headman is able to lead through common consent because his judgment is respected. Ridicule by the community is an important means of social control in bands; with ridicule, the band punishes those who violate the norms of the group. Ridicule songs are a way for Eskimos, both individually or as a group, to keep troublemakers in line. Other types of songs of a ritual nature are those with a religious function (bladder songs) and those which strengthen ties between villages (songs of the Messenger Feast and some joking partner songs).

Terms Define the following terms based on the reading from text.

14. joking partner

15. bladder festival

16. wolf dance

17. blood revenge

18. challenge songs

19. ridicule songs

20. welcoming songs

21. invitation songs

22. messenger feast

23. festival to the dead

24. trading festival

25. hoop frame drum

26. box drum

Reading Comprehension Answer the following work questions (answers at end of this chapter):

18. Joking partner songs are a type of ridicule song exchanged between people in different villages. True or False.

19. A ceremonial in which a headman of one village invites the headman of another village to attend a feast and gift exchange is called the _____.

20. A ceremonial in which the villagers appease the spirits of dead animals taken in the hunt is called the _____.

21. The Eskimos make use of a war ritual song for stirring warriors for battle. True or False.

22. One characteristic of the ridicule song type is that the person who can sing the loudest wins. True or False.

23. Box drum songs and messenger feast invitation songs are very common today. True or False.

24. The bladder festival concluded with the _____ being placed under the _____ _____.

25. In the past the loser of a ridicule song contest left his village forever. True or False.

26. Songs of violence among the Eskimos are very popular today. True or False.

27. Texts for the messenger feast invitation songs and the welcome songs

are handed down from generation to generation and sung today with great ease by all Eskimos. True or False.

Love Songs and Children Songs (Text Pages 345–346)

Purpose To identify several categories of Eskimo songs that are somewhat private in nature, such as love songs, children's songs, and other personal songs.

Guidance Certain characteristics of a culture can be seen in such personal songs as those for love and those sung by or for children. However, it is easy for a non-Eskimo to misinterpret the meaning of the texts of such songs. Non-Eskimo moral judgments (ethnocentrism) must be avoided, for example, in the song about the fatherless baby.

Terms Define or identify the following terms or areas, based on the reading from text.

27. lullaby

28. kassak

Reading Comprehension Answer the following work questions (answers at end of this chapter):

28. Which type of Eskimo songs range from a simple statement of friendship to the desire to mate? _____.

29. Eskimos do not need lullabies because the babies are rocked to sleep in their mother's parkas. True or False.

30. Many children's songs are accompanied by _____ games.

31. The Eskimos have songs to commemorate a young man's first beard. True or False.

32. Eskimo women have many songs about their illegitimate babies. True or False.

Contemporary Songs and Dances (Text Pages 347–351)

Purpose To examine the contemporary songs of present Eskimos, and to study how dance is related to Eskimo music.

Guidance Whereas traditional Eskimo songs are composed for members of the Eskimo culture, whether they be personal, supernatural, or community, contemporary songs are composed primarily for family enjoyment and entertainment. Still the music remains purely Eskimo, showing little or no resemblance to modern music of the outside world. The texts, however, may show Christian influence and/or have reference to material items or current events of the outside world, such as electricity or politics.

There are a number of types of Eskimo dances, and dance styles between men and women differ. Notice how Eskimos never touch each other while dancing, unlike American and European dancers. Some of the Eskimos dances are performed by the shaman for supernatural contact. Dance costumes may include a variety of items such as gloves, masks, finger masks, headbands, and feathered fans; a number of these items are pictured in your text and should be examined carefully.

Terms Define the following terms, based on the reading from text.

29. masks

30. finger masks

31. dance fans

32. acting dances

33. motion dances

34. muscle dances

35. common dances

36. bench dances

37. loon dances

Reading Comprehension Answer the following work questions (answers at end of this chapter):

33. The musical style of contemporary Eskimo songs is patterned after other types of music such as classical, country-western, or rock. True or False.

34. Some songs may mention Western _____ devices.

35. Contemporary Eskimo songs always focus on contemporary ideas and events. True or False.

36. Eskimo dances can be categorized in two ways, which are _____ _____ and _____.

37. Mimic dances are called _____ at Point Barrow and Wainwright, and are called _____ south of Point Hope.

38. With two exceptions only, Eskimo dancers use a limited amount of floor space when performing. True or False.

39. The role of the woman in Eskimo dance is usually one of little dance movement. True or False.

40. A common trait in Eskimo dances is that the dancers always hold hands while dancing, and they dance in a closed position. True or False.

41. The messenger feast wolf dances and the ceremonies for the bladder festival are performed twice a year, once in the spring and again at the first snowfall of winter. True or False.

42. In the messenger feast dances, it was the women who carried dance sticks with eagle feather adornment. True or False.

Musical Instruments (Text Pages 351–354)

Purpose To become familiar with the variety and function of Alaskan Eskimo musical instruments.

Guidance In Eskimo culture music is used in a variety of ceremonies that are an important aspect of Eskimo folklife. Singing and dancing are often accompanied by musical instruments. Probably due to limited natural resources there are only two major Eskimo instruments: a hand-held hoop drum (a membranophone) like a big tambourine without jingles and with a handle, and a box drum (an idiophone). Rattles are rarely used, and flutes are not found, although bone was available and at one time was used to make clappers. Aside from these two styles of percussion instruments, the only other sound maker used by the Eskimos is dance gloves that are covered with amulets or charms that rattle when shaken during dances.

The hoop drum is constructed from wood covered with a membrane. It is struck with a long and flexible stick in one of two ways: either on the wooden frame itself, which produces a tap that causes the membrane to vibrate, or on the skin and frame together. Hudson Bay Eskimos, however, use a short, thick drum stick. Study the figures 18-4 and 18-5 in the text. Although hoop drums are not tuned, the drum heads are dampened prior to and after playing in order to keep them soft. Usually played by men, although women can also play them, hoop drums are used to accompany all dance music. Drummers must know both the songs and the dances in order to provide the correct accompaniment.

The box drum, which does not have a membrane, is a hollow wooden open-ended structure that is percussed, not on the box itself, but on a striking post. For a performance it is suspended from a tripod or the ceiling pole of an Eskimo dwelling and struck. It is generally highly decorated, and as a ceremonial instrument it is considered an honor to be chosen to play it. Study Figure 18-6 for construction details.

Terms Define the following terms, based on the reading from text.

38. hoop drum

39. ritual box drum

40. clappers

Reading Comprehension Answer the following work questions (answers at end of this chapter):

43. The two traditional Eskimo percussion instruments are the _____ _____ and the _____.

44. Bones were used for making flutes in Eskimo culture. True or False.

45. Drumming is mainly a man's job, but women are not excluded from playing it as well. True or False.

46. The hoop drum is used to accompany all _____ performances.

47. The box drum is used for the ritual dances of the _____ _____.

48. Both the hoop drum and the box drum are membranophones. True or False.

49. The box drum is decorated with eagle feathers signifying the messenger feast giver. True or False.

50. The hoop drum is always struck on its skin only. True or False.

51. The handles of the hoop drums are always very plain, without design. True or False.

52. The handles of the hoop drums are always made from wood, like the frame itself. True or False.

Musical Characteristics (Text Pages 354–358)

Purpose To describe the elements of Eskimo music.

Guidance Hearing Eskimo songs out of their cultural context may lead to the ethnocentric conclusion that the music is erratic. However, the Eskimos have many melodic and rhythmic musical devices that function to regulate dance steps, establish a pitch center, and add programmatic interest. In addition, each song has a special function or personal meaning for its composer, and the musical characteristics often reflect distinct compositional techniques.

248 Musics of Many Cultures: Study Guide and Workbook

Terms Define or identify the musical terms in the reading by referring to the introduction to this study guide.

Reading Comprehension Answer the following work questions (answers at end of this chapter):

53. Meaningless syllables (vocables) can be thrown in arbitrarily in Eskimo songs. True or False.

54. Eskimo songs are usually made up of four or five pitches only. True or False.

55. The song described in the chapter that begins with the interval of a third, then a fourth, then a fifth, and then back down again is creating an arch reminiscent of a _____.

56. Rhythmical meters may be extended (such as 3/4 to 7/8) depending on _____.

57. Portamenti or sliding from one note to the next is rare but does occur in some Eskimo songs that have been influenced by Christian missionaries. True or False.

Video Viewing

1. Drum dance. Greenland Eskimo (27-1). *The JVC Video Anthology of World Music and Dance*, The Americas I, Volume 1, North American Indians and Inuit (Eskimos) (VTMV-27).
2. Drum dance. Inupiak Eskimo (Alaska) (27-5). *The JVC Video Anthology of World Music and Dance*, The Americas I, Volume 1, North American Indians and Inuit (Eskimos) (VTMV-27).
3. Drum Dance. Copper Eskimo (Canada) (27-8). *The JVC Video Anthology of World Music and Dance*, The Americas I, Volume 1, North American Indians and Inuit (Eskimos) (VTMV-27).

Sample Test Questions

Only one answer is correct.

1. Which of the following song types does *not* belong to the angakok's hunting power songs? a. boat launching songs, b. gut park songs, c. rifle power songs, d. harpoon power songs, e. skin boat stitching songs.

2. By far the most numerous of the Eskimo songs are: a. dog sled songs, b. fishing songs, c. lullabies, d. ivory carving songs, e. hunting power songs.

3. The transcription and translation of the texts of Eskimo power songs is difficult because: a. the rhythm is very syncopated, b. the shamans

sing so softly that the words are not clear, c. the songs are sung only with a humming voice, d. the songs included archaic words or secret language, e. the question is wrong, because the songs are easy to transcribe and translate.

4. The hunter's appeal to the proper spirit was made primarily through the medium of: a. drum songs sung by the hunter himself, b. drum songs sung by the hunter's wife, c. flute melodies, d. the bullroarer, e. shaking the sacred rattle and singing.

5. There are no Eskimo songs that deal with: a. weather, b. stitching, c. fire, d. air, e. seals.

6. Which is *not* an Eskimo ritual game for which there are game songs? a. blanket toss game, b. string game, c. juggling game, d. spinning top game.

7. Many texts of ritual game songs are about relationships between: a. the sexes, b. children, c. families, d. hunters and the animals, e. man and the supernatural.

8. Juggling songs are sung only by: a. women, b. men, c. children, d. shamans, e. hunters.

9. What animal gave the blanket toss ritual to the Eskimos? a. polar bear, b. raven, c. whale, d. seal, e. walrus.

10. Ridicule songs are used to: a. punish those who have offended the community, b. settle disputes between two antagonists, c. poke good-humored fun at friends in another village, d. all the above.

11. The Eskimo bladder festival included several songs. Which is *not* one of them? a. song for killing the animal from which the bladder is taken, b. song for blowing up the bladder, c. song to the bladder, d. song in honor of the wild parsnip used for purification purposes, e. none of the above.

12. Songs used to appease the souls of animals killed in the hunt are called: a. liver songs, b. kidney songs, c. heart songs, d. brain songs, e. none of the above.

13. An Eskimo hunting festival, similar to the Northwest Coast potlatch, is called: a. wolf dance festival, b. festival to the dead, c. messenger feast, d. blood revenge festival, e. bladder festival.

14. In which festival do the musicians begin practicing their new songs in total darkness? a. wolf dance festival, b. festival to the dead, c. messenger feast, d. blood revenge festival, e. bladder festival.

15. The purpose of a children's song is mostly to: a. discipline the children, b. quiet the children, c. teach the Eskimo language, d. a and b, e. all the above.

16. Which is *not* a characteristic of children's songs? a. tease children, b. have string games to go with them, c. put children to sleep, d. contain

animal calls, e. sung metaphorically by animals.

17. The boy in the Haircut Song looks like what after his hair is cut? a. polar bear, b. white man, c. seal, d. bald eagle, e. totem pole head.

18. Contemporary songs are composed primarily for family enjoyment and may be performed at village: a. Thanksgiving or Christmas programs, b. tourist shows, c. weekly social meetings, d. a and b, e. b and c.

19. Which religious influence is seen in some contemporary song texts? a. pantheistic, b. Christian, c. atheistic, d. Jewish, e. Russian Orthodox.

20. During World War II, the Eskimos learned some songs from which group of people as a result of the Little Diomede and Big Diomede Island contact? a. Siberian Eskimos, b. Russian immigrants, c. Soviet political leaders, d. Arctic missionaries, e. South Alaskan Indians.

21. Those dances which anyone may dance using whatever dance motions he or she wants are called: a. free style dances, b. shuffle dances, c. rhythm dances, d. ceremonial dancers, e. muscle dances.

22. Eskimo dances are usually structured in what way? a. they begin quietly and then become more energetic, b. they begin very vigorously and then become subdued, c. at a consistent level throughout the dance, d. with women dancing first and then joined by the men, e. with common dance movements and then with acting dance movements.

23. Eskimo dancers always wear or carry: a. rattles, b. gloves, c. decorative fans, d. feather waist bands, e. none of the above.

24. The main material object used by the shaman during his dance is: a. a dance staff, b. a bow and arrow, c. a hand rattle, d. a skin or wooden carved mask, e. medicinal herbs.

25. The hoop drum of the Eskimos in Alaska is *not* covered with which type of membrane? a. plastic, b. whale's liver, c. polar bear skin, d. walrus stomach, e. fawn skin.

26. The most important design symbolism on the box drum is of which animal? a. wolf, b. whale, c. walrus, d. eagle, e. polar bear.

27. During songs accompanied by hoop drums the preferred voice quality of the singers is: a. strident, loud, and harsh, b. soft and barely audible, c. loud, open, and with a heavy vibrato, d. falsetto, e. masked so as to imitate the animals.

28. Hoop drums are: a. not tuned, b. tuned with fire, c. tuned by tightening the hoop, d. tuned by tightening the sinew which wraps around the drum frame, e. tuned by adding a layer of wax to the head.

29. If a hoop drum is not available for private performance, the Eskimo may substitute: a. a box drum, b. a voice sound in imitation of the hoop drum, c. body slapping, d. a dustpan or garbage can lid, e. a plate that is struck with a fork.

30. The texts of Eskimo songs are predominantly: a. hummed, b. syllabic,

c. melismatic, d. improvised.

31. Eskimo songs are: a. based on continuously expanding music and text, b. strophic, with stanzas that are repeated, c. improvised, d. begun by a leader and responded by a chorus, e. sung in alternation between two choruses or groups of singers.

32. At the end of the first stanza or verse, what do the drummers do? a. take a bow, b. yell, c. get up and dance themselves, d. strike the drums vigorously, e. stop for a few seconds.

Answers to Reading Comprehension Questions

1. True
2. True
3. animals, atmosphere
4. True
5. False: they were sung only for the intended purpose
6. Blanket Toss Song
7. False: there were very few songs for polar bears or walruses
8. singing, dancing, mime, feats of magic, storytelling, sporting competition
9. True
10. with a drum
11. juggling, women
12. raven
13. True
14. False: they will not sing them
15. False: there are many versions, and some of the texts are related
16. to cause him such embarrassment that he would fall
17. archaic, meaningless
18. True
19. messenger feast
20. bladder festival
21. False: there are no war songs
22. False: dynamics are not mentioned in the text as a characteristic
23. False: they are not very common
24. bladder, sea ice
25. True
26. False: songs of violence do not exist, although there are tales of violence
27. False: they are not known today
28. love songs
29. True
30. string
31. False: Eskimos have little facial hair

32. False: there are no songs about that
33. False: it is clearly an Eskimo style
34. mechanical
35. True
36. ceremonial, social purposes of entertainment
37. acting dances, motion dances
38. True
39. True
40. False: just the opposite is true
41. False: they have not been celebrated for half a century
42. True
43. hoop drum, box drum
44. False: they were never used for flutes
45. True
46. dance
47. messenger feast
48. False: the box drum is an idiophone
49. True
50. False: it is also struck on the rim
51. False: sometimes they are ornately carved
52. False: they can be made from bone as well
53. False: they must be sung as carefully as the words
54. True
55. tossed pebble
56. dance motions
57. False: the influence has probably come from Indian songs from nearby areas

Answers to Sample Test Questions

1. c	2. e	3. d
4. a	5. c	6. d
7. a	8. a	9. b
10. d	11. a	12. e
13. c	14. e	15. d
16. c	17. b	18. d
19. b	20. a	21. e
22. a	23. b	24. d
25. c	26. d	27. a
28. a	29. d	30. b
31. b	32. d	

Listening Form

Student Name_____ I.D. Number_____
Course Name _____ Course Number_____
Date_____Chapter Number_____Listening Example Number _____
Record or Tape Number_____Name of Culture and Location _____
Name of Performer(s)_____
Instructions: place an X, ✓, or • in appropriate boxes; give types; indicate native names.

performing elements (if vocal)	solo: M/F	duo: M/F	trio: M/F	quartet: M/F	group: M/F	other: M/F
performing elements (if instrumental)	corpophone	idiophone	membrano-phone	aerophone	chordophone	electrophone	other
texture	single melody	dense unison	heterophone	imitation	parallelism	disphony	other
more texture	with drone	with time indicator	chordal	polyphonic stratification	colotomy	combination	variable
melodic contour	static	ascending	descending	conjunct	disjunct	undulating	terraced
mode or scale	number of notes	vernacular	using cipher notation (numbers), indicate the mode or scale in ascending order
meter	free	duple	triple	compound	additive	poly	other
speed	very slow	slow	moderate	fast	very fast	variable	other
amplitude	very soft	soft	moderate	loud	very loud	variable	other
timbre (tone color)	clear	breathy	nasal	open	tight	masked	other
inflections	no vibrato	slow vibrato	fast vibrato	wide vibrato	falsetto	multiphonics	other
formal structure	vernacular name	expanding	reverting	strophic	theme and variations	other
structural or performance techniques	ostinato	responsorial	antiphonal	elastic rhythm	if vocal: syllabic or melismatic	non-synchronous parts	other

Chapter 19

Text Pages 363 – 385

Symbol and Function in South American Indian Music

Dale A. Olsen

Introduction to Chapter (Text Pages 363–365)

Purpose To introduce the music of native South Americans, to identify some indigenous languages of South America, and to explore the racial origins of Amerindian people.

Guidance To attempt an understanding of the significance of any culture's musical knowledge, one must begin from the viewpoint of the culture. This is called an emic approach, or a study from within. The opposite is called an etic approach, or a study from the outside. This chapter tries to achieve a balance of the two approaches by examining what the music is like, and how it is conceived of by the Native Americans who make it. The map on page 364 includes only a small number of Native American cultures found in South America. A more complete map is entitled "Indians of South America," and has been published as a supplement to the *National Geographic*, March 1882, Vol. 161, No. 3. By consulting that map you will obtain a clear picture of cultural regions of South America, along with information about South American cultural geography and a good survey of South American archaeology.

Terms Define or identify the following terms or areas, based on readings from the text and/or other sources.

1. Find South America on a globe, and pick out the major rivers, mountains, forests, Tierra del Fuego, and other land forms. Notice the proximity that South America has with the Caribbean, Central America, and North America. Compare the size of the tropical forest (the Amazon) with the United States of America, and compare the width and breadth of the Andes with the Rockies of North America.

2. Native American and Amerindian

3. Pre-Columbian

4. Caucasoid

5. Mongoloid

Reading Comprehension Answer the following work questions (answers at end of this chapter):

1. Ethnomusicologists should always try to understand musical traditions through the eyes of the culture they are studying. True or False.

2. In South America the study of indigenous musical styles must be examined through the _____ cultures.

3. Many of the musical traditions of the Amerindian have been absorbed by the dominant culture. True or False.

4. While the number of indigenous languages spoken in pre-Columbian South America has been estimated by the linguist Loukotka to be _____ _____, today about _____ or _____ languages are spoken.

5. According to the *Handbook of South American Indians,* the four cultural areas of South America are_____ _____, _____, _____-_____, and _____.

Musical Characteristics (Text Pages 365–367)

Music Examples

shaman songs

Purpose To identify several important musical characteristics of Native South Americans.

Guidance The melodies that the Warao Native Americans use in their curing songs are short, descending in melodic contour, and are typified by becoming softer as they near their end or bottom pitches. This can be heard as the first example of shaman songs (Warao *wisiratu* shaman curing song). This descending pattern seems to be characteristic of the Warao when they sing songs for curing illness, but the opposite is true when they sing songs to cause illness: in those, the melody ascends. Many ancient native South American cultures (and also those of Central America and Mexico) made musical instruments out of clay, and these are useful for understanding about types of scales used by native people before the arrival of the conquering Spanish. The cultures mentioned in the textbook, the Nazca, Moche, and the Chancay, lived on the dry desert coast of Peru. In that dry environment many ancient wares were preserved in tombs. The Q'eros are another Peruvian culture, but one that is still living. They have preserved their ancient ways because they live in great isolation high up in the southern Peruvian Andes at over 15,000 feet. Their music is also important for study because it gives an idea of what music was probably like before the arrival of the Spanish. On page 367 a piece of music in a freestyle round or canon is called "recorded ex. 2" (of the shaman songs). This example is a Warao *hoarotu* shaman curing song, sung by three shamans. The "recorded ex. 3" (of the shaman songs), mentioned on page 367, is from a Warao shaman's harvest festival. Throughout the written musical examples or notations you will find occasional arrows pointing downward or upward. These indicate that the note is approximately a quarter tone (30 to 50 cents) flat or sharp. If the arrow is in parentheses, it is approximately an eighth tone (10 to 29 cents) flat or sharp.

Terms Define or identify the following terms or areas, based on readings from the text and/or other sources.

6. voice masking

7. song power

8. shaman

9. Warao

10. Cuna

11. Nazca

12. Moche

Reading Comprehension Answer the following work questions (answers at end of this chapter):

6. Music in many native South American cultures is _____ and vital to the culture.

7. Melodies and words have such power among indigenous South American cultures that they are almost never used together. True or False.

8. Specific melodies seem to exist for specific functions among native South American culture groups. True or False.

9. South American Indian music is pentatonic. True or False.

10. The analysis of the scales of ancient _____ _____ reveals the use of _____, or pitches that do not correspond to Western tuning.

Symbolism and Meaning (Text Pages 367–376)

Purpose To examine specific examples of how music among native South Americans is used by them for purposes of power, and to explore what music does or what the Indians believe it does.

Guidance In this section the author discusses how music is used by native South Americans for activities that continue life. These activities are often referred to as life cycle events, and they include such things as birth, puberty rites, death, the causing and curing of illnesses, controlling the weather, and many other activities that require supernatural help or communication. Most music among Native Americans, in fact, is used for life cycle events. The shaman is the most important person to participate as a person of knowledge during these events, and music is almost always used by him or her as the supernatural forces are consulted. When the Warao shaman tries to cure an illness, he must name the illness in order to remove it from a patient. This phenomenon is in a way similar to how an American psychologist works, who also names or determines what the psychological reasons are for a patient's disorder. By naming the cause (such as abuse during childhood), the American patient usually can cope with his or her problem. Among the Warao, however, the cause is believed to be the intrusion of a spiritual essence of a material object, which, when named and supernaturally removed by the shaman, makes the patient well. While the American psychologist talks to his patient, the Warao shaman sings to this.

Terms Define or identify the following terms or concepts, based on readings from the text and/or other sources.

13. chanting

14. mythology

15. the bird as symbol

16. shaman

17. trance

18. drumming related to trance

19. three types of shamanistic illnesses

20. Earth Mother

21. naming

22. women's role

23. magical protection song

24. magical love song

25. lullaby

Reading Comprehension Answer the following work questions (answers at end of this chapter):

[sidebar: *Music Examples* *lullabies*]

11. Chanting among native South American cultures is so powerful it can be used for healing. True or False.

12. The _____ is one of the most important magical animals, whose power is referred to in the music of many native South American cultures.

13. The most important function of song among native South Americans is associated with _____.

14. Voice masking, or the use of a raspy voice, is often used by Warao shamans because they believe it will scare away the evil spirits. True or False.

15. The most important tool used to reach ecstasy by the shaman, either with or without drugs, is _____.

16. An important musical instrument used as an ecstasy-inducing device by the shamans of the Araucanian Indians is the _____.

Social Function (Text Page 376)

Purpose To identify several ways how music is used socially among South American Indians.

Reading Comprehension Answer the following work questions (answers at end of this chapter):

17. Social music is often used by native South Americans in conjunction with _____ and _____ of _____.

18. Songs that give the individual Mapuche Indian an opportunity to relieve inner tension as well as to call attention to complaints about a person are known as _____ songs.

19. Among the Cuna many songs that deal with mythology are followed by an _____ _____ that attaches meanings of texts to _____.

Musical Instruments (Text Pages 376–381)

Purpose To identify the sounds, symbolism, and types of musical instruments found among some native South American cultures.

Guidance The shapes, designs, and sounds of native South American musical instruments are often filled with symbolic meaning. The fact that many instruments are associated with sexual roles and taboos indicates a strong importance on fertility, both human and agricultural. Without fertility

> *Music Examples*
>
> *musical instruments*
>
> *aerophones*
> *membranophones*
> *idiophones*

the cultures would obviously perish, and the sexual symbolism attached to the instruments strengthens their beliefs in the perpetuation of culture, more spiritually than humanly. In other words, the emphasis on sexual themes does not indicate cultural degeneration, but a highly refined system of religious communication between mortal and immortal whereby life and the cosmos is continued by sexually symbolic interaction. In addition to buzzing and whistling sounds of native clarinets and flutes, drums can imitate rushing water.

Several instruments not described in the text are elaborated upon here. The bullroarer (page 377) is a free aerophone that resembles a small, single propeller blade on a string. When swung around the musician's head, the blade twists, producing a buzzing sound. A similar instrument is used by the main character in the 1988 movie *Crocodile Dundee II*. A slit drum (page 378) is a struck idiophone made from a hollowed log (an instrument similar to the one described in the textbook is pictured on page 138; although that figure is from Tonga, similar types are found in many parts of the world where large trees are found). The panpipe discussed on page 380 is similar in shape to the instrument pictured on page 175, except that the instrument of the Aymara Indians of Bolivia consists of two halves that are played together in interlocking fashion like bellringers (this is known as hocket). Huge double flutes are used by the Amazonian Kamayurá and Kaiapó native people of Brazil for a fertility festival, and native clarinet ensembles are found in the rainforests of Guyana and French Guiana. The sounds of these musical instruments enable us to understand the whistling and buzzing sound symbolism discussed on page 381. In addition, the native clarinet players blow individual notes that they interlock (this is also known in English as hocket technique) to form a melody.

Terms   Define or identify the following terms or concepts, based on readings from the text and/or other sources.

26. Be able to identify the musical instruments in the figures

27. Three levels of sound among the Tukano

28. bullroarer

29. slit drum

30. container rattle

31. globular flute (ocarina)

32. tubular flute

33. panpipe

34. kena

35. anthropomorphic symbolism

36. iconography

Reading Comprehension Answer the following work questions (answers at end of this chapter):

20. Among many native South American cultures the _____ is considered to be a masculine symbol, while the _____ and the _____ are thought of as female symbols.

21. The three symbolic levels of sound among the Tukano Indians are _____, _____, and _____.

22. According to recent finds by ethnomusicologists, musical instruments were not very important to pre-Columbian civilizations because they were often buried rather than kept for playing. True or False.

23. The most important musical instrument among most native South American cultures is the shaman's rattle. True or False.

24. _____ are usually played by two Bolivian Aymara men using an interlocking technique known in English as _____.

25. Bark trumpets belong to the sound taxonomy recognized as _____.

Video Viewing

1. *Caxiri or Manioc Beer*. Victor Fuks. Indiana University Audio/Visual Center (1987).
2. *Plank and Slit Drumming*, Bora people, Peru. The JVC/Smithsonian Folkways Video Anthology of Music and Dance of the Americas (1995). Vol. 6, Central and South America, track 9.
3. *Horn Signal*, Manguare people, Peru. The JVC/Smithsonian Folkways Video Anthology of Music and Dance of the Americas (1995). Vol. 6, Central and South America, track 10.
4. *Festive Dance*, Bora people, Peru. The JVC/Smithsonian Folkways Video Anthology of Music and Dance of the Americas (1995). Vol. 6, Central and South America, track 11.
5. *Shepherd Song*, Q'ero people, Peru. The JVC/Smithsonian Folkways Video Anthology of Music and Dance of the Americas (1995). Vol. 6, Central and South America, track 9.
6. *Male Oratory*, Yanomami people, Venezuela. The JVC/Smithsonian Folkways Video Anthology of Music and Dance of the Americas (1995). Vol. 6, Central and South America, track 25.
7. *Flute Solo*, Panare people, Venezuela. The JVC/Smithsonian Folkways Video Anthology of Music and Dance of the Americas (1995). Vol. 6, Central and South America, track 26.

8. *Flute Solos and Duets*, Hoti people, Venezuela. The JVC/Smithsonian Folkways Video Anthology of Music and Dance of the Americas (1995). Vol. 6, Central and South America, track 27.
9. *Carrizos de Guaribe, Panpipes*, acculturated people, Venezuela. The JVC/Smithsonian Folkways Video Anthology of Music and Dance of the Americas (1995). Vol. 6, Central and South America, track 29.

Sample Test Questions

Multiple choice questions. Only one answer is correct.

1. Most Native South Americans view their music as having: a. no meaning, b. only entertainment value, c. supernatural qualities, d. functions that cannot be explained.

2. Most South American Indian music is: a. filled with symbolism, b. not important to study because other Latin American musics are much more intricate, c. monotonous and noisy, d. primitive.

3. The classification of musical styles for Native South American cultures: a. is similar to the linguistic and cultural classifications, b. contains four main groups like the phyla of the language classification, c. has not been attempted, d. is controversial because of supernatural beliefs.

4. The power of many old songs of Native South Americans remains strong even though: a. their meaning is forgotten, b. the dance form has changed, c. the words have been written down, d. only vocables are used.

5. South American Indian music often makes use of: a. pentatonic scales, b. microtones, c. a melancholic feeling, d. Western style tunings.

6. The most common term used to describe magical, religious, or ceremonial song is: a. shamanism, b. voice masking, c. chanting, d. vocal music.

7. The most important animal that affects music of Native South American cultures because of its power is: a. the bird, b. the snake, c. the lizard, d. a fish.

8. The most important function of song in Native South American cultures is with: a. dance, b. religious festivals, c. shamanism, d. hunting, e. the sun ritual.

9. Why does the Jivaro hunter often take his wife with him when he hunts? a. she brings the lunch, b. she sings to the Earth Mother, c. she prays to the Sun Father, d. she keeps the children quiet, e. she carries the arrows.

10. Among the Warao of Venezuela, voice masking: a. symbolizes the spirit's voice, b. scares away the evil spirits, c. is the supernatural itself, d. makes the person invisible, e. is how the hunter speaks to his bride-to-be.

Answers to Reading Comprehension Questions

1. True
2. individual
3. True
4. 1,492, 300, 400
5. Tropical Forest, Andean, Circum-Caribbean, Marginal
6. functional
7. False: they are almost always used together
8. True
9. False: it incorporates many types of scales
10. musical instruments, microtones
11. True
12. bird
13. shamanism
14. False: it is believed to be the voice of the supernatural itself
15. song
16. kettledrum
17. dance, drinking of homemade beer
18. assembly
19. interpretive lecture, current problems
20. flute, rattles, drums
21. whistling, buzzing, percussion
22. False: they were buried precisely because they were thought to have supernatural powers
23. True
24. panpipes, hocket
25. buzzing

Answers to Sample Test Questions

1. c
2. a
3. c
4. a
5. b
6. c
7. a
8. c
9. b
10. c

Listening Form

Student Name_____ I.D. Number_____
Course Name _____Course Number _____
Date_____Chapter Number_____Listening Example Number _____
Record or Tape Number_____Name of Culture and Location _____
Name of Performer(s)_____
Instructions: place an X, ✓, or • in appropriate boxes; give types; indicate native names.

performing elements (if vocal)	solo: M/F	duo: M/F	trio: M/F	quartet: M/F	group: M/F	other: M/F
performing elements (if instrumental)	corpophone	idiophone	membranophone	aerophone	chordophone	electrophone	other
texture	single melody	dense unison	heterophone	imitation	parallelism	disphony	other
more texture	with drone	with time indicator	chordal	polyphonic stratification	colotomy	combination	variable
melodic contour	static	ascending	descending	conjunct	disjunct	undulating	terraced
mode or scale	number of notes	vernacular	using cipher notation (numbers), indicate the mode or scale in ascending order
meter	free	duple	triple	compound	additive	poly	other
speed	very slow	slow	moderate	fast	very fast	variable	other
amplitude	very soft	soft	moderate	loud	very loud	variable	other
timbre (tone color)	clear	breathy	nasal	open	tight	masked	other
inflections	no vibrato	slow vibrato	fast vibrato	wide vibrato	falsetto	multiphonics	other
formal structure	vernacular name	expanding	reverting	strophic	theme and variations	other	
structural or performance techniques	ostinato	responsorial	antiphonal	elastic rhythm	if vocal: syllabic or melismatic	non-synchronous parts	other

Chapter 20

Text Pages 386 – 425

Folk Music of South America — A Musical Mosaic

Dale A. Olsen

Introduction to Chapter (Text Page 386)

Purpose To introduce several sociocultural concepts that help to explain the diversity of South America and its music.

Guidance Three recent movements in South America (Tenrikyo, Hallelujah, and Marxism) are mentioned but not discussed. Tenrikyo is a religion that developed in the late 1800s in Japan. Shortly after World War II the religion was brought by Tenrikyo missionaries to Brazil, where today it flourishes among thousands of the over one million Japanese immigrants and their descendants. Tenrikyo is musically very active, and its worship includes playing koto, shamisen, and gagaku. Hallelujah is a syncretic religion found in the interiors of eastern Venezuela and Guyana that comes from the mixing of Native South American shamanism with North American evangelical Protestantism. Marxist ideologies were basically found in Chile, and the important musical result was *Nueva Canción Chilena*, the New Chilean Song movement, which spawned many famous singers and musical groups.

Terms Define or identify the following terms or areas, based on readings from the text and/or other sources.

1. Find South America on a globe and study where the continent lies with relation to the United States of America. Also study the vastness of its jungle (Amazon), its mountains (Andes), and the locations and sizes of its many countries.

2. mestizo

3. mulatto

4. criollo or creole

5. zambo

6. mestization

Reading Comprehension Answer the following work questions (answers at end of this chapter):

1. Two major divisions that can be made in the oral musical traditions of South America are between the _____ and the _____ to _____ within the past _____ years.

2. List three South American countries where people of Native American descent predominate: _____, _____, and _____.

3. List two South American countries where European descendants predominate:

   _____ and _____.

4. List three South American countries where Black or African-derived characteristics are found in great number: a._____, b._____, and c._____.

5. List five South American countries where the mestizo predominates: a._____, b._____, c._____, d._____, e._____.

European-Derived Folk Music (Text Pages 386–396)

♪

Music Examples

music demonstrating sesquiáltera

tonada, joropo, marinera

Purpose To identify some of the important folk musical concepts, instruments, and forms that reveal European characteristics.

Guidance The important concept of musical preservation must be understood, along with the varying degrees of its existence. Some areas of South America function as pocket areas where old musical forms, perhaps similar to those in Spain and/or Portugal, are found. Stringed musical instruments are the most obvious importation by the Spanish and Portuguese. Harps and violins were taught to the Native South Americans by the Jesuits (Spanish missionaries), while the guitar and its many variants were learned from secular musicians. An example of harp music is shown in Example 20-15 (not 20-5 as stated in the text). Saxophones and clarinets were introduced by the military in the late 1800s and are played in ensemble with two violins and a harp in central Peru.

Two important musical concepts have to do with rhythm. They are the "colonial rhythm" and the "sesquiáltera." The first is explained well on text page 392, but the second should be elaborated upon. "Sesqui" in Spanish means one and one-half, and "áltera" means alternation. Thus, the "one and one-half alternation" refers to dividing a 3/4 measure (like a fast waltz) in half, which will equal one and one-half beats, or the same as half a measure of 6/8 time. The sequence is usually an alternation of a 3/4 measure with a 6/8 measure, and a good example of this comes from Bernstein's *West Side Story*, with the song "I like to be in America." This can perhaps be sounded out by saying "**dot** dot dot **dot** dot dot **dash dash dash**," or "**1** 2 3 **4** 5 6 **1** and **2** and **3** and" (emphasize or accent the beats that are boldfaced). If you read music, study carefully Example 20-3, which uses both rhythmic concepts.

Terms Define or identify the following terms or areas, based on readings from the text and/or other sources.

7. villancico

8. romance and romanceros

9. cuatro

10. décima

11. canción

12. tonada

13. modinha

14. tiple

15. violão

16. charango

Reading Comprehension Answer the following work questions (answers at end of this chapter):

6. Spanish-derived song forms that died out in the motherland have been preserved in isolated South American regions to this day. True or False.

7. Guitar-type folk instruments such as the cuatro, seis, cinco, and cuatro y medio are named after the _____ of _____.

8. Probably the best-known guitar-type folk instrument, distinctive because of its typical armadillo resonator, is the _____.

9. Many songs in South America are from the Spanish or Portuguese Renaissance, and they are still found in Spain and Portugal. True or False.

♪

Music Example

saxophone, clarinet, violin, and harp ensemble

aerophones and chordophones

typical orchestra from central Peru

♪

Music Examples

string instruments

chordophones

harp, cuatro, charango, guitar

10. The Spanish and Portuguese upper class were responsible for teaching their music to the South American Native Americans. True or False.

11. A type of Christmas song in South America is the _____, which literally meant "rustic song" in Spain where it originated.

12. In some cases some rural black populations in South America are responsible for the preservation of many Spanish and/or Portuguese types of lullabies. True or False.

13. An important determinant of traditional Renaissance musical characteristics in South America is _____.

14. Some lullabies in South America are sung to well-known melodies, such as national anthems. True or False.

15. List in English four regions of South America that are pocket areas for the preservation of colonial Spanish and/or Portuguese musical characteristics:

    a. _____,

    b. _____,

    c. _____,

    d. _____.

16. One reason why Iberian romances continue to be found in many regions of South America is that the romanceros included notations of the music, enabling many people to learn how to sing them. True or False.

17. A common type of song sung between two people is known in English as _____.

18. Two manners of playing the guitar in South America are known in English as _____ and _____.

19. The polka has been and still is a popular South American dance form. True or False.

20. Shoe tapping is an important element in South American dances of Iberian derivation. True or False.

African-Derived Folk Music (Text Pages 396–407)

Purpose To identify some of the major African-derived musical traditions of South America, and become familiar with their representative characteristics, styles, instruments, and song types.

Guidance Syncretism often occurs when two cultures with somewhat similar cultural characteristics come into contact with one another, developing in the process particular characteristics that are similar to both but still significantly different. The term is most often used to explain the religions of many African-derived cultures in South America and the Caribbean. Some West African cultures, such as the Yoruba (the primary culture to provide slaves for Cuba and Brazil) of Nigeria, have religions that are characterized by a pantheon of gods; these people were dominated by the Spanish and Portuguese Catholics who have a pantheon of saints, leading to a synchronization or fusion of their representative supernatural entities within the new religions known as *lucumí* or *santería* in Cuba and Miami, and *candomblé, macumba,* and *umbanda* in Brazil. Musical syncretism also took place, as African call-and-response joined with Catholic call-and-response, African scales merged with European scales, and so forth. Music of the African Diaspora (scattering) should be studied as a unit that includes all the areas where Black slaves were brought, including South America, Central America, the Caribbean, and North America. Similar syncretic cultures developed in South America and the Caribbean, for example, while a totally different development occurred in North America because of Protestantism. On text page 407 a common drum is described briefly as a friction drum. The most usual name for this instrument is *cuíca*, and it is characterized by having a smooth stick fastened to its single head inside the drum's body. This stick is rapidly rubbed by a wet rag in the player's hand, which creates a groaning or whining sound so familiar to carnival music in Rio de Janeiro. In the glossary the definitions for the *agida* (p. 418) and the *apinti* (p. 419) are reversed. The apinti resembles the Ghanaian *apintema* drum from which it is derived.

Terms Define or identify the following terms or areas, based on readings from the text and/or other sources.

17. syncretism

18. apinti

19. mina

20. currulao

21. batucada

22. cuíca (also puíta)

23. macumba

Music and Dance Examples

African-derived festivals

various celebrations from Brazil and Venezuela

> **Music Example**
>
> *samba and samba-related music*
>
> *Afro-Brazilian percussion ensemble, choro, bossa nova*

24. candomblé

25. capoeira

26. berimbau

27. marimba

28. samba (samba de morro, samba da roda)

29. samba school (escola de samba)

30. folk Catholicism

Reading Comprehension Answer the following work questions (answers at end of this chapter):

21. South American slave-owners were more determined than their North American counterparts in destroying the African's cultural identity. True or False.

22. An important African characteristic, in which a leader alternate with a chorus, is known as _____.

23. Syncopation is a reliable indicator of African influence in Afro-South American music. True or False.

24. A dance that is derived from the days when shackled slaves could only kick their oppressors is the _____.

25. The _____ is a popular rhythmic dance associated with the carnival in Rio de Janeiro, Brazil.

26. The _____ is the favored musical instrument of the blacks living in the Pacific littoral of Colombia, for the currulao dance.

27. The _____ is the favored musical instrument of the Blacks living in Bahia, Brazil, for the capoeira dance.

28. In the music for the Saint John festival in Curiepe, Venezuela, the small drum (curbata) plays the _____ while the large drum (mina) plays _____.

29. The most important overall characteristic of Afro-South American music is _____.

30. List four important characteristics of South American dance that reveal African influences:

a. _____,

b. _____,

c. _____,

d. _____.

Amerindian-Derived and -Influenced Musical Folklore (Text Pages 407–416)

Purpose To examine several types of South American music that show strong Native American influences.

Guidance This section can perhaps be seen as a continuation of Chapter 19 by thinking in terms of a continuum for native South American music. The information here discusses musical change among Native South Americans, especially in those areas where cultural and musical mixing has taken place for centuries, such as in the Peruvian and northern Chilean Andes. An error in musical notation occurs on line 12 of text page 410, where the final note should be an eighth note, similar to the second halves of the two notations in Example 20-13. The reason for the differences in terms for the panpipes in the Andes is that *antara* is Quechua (the predominant culture in Peru), *sicu* is Aymara (the predominant culture in Bolivia, parts of southern Peru, and parts of northern Chile), and *zampoña* is Spanish (the predominant language in Chile). It must be pointed out, however, that Native American cultures are not relegated to particular political boundaries, and Aymara people are found in southern Peru and northern Chile, and some Quechua are found in Bolivia. The dancing *chino* flute players in Chilean festivals play their individual notes in hocket, which is similar to the interlocking technique discussed in Chapters 7 and 19.

> ♪
> *Music and Dance Examples*
>
> *Amerindian-derived festivals*
>
> *celebrations from Peru*

Terms Define or identify the following terms or areas, based on readings from the text and/or other sources.

31. Inca

32. Nazca

33. Moche

34. Quechua

35. Aymara

36. wayno

37. yaraví

38. sicu (*siku*; also zampoña)

39. quena (*kena*)

40. Hallelujah

41. caboclo

Reading Comprehension Answer the following work questions (answers at end of this chapter):

31. The pentatonic scale was the only one in use in Inca territory before the Spanish conquest. True or False.

32. The process by which tritonic and pentatonic scales came to more closely resemble Western scales is called _____.

33. A two-step Native American-derived dance that can also be a narrative song form is called the _____.

34. A slow, lamenting Native American song form from the Andes, and often played on the Peruvian harp is the _____.

35. In Brazil, people of mixed Native American and Portuguese heritage are called _____.

36. A folk religion based on North American Protestantism in the Guinea Highlands of South America is called _____.

37. Certain festivals are held in Chile (and throughout Latin America) in honor of _____ or the _____ , and these are characterized by cultural and musical blending.

38. In the Andes, panpipes are known as _____ in much of Peru, _____ in Bolivia (and parts of southern Peru), and _____ in Chile.

39. The chino flutes in certain Chilean festivals play beautiful, lyrical melodies on their instruments. True or False.

Musical Synthesis—The Center of the Mosaic
(Text Pages 416–418)

Purpose To examine certain South American musics that represent a synthesis of African, European, and Amerindian elements.

Guidance One could perhaps graphically think of the musics of each South American country (or any country) as a bicycle wheel. At the center of the wheel, the hub, would be the various types of music that are considered by each country as its nationalistic musical and dance expressions. Radiating into the hub are numerous spokes, each representing one of the numerous musical forms from indigenous cultures, African-derived cultures, European cultures, Asian cultures, American, and so forth. Each spoke can be seen in itself as a continuum representing the development of a particular musical form, and in some cases, perhaps, the spokes (musical forms) themselves intertwine and influence one another. One of the most important of these expressions at the hub of the musical wheel is the *Nueva Canción Chilena*, which is briefly explained on text page 418 as the new protest song movement led by Victor Jara. The movement was begun in the 1960s by Violeta Parra, continued by her children Angel and Isabel, given international fame by the groups Inti Illimani and Quillapayún, and ended with the murder of Victor Jara by the Chilean military in 1973. The music of the New Chilean Song movement continues to be an important expression for many oppressed people of Latin America.

Music Examples

Nueva Canción Chilena

protest songs from Chile

Each country in South America has developed its own unique types of pop music, some of it influenced by European and American rock, some based on Caribbean styles such as reggae and merengue, and still others founded on nationalistic musics. Brazil, which rivals the United States in population, size, and technology, has produced such international pop musicians as Roberto Carlos and Milton Nascimento, while other countries have regional artists who appeal to the hundreds of thousands in their own countries, but are virtually unknown beyond their own borders.

One of the most important pop music movements in Brazil in recent years is known as MPB (música popular brasileira). While there are literally hundreds of artists who produce recordings and tour throughout that country, Chico Buarque is one of the geniuses of Brazilian pop music. He has also written operas, poetry, and books, and has been imprisoned for his expression of political ideas through music. Another extremely popular form of music in Brazil in the 1990s is *música sertanêja*, music originally from the Sertão or Northeast of the country. This is essentially Brazilian country music, and it is currently sweeping the country, urban and rural areas alike. Although Brazilian country music has been around for a long time, it has recently become sophisticated with the technological and marketing advancements of the Brazilian Nashville-like recording industry. *Forró* is another form that originated in Brazil's Northeast. It features an accordian and percussion.

Argentina, the second largest country in South America, still has its tango, which has been modernized and jazzed-up by the late Astor Piazzolla, and experimented with until "tango-rock" was one result. More recent forms are "trash rock" in Buenos Aires and *música cuartetera* in Córdoba. The latter form is a real people's music with a slight Caribbean beat. Argentine jazz/rock tenor saxophonist Gato Barbieri has recorded important fusion albums both in Argentina and the United States. While not a performer on traditional musical instruments himself, he has joined forces with many of South America's greatest folk musicians. "Juana Azurduy," composed by Argentinian composer Ariel Ramirez and recorded in Buenos Aires, features many

South American musicians playing such traditional instruments as quena, indigenous harp, charango, siku, erke, and others, as well as electric guitars, bass, and a large battery of drums, all backing up Barbieri's progressive jazz improvisations.

The "Caribbeanization" (influences of reggae, cumbia, merengue, and salsa) of pop music in many parts of South America is a very important phenomenon. Peru has developed its *cumbia andina* or *chicha* music, which is wayno music with a Caribbean beat; Bahia, Brazil has its *samba-reggae* style which is very popular; and salsa can be heard in most urban areas throughout South America. In Colombia the cumbia and a cumbia-styled rural form of music known as *vallenato* is very popular.

Venezuelan *música llanera* (inspired by the Venezuelan plains or llanos) has been modernized by the group Gurrufío, which performs with the traditional *cuatro* and several more urbanized instruments in a highly percussive, harmonically progressive, and virtuosic style. Another current Venezuelan ensemble with a contemporary fusion style is Maroa.

Since the return of democracy in Chile, Andean instruments that were made popular by urban groups such as Inti-Illimani and Quilapayún and outlawed by the oppressive government of the 1970s and 80s, have returned. One of the most recent groups is a fusion rock band known as "Los Jaivas," which uses Andean sikuri panpipes and kena flutes along with electric guitars and synthesizers. Inti-Illimani, after fifteen years of fusing its Andean music with Italian music, is continuing to record contemporary Andean styles in Chile.

Many South American jazz and pop artists living in the United States are either developing important musical fusions or contributing to them. Bernardo Rubaja, from Argentina, composes and performs a type of "pan-American" music that he hopes will unite the Americas. Brazilian Junior Homrich, who composed the film score for *The Emerald Forest*, was the Native American music advisor for the film *Medicine Man*, and who is an honorary member of the Xavante tribe, fuses many Brazilian musical instruments and characteristics into his musical palate.

Terms Define or identify the following terms or areas, based on readings from the text and/or other sources.

42. cueca

43. marinera

44. cumbia

45. tango

46. Victor Jara

47. Nueva Canción Chilena

Reading Comprehension Answer the following work questions (answers at end of this chapter):

40. A Colombian dance with erotic choreography and with African influence is the _____.

41. Which dance form was written about in 1914 as being "...a reversion to the ape, and a confirmation of the Darwin theory": _____ _____.

42. The *Misa Incaica* and the *Misa Criolla* are examples of the _____ _____.

43. The Nueva Canción Chilena is the _____ movement that began in the country of _____.

44. The Chilean song and dance form known as the _____ shows musical or dance elements from which three cultures or cultural areas: _____, _____, and _____.

45. Two dance forms that are expressions of the urban elite in Brazil and Argentina respectively are the _____ and the _____.

Video Viewing

1. *Mountain Music of Peru.* John Cohen, director and producer.
2. *The Music of the Devil, the Bear, and the Condor.* Mike Akester, director and producer. The Cinema Guild, Inc.
3. *Shotguns and Accordions. Music of the Marijuana Regions of Colombia.* Beats of the Heart series. Jeremy Marre, director and producer.
4. *Spirit of Samba. The Black Music of Brazil.* Beats of the Heart series. Jeremy Marre, director and producer.
5. *Creation of the World: A Samba-Opera.* Vera de Figueiredo, director and producer. The Cinema Guild, Inc.
6. Capoeira dance (Brazil) (28-8). *The JVC Video Anthology of World Music and Dance*, The Americas II, The Music of Latin America (VTMV-28).
7. Candomblé (Brazil) (28-9). *The JVC Video Anthology of World Music and Dance*, The Americas II, The Music of Latin America (VTMV-28).
8. Modern folk song: "Qunapaqui" ("Why?") (Bolivia) (28-10). *The JVC Video Anthology of World Music and Dance*, The Americas II, The Music of Latin America (VTMV-28).
9. Modern folk song: "El Cóndor Pasa" ("The condor passes") (Bolivia) (28-12). *The JVC Video Anthology of World Music and Dance*, The Americas II, The Music of Latin America (VTMV-28).
10. Modern folk song: "Mañañachu" ("No longer") (Bolivia) (28-13). *The JVC Video Anthology of World Music and Dance*, The Americas II, The Music of Latin America (VTMV-28).
11. Tango: "El Choclo" ("Corn") (Argentina) (28-15). *The JVC Video Anthol-*

ogy of World Music and Dance, The Americas II, The Music of Latin America (VTMV-28).

12. *Harawi*, Andean Peru. The JVC/Smithsonian Folkways Video Anthology of Music and Dance of the Americas (1995). Vol. 6, Central and South America, track 13.
13. *Song from Dance of the Pallas*, Andean Peru. The JVC/Smithsonian Folkways Video Anthology of Music and Dance of the Americas (1995). Vol. 6, Central and South America, track 14.
14. *Michicoq (Water Guiding and Cleansing Ritual)*, Andean Peru. The JVC/Smithsonian Folkways Video Anthology of Music and Dance of the Americas (1995). Vol. 6, Central and South America, track 15.
15. *Ritual Music and Dance for Marking Cattle, Festival of Santiago*, Andean Peru. The JVC/Smithsonian Folkways Video Anthology of Music and Dance of the Americas (1995). Vol. 6, Central and South America, track 16.
16. *Dance of the Chunchus*, Peru. The JVC/Smithsonian Folkways Video Anthology of Music and Dance of the Americas (1995). Vol. 6, Central and South America, track 17.
17. *Andean Carnival Music*, Peru. The JVC/Smithsonian Folkways Video Anthology of Music and Dance of the Americas (1995). Vol. 6, Central and South America, track 18.
18. *The Festejo, María Ballumbrosio*, Afro-Peru. The JVC/Smithsonian Folkways Video Anthology of Music and Dance of the Americas (1995). Vol. 6, Central and South America, track 19.
19. *Festejo*, Afro-Peru. The JVC/Smithsonian Folkways Video Anthology of Music and Dance of the Americas (1995). Vol. 6, Central and South America, track 20.
20. *Zapateo*, Afro-Peru. The JVC/Smithsonian Folkways Video Anthology of Music and Dance of the Americas (1995). Vol. 6, Central and South America, track 21.
21. *Hatajo de Negritos (Afro-Peruvian Christmas Dance)*, Afro-Peru. The JVC/Smithsonian Folkways Video Anthology of Music and Dance of the Americas (1995). Vol. 6, Central and South America, track 22.
22. *Pregón*, Afro-Peru. The JVC/Smithsonian Folkways Video Anthology of Music and Dance of the Americas (1995). Vol. 6, Central and South America, track 23.
23. *Marinera, "Palmero, sube a la palma,"* Afro-Peru. The JVC/Smithsonian Folkways Video Anthology of Music and Dance of the Americas (1995). Vol. 6, Central and South America, track 24.
24. *Joropo, Pajarillo*, Venezuela. The JVC/Smithsonian Folkways Video Anthology of Music and Dance of the Americas (1995). Vol. 6, Central and South America, track 28.
25. *Diablos Danzantes (Devil Dance)*, Venezuela. The JVC/Smithsonian Folkways Video Anthology of Music and Dance of the Americas (1995). Vol. 6, Central and South America, track 30.

Sample Test Questions

Multiple choice questions. Only one answer is correct.

1. The villancico and aguinaldo in South America are examples of: a. Christmas songs, b. challenge songs, c. narrative songs, d. lyrical songs.

2. Which is *not* an important characteristic of oral tradition, and one that is useful to the musicologist attempting to find derivation of South American folk musics from Spanish or Portuguese prototypes? a. texts often survive with little change, b. melodies are still recognizable, c. instruments are similar, d. cultural contexts are often similar.

3. From the Spanish romance are derived many kinds of Latin American: a. challenge songs, b. amorous songs, c. narrative songs, d. funerary songs.

4. A South American musical genre that requires spontaneous textual and melodic improvisation, as well as a quick wit, is the: a. romance, b. cowboy song, c. challenge song, d. lullaby.

5. South American narrative songs are commonly used for: a. historical and current events, b. romantic love, c. genealogical histories, d. supernatural powers, e. social control.

6. The charango is unique to: a. Brazil, b. Venezuela and Colombia, c. coastal Argentina and Chile, d. mountains of Peru and Bolivia, e. all of the above.

7. The berimbau is unique to: a. Brazil, b. Venezuela and Colombia, c. coastal Argentina and Chile, d. mountains of Peru and Bolivia, e. all of the above.

8. The guitar is unique to: a. Brazil, b. Venezuela and Colombia, c. coastal Argentina and Chile, d. mountains of Peru and Bolivia, e. all of the above.

9. The cuatro is unique to: a. Brazil, b. Venezuela and Colombia, c. coastal Argentina and Chile, d. mountains of Peru and Bolivia, e. all of the above.

10. In South America, rituals associated with the Roman Catholic feasts of the Lord and the commemoration of the Saints' days were largely introduced by: a. recent missionaries, b. Jesuits, c. Spanish conquerors, d. early minstrels, e. African slaves.

11. In Latin America, the term used to explain the joining of Roman Catholic religious beliefs with those of African slaves is: a. heterophony, b. syncretism, c. enculturation, d. interlocking technique, e. hybridization.

12. Some lullabies in Venezuela have melodies that are based on: a. American rock tunes, b. the national anthem, c. themes by Mozart and Beethoven, d. Brazilian melodies, e. none of the above.

13. The most characteristic African quality of present Afro-South American music is: a. melody, b. reference to African deities, c. percussion, d. cultural context.

14. The marimba dance in Colombia consists of: a. calling the spirits of African deities, b. a tug-of-war between opposing shamans, c. miming the first amorous advances of a couple, d. opponents trying to place blows on each other with their feet, e. use of a handkerchief or scarf by one of the dancers.

15. The capoeira dance in Brazil consists of: a. calling the spirits of African deities, b. a tug-of-war between opposing shamans, c. miming the first amorous advances of a couple, d. opponents trying to place blows on each other with their feet, e. use of a handkerchief or scarf by one of the dancers.

16. The candomblé dance in Brazil consists of: a. calling the spirits of African deities, b. a tug-of-war between opposing shamans, c. miming the first amorous advances of a couple, d. opponents trying to place blows on each other with their feet, e. use of a handkerchief or scarf by one of the dancers.

17. The cueca dance in Chile consists of: a. calling the spirits of African deities, b. a tug-of-war between opposing shamans, c. miming the first amorous advances of a couple, d. opponents trying to place blows on each other with their feet, e. use of a handkerchief or scarf by one of the dancers.

18. Original Native American musical instruments in the Andes do *not* include the: a. kena, b. siku, c. charango, d. drums.

19. A syncretic religious form in South America that is a mixture of Native American shamanism and American Protestantism is: a. macumba, b. Hallelujah, c. candomblé, d. yaraví, e. wayno.

20. Tritonic scales are found more in the South American: a. lowlands where Spanish influence is the greatest, b. the highlands where Indian traditions are stronger, c. coasts where African traditions exist, d. cities where musical mixing has taken place.

21. The yaraví is a: a. quick two-step Native American dance, b. slow mournful Native American song, c. a type of diatonic harp, d. a couple dance featuring colonial rhythm.

22. The new protest song movement of the 1960s took place in which South American country? a. Chile, b. Brazil, c. Argentina, d. Colombia, e. Ecuador.

23. The tango dance craze of the 1910s began in which South American country? a. Chile, b. Brazil, c. Argentina, d. Colombia, e. Ecuador.

24. The cumbia dance craze of this century began in which South American country? a. Chile, b. Brazil, c. Argentina, d. Colombia, e. Ecuador.

25. The Brazilian puíta or cuíca is: a. a friction drum played by rubbing a stick attached to its single skin, b. a musical bow made of wood, with a wire string, c. a small, closed and elongated wicker basket rattle, d. a small guitar with four strings, e. a diatonic xylophone.

Answers to Reading Comprehension Questions

1. Native Americans, immigrants, South America, five hundred years
2. Bolivia, Ecuador, Peru
3. Argentina, Chile (also Uruguay)
4. Brazil, Colombia, Venezuela
5. Brazil, Chile, Colombia, Paraguay, Venezuela
6. True
7. number, strings
8. charango
9. False: they have long since died out in their native country
10. False: they were taught by members of the lower classes, such as the conquistadores or conquerors, and the immigrants that followed, plus the Catholic clergy
11. villancico
12. True
13. modality
14. True
15. a. a state located in the dense rain forest of the northern Pacific littoral of Colombia, b. the Caribbean coast of Colombia, c. the dry northeast of Brazil, d. in the mountains of Chile
16. False: the music was never printed, only the words were
17. challenge, duel, or competition song
18. picking, strumming
19. True, although today it has often merged with other dance forms
20. True
21. False: most important to the Catholic South American slave-owners was the soul of the slave; after the slave was converted, he was often allowed to continue many of his African-derived folkways; the North American slave was often not considered to have a soul, so his culture was virtually destroyed
22. call-and-response or responsorial
23. False: it is found in many types of music, not only African-derived
24. capoeira
25. samba
26. marimba
27. berimbau
28. the ostinato or basic rhythm (steady beat), improvised patterns
29. percussion
30. a. collective ring or circle dancing, b. one person dancing solo in the

center of a circle of spectators, c. the dancers half raising their arms, d. dancing in a slightly bent posture (two others listed on text page 401)
31. False: a tritonic scale and microtonal scales were also used
32. hybridization
33. wayno
34. yaraví
35. caboclo
36. Hallelujah
37. patron saints, Holy Virgin
38. antara, sicu, zampoña
39. False: they collectively play only two notes in hocket (interlocking fashion)
40. cumbia
41. tango
42. folk Mass movement
43. new protest song
44. cueca, African, Spain, Moorish
45. samba, tango

Answers to Sample Test Questions

1.	a	2.	b
3.	c	4.	c
5.	a	6.	d
7.	a	8.	e
9.	b	10.	b
11.	b	12.	b
13.	c	14.	c
15.	d	16.	a
17.	e	18.	c
19.	b	20.	b
21.	b	22.	a
23.	c	24.	d
25.	a		

Listening Form

Student Name _____ I.D. Number _____
Course Name _____ Course Number _____
Date _____ Chapter Number _____ Listening Example Number _____
Record or Tape Number _____ Name of Culture and Location _____
Name of Performer(s) _____
Instructions: place an X, ✓, or • in appropriate boxes; give types; indicate native names.

performing elements (if vocal)	solo: M/F	duo: M/F	trio: M/F	quartet: M/F	group: M/F	other: M/F
performing elements (if instrumental)	corpophone	idiophone	membrano-phone	aerophone	chordophone	electrophone	other
texture	single melody	dense unison	heterophone	imitation	parallelism	disphony	other
more texture	with drone	with time indicator	chordal	polyphonic stratification	colotomy	combination	variable
melodic contour	static	ascending	descending	conjunct	disjunct	undulating	terraced
mode or scale	number of notes	vernacular	using cipher notation (numbers), indicate the mode or scale in ascending order
meter	free	duple	triple	compound	additive	poly	other
speed	very slow	slow	moderate	fast	very fast	variable	other
amplitude	very soft	soft	moderate	loud	very loud	variable	other
timbre (tone color)	clear	breathy	nasal	open	tight	masked	other
inflections	no vibrato	slow vibrato	fast vibrato	wide vibrato	falsetto	multiphonics	other
formal structure	vernacular name	expanding	reverting	strophic	theme and variations	other
structural or performance techniques	ostinato	responsorial	antiphonal	elastic rhythm	if vocal: syllabic or melismatic	non-synchronous parts	other